Inalienable Properties

LAW AND SOCIETY

Law and Society Series
W. Wesley Pue, Founding Editor

We pay tribute to the late Wes Pue, under whose broad vision, extraordinary leadership, and unwavering commitment to sociolegal studies our Law and Society Series was established and rose to prominence.

The Law and Society Series explores law as a socially embedded phenomenon. It is premised on the understanding that the conventional division of law from society creates false dichotomies in thinking, scholarship, educational practice, and social life. Books in the series treat law and society as mutually constitutive and seek to bridge scholarship emerging from interdisciplinary engagement of law with disciplines such as politics, social theory, history, political economy, and gender studies.

Recent books in the series:

Amanda Nelund, *A Better Justice? Community Programs for Criminalized Women* (2020)
Trevor C.W. Farrow and Lesley A. Jacobs, eds., *The Justice Crisis: The Cost and Value of Accessing Law* (2020)
Jeremy Patrick, *Faith or Fraud: Fortune-Telling, Spirituality, and the Law* (2020)
Obiora Chinedu Okafor, *Refugee Law after 9/11: Sanctuary and Security in Canada and the United States* (2020)
Anna Jane Samis Lund, *Trustees at Work: Financial Pressures, Emotional Labour, and Canadian Bankruptcy Law* (2019)
Shauna Labman, *Crossing Law's Border: Canada's Refugee Resettlement Program* (2019)
Peter McCormick and Marc D. Zanoni, *By the Court: Anonymous Judgments at the Supreme Court of Canada* (2019)

For a complete list of the titles in the series, see the UBC Press website, www.ubcpress.ca.

Inalienable Properties

The Political Economy of Indigenous Land Reform

JAMIE BAXTER

UBCPress · Vancouver · Toronto

29 28 27 26 25 24 23 22 21 20   5 4 3 2 1

Printed in Canada on FSC-certified ancient-forest-free paper (100% post-consumer recycled) that is processed chlorine- and acid-free.

Library and Archives Canada Cataloguing in Publication

Title: Inalienable properties : the political economy of Indigenous land reform / Jamie Baxter.
Names: Baxter, Jamie, 1982– author.
Series: Law and society series (Vancouver, B.C.)
Description: Series statement: Law and society | Includes bibliographical references and index.
Identifiers: Canadiana (print) 20200193201 | Canadiana (ebook) 20200193228 | ISBN 9780774863421 (hardcover) | ISBN 9780774863445 (PDF) | ISBN 9780774863452 (EPUB) | ISBN 9780774863469 (Kindle)
Subjects: LCSH: Indigenous peoples—Land tenure—Canada. | LCSH: Indigenous peoples—Legal status, laws, etc.—Canada. | LCSH: Land use—Canada. | LCSH: Indigenous peoples—Canada—Politics and government. | CSH: Native peoples—Canada—Claims.
Classification: LCC E98.L3 B39 2020 | DDC 333.2—dc23

Canadä

UBC Press gratefully acknowledges the financial support for our publishing program of the Government of Canada (through the Canada Book Fund), the Canada Council for the Arts, and the British Columbia Arts Council.

This book has been published with the help of a grant from the Canadian Federation for the Humanities and Social Sciences, through the Awards to Scholarly Publications Program, using funds provided by the Social Sciences and Humanities Research Council of Canada.

Printed and bound in Canada by Friesens
Set in Bodoni and Baskerville10Pro by Apex CoVantage, LLC
Copy editor: Frank Chow
Proofreader: Caitlin Gordon-Walker
Indexer: Cheryl Lemmens
Cover designer: JVDW Designs

UBC Press
The University of British Columbia
2029 West Mall
Vancouver, BC V6T 1Z2
www.ubcpress.ca

For Sachi

Contents

Acknowledgments

I AM GRATEFUL to Susan Rose-Ackerman for her guidance and insight on this project, as well as to Kim Brooks, Robert Ellickson, and David Singh Grewal for their generous input.

And of course, to my family for all their love and support.

Inalienable Properties

1

Keeping the Land, Making the Market

The Nisga'a Nation, whose people have lived in the Nass River Valley since a time "before memory,"[1] has made national headlines over the past decade by creating a new regime of "alienable" rights in Nisga'a lands.[2] These changes gave Nisga'a citizens the option to own small tracts of land in Nisga'a territory – including the right to transfer ownership of those lands to individuals who are not members of the Nisga'a Nation. Set against a long history of legal restrictions on buying and selling of Indigenous lands in Canada, the decision to create transferable land rights in the Nisga'a Nation marked what seemed, to some, a dramatic break from past law and practice.

The people of the Mi'kmaw Nation have lived on Unama'ki (Cape Breton Island) and throughout Mi'kma'ki (the Atlantic region and the southern Gaspé Peninsula) since "time immemorial."[3] In 1916, the Exchequer Court of Canada authorized a forced surrender of a Mi'kmaw community's reserve lands at Kun'tewiktuk (Kings Road Reserve).[4] The community had long resisted displacement from their lands at the entrance to the rapidly industrializing city of Sydney, but powerful commercial and local political interests ultimately won out, persuading the court to relocate the community to its current lands at Membertou, then on the city's outskirts. Despite its history of economic struggle on these lands over the past century, the Membertou First Nation has made remarkable strides in economic and business development, even as it continues to maintain community control of its lands instead of "liberalizing" its land base.

Nisga'a leaders have championed the nation's reforms as a way to catalyze community economic development.[5] Supporters argue that alienable property rights will attract needed outside investment and reduce barriers to credit markets for financing new housing and public infrastructure.[6] Others hold up the Membertou approach as a model of economic success that balances development against concerns that, by abandoning historical constraints on buying and selling land, the Nisga'a Nation and others may be opening themselves up to exploitation by powerful interests and to interconnected risks of cultural, environmental, and economic loss and social fragmentation.[7]

The consequences of these changes in land rights for the Nisga'a, Membertou, and other Indigenous communities in Canada are still unfolding.[8] But whatever their ultimate successes or failures, these two contrasting approaches to community land rights raise unanswered questions about how property regimes persist and change. Why did the Nisga'a introduce property rights that can be traded in the market? And how have communities such as Membertou maintained control over their lands in the face of economic pressures and incentives that favour new regimes for saleable rights?

Answers to these questions in studies of institutional change throughout Indigenous-settler history have mainly relied on the political economy of colonial settlement.[9] Colonial governments, land speculators, and other powerful interests allied with one another to impose formal limits on the sale of Indigenous peoples' lands, while using those same legal restrictions to channel land ownership into the hands of private settlers.

Today, however, as many Indigenous communities move increasingly toward self-governance and self-determination, and their own approaches to land rights and community development, new dynamics of political economy complicate our understanding of changing property regimes in these contexts.

This book explores the contrasting approaches to land rights illustrated by the Nisga'a and Membertou Nations in order to develop and test a theory of property transitions that helps us understand why Indigenous communities in Canada are making different choices about whether, or how, their lands should remain inalienable. Much has been written in the media and in the academic literature about how First Nations *should* reform their property regimes to best pursue economic change and community well-being. In this study, I am interested in a different kind of inquiry. Taking it as given that goals for legal and economic reform will be set by and within Indigenous communities, I aim to understand – from an institutionalist and transactional perspective – how those goals might come to be established and sustained.

The Puzzle of Inalienability

A sizeable literature has developed over the past few decades around normative debates about "inalienability," defined as limits on the range of permissible market transactions for a legal entitlement. These debates arise in the context of Indigenous peoples' lands, as well as in relation to other important resources.[10] In this book, I take up the question that has largely evaded research in property law and institutional analysis: *why* does inalienable property persist in some settings but not in others?[11] More specifically, how are both formal and informal limits on the free alienability of land rights sustained by self-determining political communities over the long term?

Framed in these terms, the central puzzle of this book is part of a broader set of questions about how property rights – and legal rules and norms more generally – change over time in different settings. As a way to engage this broader set of questions, my focus on inalienability may seem like an odd choice. Inalienability has always occupied a fitful position in research on property, where legal scholars have mostly dismissed the concept as having little to do with big questions of efficiency, fairness, and social change.[12] That position has been reinforced over the past few decades by the dominant tide of law-and-economics scholarship that centres its attention on owners' rights to exclude, while consigning other dimensions of property to second-order concerns about "governance."[13] At the same time, some of the most contested social and political issues related to property turn on the rules and norms that limit owners' participation in the marketplace. Limitations on the transfer and use of land, human tissues,[14] legal claims,[15] sacred objects and cultural property,[16] parental and voting rights,[17] ideas and information,[18] and human capital[19] are regularly debated in politics, in the press, and in voluminous popular and social science literatures.

Why this disconnect? Why does inalienability appear to pervade social and economic life and political discourse yet receive so little sustained attention when we turn to some of the most basic questions in property law and legal theory?

One answer is that popular ideas about the "evolution" of property rights reinforce the assumption that inalienable rights will inevitably give way to institutional arrangements thought to be more suitable to business development and economic growth. As Claire Priest has observed, "the emergence of the modern system of private property is ... often described as a steady march toward free alienability" – a position that takes "the freely alienable fee simple estate as the paradigmatic form of land tenure."[20] To the extent that free alienability has become inextricable from modernist private property, inalienability has rarely been studied as a distinctive set of rules or practices with their own dynamics of persistence and change. But because we lack a dynamic theory of how inalienability actually changes over time, our stories about this set of institutions tend to be swamped by encompassing narratives about evolutionary property – stories in which all legal systems inexorably move toward regimes of individuated, exclusionary, and transferable rights.[21]

As I explain in later chapters, there are substantial problems with the theory that alienable land rights are inevitable. Nevertheless, a community's ability to sustain inalienable property remains – in some cases – a difficult puzzle to explain. Under certain conditions, communities can face intense pressures to create new options for market exchanges in real property rights. Some of those pressures are likely the result of external economic and political forces – combined with pre-existing institutional conditions – that pull individual community members' incentives in favour of alienability. In these cases, it is not obvious how communities can successfully sustain the legal architecture to support inalienability over the long term.

At least since Susan Rose-Ackerman's work on inalienability rules in the mid-1980s, it has been well understood that these rules can benefit groups when market failures occur due to externalities, incomplete information, and coordination problems.[22] But even when inalienability is collectively beneficial in economic terms, the associated costs of restricting market exchange may be felt acutely by current and prospective owners who forgo their expected gains from trade as well as, in the case of land, the benefits of collateralization. Land market liberalization can also create the prospect of windfall gains for some group members, increasing political pressures for reform. Moreover, in the context of the land rights studied in this book, inalienability may approach a pure cost to current owners when the benefits of inalienability accrue mainly to future generations – as when inalienable land rights serve primarily to preserve community control over its land base for the future. In these situations, community members not only face the challenge of coordinating their actions to achieve collective ends but must also agree to sacrifice current private benefits as contributions to an intergenerational public good enjoyed by others at some indeterminate point in the future.[23]

Under such conditions, how do communities successfully sustain regimes of inalienable entitlements as a matter of economic incentives? And what distinguishes those communities from others, facing similar conditions, who have taken up free alienability and pursued new markets for formerly inalienable rights?

These questions are raised squarely by changes in Indigenous land rights in Canada over the past half-century. As in other former colonies of the British Commonwealth, strict constraints on the transfer of property in Indigenous peoples' lands in Canada had long been imposed by colonial law, and inalienability remains the default position under that law for most First Nations to the present day. At least since the later part of the twentieth century, however, as federal and provincial governments have gradually come to offer measured support for First Nations' self-determination and self-governance, some of these restrictions on alienability have been relaxed and communities have encountered a range of new options that make various forms of alienable land rights available. Given the dynamics of collective action sketched above, we might expect to see more First Nations moving away from longstanding inalienability rules. To date, however, few communities have done so – even among those who have taken other active steps toward land tenure reform.[24]

Defining Inalienability

"Inalienability" is used throughout the book to describe a set of institutions – by which I mean formal legal rules or informal norms – that limit the range of permissible market transactions for an entitlement. These institutions might prohibit transfers directly, such as by excluding sales or gifts, or indirectly, such as by setting transaction fees or limitations on price. They might also constrain markets for an entitlement by limiting transfers to a defined class of owners or for a defined class of uses.[25] This definition of inalienability is considerably broader than the one used by some researchers who focus on rules dealing directly with transfers but who ignore any constraints that limit the general marketability of a resource.[26]

I adopt the broader definition of inalienability here for three reasons. First, from a functional perspective, all restrictions that limit marketability – whether those placed on transfers or those that constrain the universe of willing buyers – raise the same basic problem of political economy because they require current owners to forgo potential gains from trade compared with a regime in which entitlements are freely alienable. Because I am interested in how long-term community support for such restrictions is sustained under these conditions, the broader definition of inalienability allows me to cast a wider net for case studies and empirical data to test the theoretical model described in Chapter 3.

Second, a broader definition of inalienability that captures not only direct limitations on land transfers but also a range of other mechanisms through which property entitlements are adjusted, modified, and customized goes to the heart of a central question about Indigenous land tenure reforms: will the likely result of property transitions for First Nations in Canada be legal uniformity, or can variety and diversity among property regimes be sustained? What, in other words, does the political economy of land reform tell us about prospects for the future of legal pluralism in Canada?

According to one influential line of thinking in property theory, those prospects look dim. If a defining feature of property is that it mediates relationships between individuals who are often strangers to one another, then one of its key functions is to reduce the costs of generating and disseminating information about rights to resources.[27] One consequence of this argument is that "idiosyncratic" rules – as defined from the perspective of those operating in the predominant legal system – will raise transaction costs and ultimately diminish the value of reforms for owners and investors who face increased uncertainty.

Inalienability, defined broadly, includes those rules and norms that reduce the marketability of Indigenous peoples' lands simply because the rules and norms themselves diverge from others that are more familiar to potential buyers or investors. The broader definition of inalienability above engages questions about whether – in the context of Indigenous land rights – this "standardization thesis" holds as a positive matter of institutional change, and if not, how communities can continue to sustain so-called nonstandard property regimes in the face of substantial pressures for reform.[28]

Third, as Lee-Ann Fennell has observed, "it is essential to recognize that alienability is not a binary switch to be turned on or off, but rather a dimension of property ownership that can be adjusted in many different ways."[29] A broader definition of inalienability better captures this spectrum of options. For example, while the Nisga'a made the initial choice to introduce a limited form of alienable property, this choice itself has opened the door to a new set of legal options concerning future constraints that might be placed on Nisga'a land ownership to balance competing interests and aims and to mitigate risks from alienability. Not only is the Nisga'a Nation empowered to establish new proprietary entitlements in its lands but Nisga'a lawmakers also wield governance and regulatory powers over land use, transfer, and expropriation.[30] How those powers will be exercised to determine who can own Nisga'a lands, how Nisga'a lands can be used, and when and how ownership can be transferred to others will ultimately shape the meaning and consequences of "alienability" in the Nisga'a Nation.

Explaining Inalienability

Both constitutionally protected Aboriginal title – based on Indigenous peoples' prior occupation of their lands – and federal statutory land rights in Canada are today subject to strict constraints on alienation.[31] While an early period of colonial law sanctioned private exchanges between Indigenous communities and settlers in British North America, bureaucratic control over land markets was eventually centralized and private transactions with First Nations were prohibited. At the same time, even as colonial governments moved toward stronger restrictions on private markets for Indigenous lands, these legal changes made possible the transfer of Indigenous land rights to the very settlers who were prohibited from purchasing them directly.

Perhaps no other history illustrates so well the two conflicting stories that legal scholars often tell about what drives property rights and regimes to change over time. The most influential of these narratives is Harold Demsetz's theory that property regimes evolve from systems of inalienable, communal property to systems of private and freely alienable rights.[32] For Demsetz, the pace and timing of property's evolution depend on the aggregate, *ex post* costs and benefits of reform – driven either by resource scarcity or by factors like geography and changing technology. But a growing suspicion that the Demsetzian narrative lacks any real explanatory power has led some to embrace a different kind of story, one focused on the politics of elite power.[33] In this alternative "interest-group" account of change, property rights do not simply emerge or change on their own but are pushed and pulled in directions determined by the aims and coordinative abilities of powerful and well-resourced people or subgroups in society.

The history of inalienable Indigenous land rights in Canada seems at once to refute and support both of these stories about property. On the one hand, legal rules were developed to constrain the transfer of Indigenous lands and to position the colonial administration as the sole intermediary in all land transfers, even as the pace of colonial settlement and the demand for land among settlers increased. As restraints on alienation were carried forward from the era of large-scale treaty making, they worked to prohibit transactions around most of the land rights that remained to Indigenous peoples. This is exactly the inverse outcome predicted by Demsetz's evolutionary theory, but it can be explained, to a degree, by historical shifts in the configuration of influential colonial interests driving support for inalienability over time.

On the other hand, formal restraints on alienation directly to private interests apparently facilitated transfers of Indigenous land rights to the colonial government, which then granted those rights to private settlers, thereby helping to meet the growing demand for land as settlement spread west across the continent. In this sense, formally inalienable lands became functionally tradable in the marketplace at precisely the same time that land available for colonial settlement was becoming scarce. Demsetz's evolutionary theory arguably predicts, in general terms, the practices of alienability and inalienability on the ground.

In Chapter 2, I describe why an evolutionary theory cannot provide an adequate account of institutional change, and I argue that the interest-group story does a better job of explaining the legal history of inalienability in Canada under the colonial balance of power. But this history also exposes the limitations of a theory of political economy that neither accounts for changes in the interests of actors themselves nor addresses the diversity of First Nations' own approaches to inalienability in an era of increasing recognition and support for Indigenous self-governance. While interest-group theory helps to explain how inalienability rules emerged and were sustained under the power relationships between colonists and Indigenous peoples, it needs to go further to capture the complex settings of self-governing communities, where local political dynamics and their interactions with the Canadian state are significant determinants of legal and economic outcomes.

In order to understand property transitions in these settings from the perspective of political economy, we need new approaches that directly address actors and institutions within First Nations themselves. As recent scholarship on Indigenous law has shown so powerfully, First Nations have long sustained diverse legal orders and systems of governance that are integral to their communities.[34] As more and more communities build their capacities for self-governance, any viable political economy of legal change in these contexts must account for community dynamics and situate these within overlapping, polycentric systems of land rights and lands governance.[35]

Leadership and Political Institutions

To develop an answer to the puzzle of inalienability described above, I turn to the roles and commitments of community leaders who help to shape the politics and political structures of their communities. I explore these aspects of property transitions to explain why some Indigenous communities in Canada have sustained inalienable land rights while others have opted to liberalize land markets as a means of attracting outside investment, new forms of collateralization, and non-member population growth.

Departing from predominant attempts to explain property transitions using theories about legal evolution or powerful interest groups, the framework I apply draws from an emerging body of research on leadership and political institutions as determinants of institutional stasis and change. Following recent efforts by organizational theorists to understand these processes in settings like labour unions and business corporations,[36] I model Indigenous land reform as a special type of the public goods problem analogous to team production within a firm. In their collective efforts to plan, design, and implement property regime changes, this model assumes that community members look to a leader with privileged and valuable information that can help them coordinate their land reform activities. In this model, community members agree to incur the individual costs of inalienability as one form of compensation or "rents" to the leader insofar as that leader continues to deliver the collective benefits of "good" leadership.

Following earlier studies in this vein, my approach reveals that different forms of leadership rents – representing different political, cultural, or ideological commitments on the part of leaders – may be a crucial factor in explaining institutional dynamics. In particular, for those leaders committed to inalienable land rights and the preservation of the community's land base for the future, their instrumental value as leaders could be the key to unlocking group members' willingness to sacrifice some of their potential private gains from liberalization. Inherent information asymmetries in the land reform process therefore set the conditions under which leaders and community members can forge a distinctive type of social contract – a bargain that sustains a system of law and practice requiring members to forgo some of the returns they might expect from undertaking land reform in the first place.

There is, of course, considerable uncertainty and instability associated with making difficult-to-sustain property regimes contingent on individual leaders. But when such prominent individuals act at pivotal historical moments in a community's land reform process, they may also have opportunities to shape political institutions – that is, rules for collective decision making – to address the dual challenges of uncertainty and instability and achieve a kind of long-term institutional equilibrium.[37] Those political institutions generate a new set of structural conditions going forward and determine how communities make future decisions around land reform after individual leaders are gone. As a result, in communities that sustain inalienability, we would expect to see certain forms of collective decision making that differ from those in communities pursuing liberalization.

This type of model analogizes community land reform to a collective enterprise more closely resembling co-production in an organization than the contested terrain of national electoral politics. It offers a way to connect the economic logic of individual interests and incentives with a genuine role for shared goals and successful collective action. In doing so, it escapes some of the latent pessimism in property theory about a community's prospects for maintaining lasting control over their lands.

At the same time, this model turns on two assumptions: first, that individual community members face uniform private incentives to favour liberalized land regimes, and second, that community members' preferences for land reform are well defined from the outset. Clearly, both assumptions can serve only as initial generalizations that oversimplify the diversity of preferences and certainty of knowledge related to land reform within any given community. While these assumptions may yield good predictions in some cases, they are much less likely to hold in others. In later chapters, I relax both assumptions, making way for a closer study of how ideas, beliefs, and public discourses bear on community decisions about land rights and supporting political institutions. While the precise role of ideas in institutional change has long eluded social scientists, new approaches to studying the interaction of ideas and interests have opened promising ways to study these phenomena – especially where ideas are put forward by leaders or "political entrepreneurs" who use their positions of influence to shape public discourse and beliefs about the costs, benefits, and risks associated with change.

A Brief Map of the Argument

This study contributes to research on the political economy of legal change by using tools in game theory and institutional analysis to move beyond conventional stories about the driving forces of property regimes and economic change. It also contributes to a growing body of empirical work on land reform in Indigenous communities in Canada and globally, using a series of community-level case studies as "analytical narratives" to develop and evaluate a theory of change centred on the role of leadership and political institutions.[38] This introductory chapter identified the central puzzle of inalienability explored in the book and sketched out my approach to answering that puzzle from an institutionalist perspective.

Chapter 2 establishes the theoretical and historical background for the book. Indigenous communities in Canada have, for most of colonial history, confronted strict constraints on the alienability of their land rights. In this chapter, I assess how well property scholarship's conventional stories about land regime change explain this history. Chapter 2 also introduces the modern era of Indigenous land tenure reform and the divergence in approaches to inalienability that appears to be emerging across different communities.

It is this divergence that the formal model developed in Chapter 3 seeks to explain by bringing new attention to the role of community leaders in determining paths of institutional stasis and change. Before describing the model, I canvas a small but growing literature on the role of leaders within the field of law and development and point to existing gaps in our understandings of what it is that leaders actually "do" to influence or change institutions. To a degree, the model developed in Chapter 3 addresses these gaps and offers a new perspective on property transitions that can be used to explain why First Nations in Canada have taken such divergent approaches to inalienability. Chapter 4 then develops two comparative case studies to evaluate the predictions of the theoretical model.

In Chapter 5, I modify and extend the baseline model developed in Chapter 3 to account for situations in which community members' preferences for land reform are undefined or uncertain. To do so, I integrate new research on ideas and public discourses from institutionalist theory to show how key leaders not only offer instrumental value but also work to persuade their followers about the benefits and costs of inalienability as a precondition for broader community agreement to pursue leaders' aims. I develop – more briefly than in Chapter 4 – two additional case studies to evaluate some of the predictions from this revised model. Chapter 6 concludes with a summary of my findings and discusses several directions for future work.

2

Property Stories

STORIES ABOUT EVOLUTIONARY legal change have long been a staple of property theory, and for just as long have been bound up with stories about Indigenous peoples' lands.[1] Harold Demsetz's early work popularizing the idea that property regimes evolve toward systems of individualized, alienable rights was based on his historical narrative about the emergence of private property among the Innu peoples of northern Quebec in the early eighteenth century.[2] Increasingly, such evolutionary accounts have come under attack – not just because, as Claire Priest claims, historical "depictions of a steady march toward alienability and modernity are inaccurate,"[3] or because they tend to privilege certain cultural systems and legal orders, but also because these theoretical accounts appear to be fundamentally incomplete, making it impossible to assess their validity or invalidity on functional grounds.

As Demsetz himself described it, the "literary hook" in his story about institutional evolution was a "puzzle concerning property rights to land among Native American tribes."[4] That puzzle was to explain the causal relationship between two historical events: the shift toward a regime of exclusionary property in hunting and trapping lands by some Indigenous communities and a concurrent rise in the price of beaver pelts in the European retail market. Demsetz's answer was that rising prices reflected a growing scarcity of wild beaver and therefore new incentives for trappers and family groups to establish exclusive trapping territories on community lands. Given the option of regime change, Demsetz argued, individual trappers would respond to these market dynamics by attempting to maximize their share of the collective resource.

For Demsetz, this was a success story: Innu laws and practices responded to changes in the marketplace and to the demands of resource users by efficiently allocating rights over the available supply of lands. His narrative was also, of course, intended to be a certain kind of story about "progress" and modernization – one that viewed the Innu as developing a new property regime to meet changing market demands and to maximize social wealth in a globalizing world.

At the core of Demsetz's story was the assertion that "property rights develop to internalize externalities when the gains of internalization become larger than the costs of internalization."[5] That is, institutional change will occur when the social benefits of moving away from the status quo exceed social costs.[6] In a theory that has been called alternatively "optimistic"[7] and "naive,"[8] Demsetz located resource scarcity as the crucial driver of individual, exclusionary rights. As resources become more difficult to appropriate, he argued, opportunities to capture economic rents from those resources increase, making exclusionary regimes more valuable for rights holders and potential claimants compared with earlier forms of collective ownership and resource management. When those benefits exceed the costs of transitioning to a new regime, Demsetz argued, property rights should naturally evolve.

Demsetz's story about the Innu focused on the emergence of exclusionary rights in their hunting and trapping grounds, but said nothing directly about whether or not the Innu themselves developed transferable rights or actual markets to trade their lands once the boundaries of private property had been drawn. Elsewhere in his study, however, Demsetz recognized the application of his theory to the emergence of free alienability. Accordingly, "in a lawful society the prohibition of voluntary negotiations makes the cost of transacting infinite. Some costs and benefits are not taken into account by users of resources whenever externalities exist, but allowing transactions increases the degree to which internalization takes place."[9] As a result, like exclusionary rights,

Demsetzian analysis predicts that new markets for property will emerge when the benefits of alienability outweigh its social costs.

Benefits and Costs

The benefits and costs of alienability have been well catalogued in the now extensive literature linking property rights to development and economic growth.[10] Two general types of benefits associated with alienable property rights emerge from this literature.[11] First, when property is tradable, land can move from less efficient users to more efficient users, thereby creating mutually beneficial gains from trade.[12] From the perspective of owner-sellers, the potential for future trades increases incentives for investment by enabling owners to capitalize future benefits into their present investment decisions. From the perspective of buyers, the acquisition of underproductive lands presents opportunities to increase productivity and realize surplus gains.[13]

Second, alienable property arguably improves access to credit markets by making land available as collateral.[14] Financial lenders will be willing to provide access to credit only if title, serving as security, is saleable in the event of foreclosure. When credit is more accessible, owners of alienable property can generate the resources needed for new capital investments and the development of new technology, leading to additional increases in productivity.

Each of these conceptual benefits from making property alienable has also been discussed at some length in relation to Indigenous land tenure reform. Some have suggested – in line with Demsetz's theory – that these benefits will ultimately encourage a growing number of First Nations to adopt regimes of alienable land rights, at least where exogenous factors such as rising resource values provide the necessary shocks.[15]

But where alienable land rights impose or risk imposing relative costs over benefits, Demsetz's theory also predicts that inalienability rules will be self-sustaining. While positioning inalienability as a second-best response to conditions of market failure,[16] researchers have identified several reasons why a move toward alienable rights may raise substantial social costs. The most relevant costs here relate to negative externalities and to the corresponding coordination failures that can result.[17]

In the context of Indigenous land rights, observers have noted that pre-existing regimes of inalienable rights – or regimes in which rights are alienable only to other members within a community – can generate positive spillovers in terms of cultural and community cohesion, support for Indigenous self-governance, and social equality.[18] As Sari Graben observes, a transition from a land tenure regime based on "membership" to one based on "ownership" may work to reduce some or all of these spillovers in some cases.[19] Whereas some existing regimes of inalienable Indigenous land rights in Canada have conventionally afforded community members the right to occupy property by virtue of their membership, reforms that introduce alienable rights may reduce the quantity of lands available to community members. A new influx of non-members or absentee landlords could create problems for the community as a whole, particularly when incoming owners "have almost no social, economic, or political relationship with the tenant, nor social or physical attachment to the land or the community in which that land is located."[20]

Likewise, introducing a regime of inalienable rights may have consequences for Indigenous self-governance to the extent that land ownership is tied to issues of political jurisdiction and formal or informal political power. Finally, increased transactions in land rights could create or exacerbate unequal distributions of wealth within some communities, resulting in some of the detrimental effects on communities linked to increased social inequality.[21]

Demsetz's Dilemma

Demsetz's theory has been compelling for many because it suggests that changes in inalienability rules can be predicted in a straightforward manner from changes in the schedule of costs and benefits described above. Intuitively, this theory appears best suited to cases in which a community confronts exogenous shocks that substantially alter the relative benefits of free alienability for entitlement holders. For Indigenous communities in Canada, those shocks might include changing prices for natural resources such as timber, minerals, or oil and gas, or – for urban and peri-urban communities – changing real estate values and housing markets.

But even when such shocks occur, the bridge between the social benefits and private costs of transition in Demsetz's account contains a crucial gap that limits its explanatory power. Given the administrative, organizational, and informational demands that such transitions entail, the Demsetzian theory of change produces its own public goods problem – one in which individuals face incentives to become free-riders on the provision of the new property regime.[22] While Demsetz's theory points to the external cost-benefit conditions that might influence institutional change, it fails to identify the necessary mechanisms of coordination, cooperation, and decision making through which communities can effectively achieve collective action. As Carol Rose has pointed out, this is a problem that confounded classical theorists of property from Blackstone to Locke.[23] Likewise, similar gaps in logic have troubled foundational theories of change among neo-institutionalists, from Douglas North to Oliver Williamson.[24]

In fact, the more general problem with Demsetz's "just so" story, according to Jules Coleman, is one that has plagued functionalist arguments about the efficiency of law.[25] In Coleman's diagnosis, this problem has a direct analogue in evolutionary biology:

> The leopard's spots, we know, have the effect, or produce the outcome, of camouflaging the leopard, thereby increasing its success as a hunter. We might then conjecture that the existence and – quite literally – the shape of the leopard's spots are explained by reference to this effect or outcome; that is, we might regard "camouflage efficiency" as the purpose or function of the spots. But so far, this conjecture remains a Just So Story and not a genuine functional explanation. Missing is the causal mechanism that would support the counterfactual, "Were they

> not camouflage-efficient, the leopard's spots would not be" (or, "... would not be the shape they are"). Random mutation and natural selection (jointly) suffice as a plausible causal mechanism supporting that counterfactual, and thus suffice to turn our Just So Story into a formally adequate functional explanation.

Coleman's critique suggests that this same causal mechanism is missing from Demsetz's evolutionary story. Meanwhile, the collective action problems raised by any transition between property regimes provide a compelling reason to think that efficiency alone cannot fully or accurately explain how, or when, property regimes will change.

This is not to say that Demsetz's account will necessarily fail to predict the emergence of alienable property rights in any particular case.[26] But evolutionary theories of property generally lack any real explanatory power because they merely assume that alienable property is presumptively efficient whenever it is observed.[27] Perhaps more importantly, the predictive power of Demsetz's account suffers from a basic methodological problem: if those property regimes that tend to survive are the more efficient ones, then our observational data will be biased by the absence of sufficient variation.[28] In any case, several studies have suggested that rising resource values fail to consistently predict transitions to more efficient regimes and, inversely, that property transitions still occur in situations where regime change is clearly inefficient.[29]

Interest Groups and Political Power

Notwithstanding the basic problems of analytical completeness and collective action that plague Demsetzian property transitions in theory, people of course cooperate around and contest property as a matter of course in political life. An alternative source of Coleman's causal mechanism, then, may be found by analyzing the politics through which property is generated, challenged, adapted, and changed.[30] If we define political economy narrowly as the analysis of collective decision making from the perspective of individual choice, and therefore as the study of pervasive collective action problems,[31] then this lens represents a promising candidate to address the gap left unfilled by Demsetz's account.

The key analytical move in this approach rejects Demsetz's singular concern with the aggregate gains of property transitions and focuses instead on the *distribution* of expected gains and losses among different groups. So-called public choice theories embrace the frame of political actors who behave according to strategic self-interest, rejecting the assumption that politicians and their agents behave like benevolent rulers. Here, "interest groups" who wield the most political clout in terms of votes, donations, or other goods desired by politicians will ultimately determine outcomes in the political market for property. Interest-group theory generally takes the collective choice – or "political" – institutions through which property rights are supplied as a given, and explores the consequences of different stakes and distributions of resources in altering or sustaining the existing allocation of rights. Political institutions in this approach are "largely transparent to the underlying political and economic forces" driving change.[32]

The key message of most interest-group studies of property transitions is this: there is no necessary correspondence between changing property rights in a particular resource and maximizing social wealth (or the realization of other collective ends or values, for that matter). To the extent that Pareto-improving property rights are actually supplied through political processes, this occurs only incidentally or indirectly – when the interests of powerful groups who benefit from transition happen to be aligned with those of society overall, or when the costs of bargaining are low enough for powerful groups to be compensated by everyone else. Symmetrically, property regimes – whether efficient or not – persist over time because they continue to benefit vested interests, even when changes in relative prices alter the aggregate calculus and make transitions socially beneficial.[33]

Interest-group theory recognizes that property transitions can sometimes generate considerable over-cost benefits – that is, resource rents – for prospective rights holders.[34] Individuals who stand to gain from these transitions are most likely to expend their own resources to encourage political decision makers to grant new rights or to change existing ones. Likewise, politicians, bureaucrats, and other public actors stand to gain in terms of power, prestige, or position by rewarding influential groups with new entitlements.[35] Under systems of majoritarian rule, such rent-seeking activities do not necessarily generate optimal outcomes because large, dispersed groups generally face much higher organizing costs compared with smaller, concentrated groups, thereby encouraging free-riding behaviour among individuals within the larger majority and placing de facto political power mainly in the hands of more concentrated special interests.[36] Small groups with high potential payoffs and access to sufficient material resources generally get their way, resulting in property transitions that have no necessary correlation with aggregate social wealth. Moreover, once such interest-group-induced transitions are in place, they generate institutional inertia, or path dependency, that inhibits future change.[37]

As a result, interest-group theories tend to perform especially well in explaining institutional stasis rather that change.[38] The main effect of concentrated political power in most settings, most of the time, appears to be a heavy bias toward the status quo – especially when existing property arrangements protect the favourable distribution of resource entitlements and underwrite the political influence of powerful interests. In part, this emphasis on institutional inertia describes the reality of property much of the time.[39] By definition, institutions include a certain degree of permanence or stickiness to provide predictable guides for behaviour.[40] And because the legitimacy and the workability of property regimes depend heavily on social respect for property rules and norms, we do not generally observe rapid or sustained change in these regimes – except perhaps in highly unstable polities, through ongoing periods of crisis, or during foundational moments and critical junctures of reform.[41]

But absent some exogenous shock that reconfigures either the payoffs of a new property regime or the distribution of power and resources between groups, theories of interest-group politics have more difficulty explaining property transitions when they actually occur.[42] In cases where institutions do change, interest-group theories more often than not regress to Demsetzian explanations by assuming that long-standing property regimes may change, even in the face of interest-group pressures, when the aggregate gains from transition are simply large enough to overcome distributional conflicts.[43]

Some interest-group theorists have tried to address the problem of explaining change by identifying opportunities for "political bargaining." Gary Libecap, for example, develops a model in which parties engage in "private negotiations within groups to adopt or to change group rules and customs regarding the allocation and use of property, as well as lobby efforts involving private individuals, government officials, politicians and judges to implement or alter more formal property laws and administrative rulings."[44] Where transaction costs are low enough to permit bargaining, a "political consensus" may emerge in which the majority agrees to increase the share of gains to influential groups in exchange for their acquiescence in the transition to a new property regime.[45]

Libecap's work in various transitional contexts has focused on the factors that may be conducive to such "contracting for property rights," including the size of aggregate expected gains from transition, the number and heterogeneity of the parties, the "skewness" of distributional shares, and the presence of information problems.[46] Because Libecap's theory allows for the possibility that property transitions are efficient when transaction costs are sufficiently low, one commentator has described it as an attempt to extend the Demsetzian model by "introducing a passive government that provides the framework for bargaining among affected parties."[47]

But just as Libecap's account aims to reconcile the interest group and evolutionary stories, it also reproduces another crucial gap in the analysis. His social contracting model has been criticized as an unsustainable "political Coase theory" – not only because it depends heavily on low transaction costs to political bargaining but also because insurmountable commitment problems on the part of political leaders and influential elites will generally prevent what one commentator calls "efficient predation."[48] Interest-group theory takes as its starting point the idea that political decisions about property rights are heavily determined by special interests, but it offers no mechanism by which those same interests might credibly commit not to renege on their contracts after they have secured redistributive payments. Likewise, politicians may face incomplete contracting problems that prevent successful bargains in the face of future uncertainty. For Libecap's social contracting model to provide a comprehensive theory of institutional persistence and change, it would need to identify some means to deal with these challenges of credible commitment and incomplete contracting. I return to these problems and potential solutions in the theoretical model introduced in Chapter 3.

Inalienability in Colonial History

Against this conceptual background, the remainder of this chapter covers a brief history of inalienability in the context of Indigenous land rights in Canada and British North America from the perspective of interest-group theory. Because colonial-Indigenous relations have historically been characterized by different positions of military and economic power, a theory that emphasizes the alliance of powerful elites appears to do relatively well in explaining why inalienability persisted throughout this period. But as the history below also shows, these underlying interests and alliances themselves also shifted over time. Overall, the lens of interest-group theory helps us to see not only how colonial elites used inalienability as a tool to acquire land wealth and promote assimilationist social policies but also why the different forms of inalienability in modern title and reserve lands took on their particular legal forms.

Before examining these interest-group dynamics, it is important to recognize that this section focuses on colonial land policies and laws without addressing the question of what role inalienability played or continues to play in the legal orders that Indigenous communities have developed and enforced since long before European settlement. Indigenous communities have long defined the contours and meaning of their relationships to land within their own communities, with other First Nations, and with colonial governments – even if those relationships and their meanings have only rarely been acknowledged by the latter. Writings by contemporary Indigenous legal scholars suggest that inalienability, as I have broadly defined it, may figure prominently in some of these systems in some form.[49] But while I do not engage these questions here, I return to the topic, in part, in Chapter 4 when discussing the institutional trajectory of inalienability in some contemporary settings of Indigenous land regime change.

Proclamation and Preemption

Despite their enduring role today, Indigenous legal orders during the early colonial period existed at the "borders of the Canadian legal imagination."[50] Land rights defined by European colonial governments "bracketed" these systems and engrafted their own evolving understandings of property, possession, and transfer onto the process of colonial land settlement.[51] Nevertheless, the prior occupation of British North America by Indigenous peoples with developed legal traditions posed a legal challenge for colonial governments, who relied on the doctrine of discovery to assert sovereignty and radical title to the land. In order to rationalize colonial settlement under the discovery doctrine, colonial law and legal institutions have long adopted the fiction – and its accompanying racist assumptions – that Indigenous peoples' lands were vacant, or *terra nullius*.[52]

While the doctrine of discovery has been at least partially rejected by Canadian courts, its consequences continue to pervade the basic structures of Indigenous land rights as they have been interpreted in Anglo-Canadian law. One consequence of the discovery doctrine was that Indigenous land rights were conceived as "burdens" on underlying Crown title.[53] This construction denied

Indigenous peoples recognition of their territorial rights even as it controlled land transactions by requiring private settlers to formally acquire property rights in Indigenous lands, either by sale or gift, from Indigenous peoples themselves. While coercion and foul play by settlers often went unchecked on the ground, lands remained formally in the possession of First Nations unless and until they were sold or given away according to the processes of colonial law.

As a result, until the middle of the eighteenth century, Indigenous land rights were considered to be freely alienable in much the same way as common law estates. This legal status changed in 1763, when the British Crown issued its Royal Proclamation establishing the Crown right of preemption – the rule that Indigenous land rights were inalienable to private settlers and could be ceded only, if at all, directly to the Crown.[54] Once ceded, the Crown was free to issue patents granting the fee in those lands to private settlers. Thus, while the Royal Proclamation did not prevent First Nations from selling their lands or prevent settlers from possessing title to those lands, the Crown's preemptive right ultimately had the effect of interposing the Crown between Indigenous peoples and the market. To the extent that First Nations chose, or were coerced into, land sales after 1763, any valid exchange needed to conform with terms negotiated by or through the Crown – though there are several cases in which Indigenous peoples were simply displaced by colonial governments without the pretence of a formal sale.[55] It was the Royal Proclamation's framework for land transactions that set the stage for the subsequent era of treaty making and colonial expansion from the Eastern United States and Upper Canada to much of the West.

From a Demsetzian perspective, the timing of the preemption doctrine is difficult to interpret. The British appeared to intervene in land markets and to limit the alienability of Indigenous lands at exactly the moment when the demand for land was growing and the availability of land for settlement was becoming increasingly scarce. All else being equal, Demsetz's theory predicts that Indigenous land rights under colonial law should have become more, rather than less, freely alienable under these circumstances.

Several explanations have been offered for the Royal Proclamation's inalienability rule.[56] Certainly, the relative military strength of First Nations at the time and their importance as British allies against the French and later against American revolutionary forces provided strong incentives for the British to address, in the words of the Royal Proclamation itself, the "great Frauds and Abuses" committed by settlers and land speculators in purchasing Indigenous lands.[57] A related reading is that British policy makers paternalistically regarded Indigenous peoples as lacking the competence or capacity to engage in land transactions and therefore in need of oversight by the Crown – what Kent McNeil has described as the "protection rationale."[58] Alternatively, McNeil himself has argued that the Royal Proclamation's restrictions on transfers to private settlers is consistent with a view, at the time, that Aboriginal title was in fact more than a property right – that Indigenous land rights contained a "governmental aspect" that could be the subject of exchange only between mutually authoritative national states.[59] From this perspective, the Royal Proclamation's inalienability rule was primarily a consequence of *settlers'* legal incapacity to acquire sovereign or jurisdictional entitlements to Indigenous lands.

While each of these explanations may contain elements of a functional story about how the Royal Proclamation's inalienability rule emerged, it is here that interest-group theory provides the scaffolding for a more complete political economy of colonial land policy during this period. From this perspective, the Crown's right of preemption was a mechanism by which powerful colonial elites – especially government administrators and British landowners – engaged in profitable rent seeking.

This argument has been made persuasively by Stuart Banner based on his comparative histories of land policies across the British colonies.[60] By the time the Royal Proclamation was issued in the mid-1700s, the English settler population in British North America was skyrocketing, driving intense demand for new settlement lands.[61] "Anyone," according to Banner, "could see that there were immense profits to be made in acquiring blocks of land" from Indigenous peoples and then selling that land to colonists.[62] But high demand for settlement lands also created strong incentives for private land speculators to engage in fraudulent and sometimes violent behaviour. While some actors may have been driven to support the preemption doctrine out of a genuine concern about these activities, colonial governments also had a strong self-interest in interposing themselves between Indigenous peoples and the market. "Establishing colonial governments as the sole lawful purchasers of Indian land," according to Banner, "would allow the governments to capture the profits from reselling the land to settlers, profits that under private purchasing flowed to individual speculators."[63] The opportunity to capture these land rents in the name of protecting Indigenous communities and settlers from corrupt speculators proved especially attractive.

That opportunity was perhaps nowhere better illustrated than in colonial New Zealand, where Banner's data show precisely how elites within the administration used preemption rights to segment the market for Māori lands as an effective means of capturing large rents. As both a monopsonist buyer and a monopolist seller under the preemption doctrine, the colonial government set below-market prices to purchase lands from the Māori while supplying those same lands to settler-purchasers at inflated prices. In buying low and selling high, the government generated substantial profits. Banner estimates that from first contact until 1844, the British government in New Zealand paid approximately five thousand pounds in total for all the Māori land rights it acquired, while collecting more than ten times that amount from land sales to speculators and other private settlers over the same period.[64]

"Preemption's long life as part of British colonial law," according to Banner, "was doubtless due in large part to the advantage it gave to the government rather than to any benefits it provided for the native population."[65] In addition to the obvious hardships that such a regime imposed on the Māori, the preemption doctrine also had important distributional consequences that favoured an alignment of interests between colonial elites and their constituents. Because "most of the British residents of New Zealand were land purchasers at one time or another ... the net effect [of preemption] was very nearly a wealth transfer from the Maori to the British."[66] These consequences were magnified by informational advantages of the British in predicting future changes in land settlement and prices, and were ultimately facilitated by the relative political fragmentation of the Māori.[67] It was this set of interest-group dynamics that would, counterintuitively, cement the inalienability of Indigenous land rights throughout the period of most rapid settlement and highest demand for those same rights.

Reserve Lands

Crown preemption ultimately did little to prevent the transfer of Indigenous lands to private land speculators and settlers. The era of treaty making that followed the Royal Proclamation resulted in the transfer of control over large tracts of British North America and the displacement of Indigenous communities to designated reserve lands.[68] These reserve lands remain subject to a strong inalienability rule, including the preemption constraint that reserve lands may only be transferred directly to the Crown. But while the federal *Indian Act* – which continues to govern property entitlements in most reserve lands – retains the essential architecture of Crown preemption, its legislative and social history suggests that a different set of interests and alliances underlies the inalienability of reserve lands. If the British colonial government limited land markets through the Royal Proclamation mainly as a way of extracting land rents and redistributing land wealth from Indigenous peoples to settlers, the constraints placed on reserves were driven by an alignment of interests between colonial bureaucrats and missionary organizations around the assimilationist social policies that came to the forefront in the nineteenth century.

The earliest rationales for designating reserve lands as inalienable no doubt ensured that the colonial government's broader program of land acquisition could proceed apace. Preserving small land areas for Indigenous communities against further encroachment from settlement helped to maintain, for a time, the colonial narrative that land deals were mutually advantageous: Indigenous communities retained protected entitlements in the form of reserves, while "surplus" lands were made available for settlement by colonists.

By the early nineteenth century, however, any unifying logic of inalienability among the colonial powers responsible for the reserve system was disintegrating. After the War of 1812, the British were less dependent on the military cooperation of Indigenous peoples in North America, and wartime operations elsewhere in the world shifted attention away from imperial relationships with First Nations.[69] Because the British Indian Branch was effectively an arm of the British military, changing global military priorities reduced centralized funding, personnel, and other support for colonial operations dealing with land policy in British North America.[70] In the vacuum left by London's withdrawal, a cleavage in perspectives on the reserve system among colonial administrators began to emerge, often along regional lines.

Some bureaucrats regarded reserves as the expression of a "civilizing" logic intended to Christianize and assimilate Indigenous peoples to colonial society. Here, bureaucratic interests were aligned with religious organizations who administered the missionary operations that saw church officials become deeply enmeshed in the reorganization of Indigenous religious and social life. As competing Christian sects vied for access and influence, each saw new opportunities in the trend to re-create reserves as "model" agrarian communities based on small-scale agriculture and overseen by church officials.[71] For those pursuing an agenda of religious conversion and social assimilation, the inalienability of reserve lands became a means to exercise a level of control over the day-to-day affairs of First Nations that would achieve these ends.

But others in the colonial administration regarded with skepticism claims that all Indigenous peoples would be converted to a sedentary agrarian lifestyle. A competing group of influential colonial elites argued that the reserve system should be used to "remove and fortify" Indigenous peoples so as to minimize their contact with settlers.[72] From this perspective, the inalienability of reserve lands served more to confine Indigenous peoples to isolated enclaves than to further assimilation.

For assimilationists, isolationist arguments also exposed a central contradiction: how would Indigenous peoples assimilate to colonial society if their lands – and thus their primary sources of material wealth – were effectively cut off from outside capital and credit markets? The response to this apparent contradiction was a legal framework for reserve lands that linked "full" landownership with rights of political citizenship. In 1857, the legislature of the United Canadas enacted the *Gradual Civilization Act,* creating a voluntary regime for individuals to surrender their official Indian status in exchange for political rights.[73] In doing so, an enfranchisee gave up the right to live on reserve as well as to certain social entitlements. This legislation "was based on the assumption that the full civilization of tribes could be achieved only when Indians were brought into contact with individualized property."[74] In exchange for relinquishing their formal rights to community membership, English-speaking male individuals of "good moral character" and free of debt were allotted up to fifty acres of reserve land. Enfranchisees who met these requirements would take their allotment as a common law life estate, with the remainder interest going to their children.[75] The combined effect of this regime would thus create "a gateway through which individual Indians would pass into the civilized world."[76]

Since it was a voluntary regime, however, few individuals elected to take this path. Between 1857 and the enactment of the first official *Indian Act* in 1876, there is record of only one person completing the process of enfranchisement.[77] The subdivision of reserve lands through enfranchisement or other means was also strongly resisted by Indigenous leaders.[78] In the face of such resistance and the deep unpopularity of voluntary enfranchisement among potential enfranchisees, the link between individual political and land rights forged by the *Gradual Civilization Act* of 1857 was eventually severed through amendments to the *Indian Act* in 1918.[79] Under these changes, enfranchisement remained an option but was no longer accompanied by private individual allotments hived off from a community's reserve lands.

Other changes in reserve land tenure that encapsulated the tensions in colonial land policies would be taken up more broadly. Soon after the federal government asserted jurisdiction over "Indians and lands reserved for Indians" at Confederation in 1867,[80] it introduced the location ticket system on reserve lands as a new regime of possessory interests with some features of alienable property. Under the *Gradual Enfranchisement Act* of 1869, individual band members could, on application to their band council, acquire a location ticket to an allotment of reserve land that recognized individual rights of possession and granted exemption from taxes and legal seizure.[81] Location tickets also gave holders limited rights to transfer their possessory interests, including through inheritance. Without fully embracing rights of alienation to reserve lands, this legislation created the legal basis for limited internal lands markets. It seems unlikely that colonial administrators designed this regime with the expectation of supporting on-reserve economic development by inducing investment. More likely, location tickets were created with the goal of promoting norms of market exchange while enabling the federal government to retain effective control over on-reserve affairs. The location ticket provisions of the *Gradual Enfranchisement Act* were retained in the first *Indian Act* when it was introduced in 1876 as a more complete regime for on-reserve governance, and this system became the precursor to the current regime of possessory rights on reserves still in force today.

A second aspect of the *Gradual Enfranchisement Act* of 1869 was its overhaul of on-reserve governance and the new set of political institutions it established for electing band leadership. Based on experiences with the *Gradual Civilization Act,* colonial administrators began to look for ways to circumvent the authority of Indigenous political leaders.[82] The 1869 legislation implemented a new set of procedures – determined by the Superintendent General of

Indian Affairs – for Indigenous communities to elect a chief and council, and it empowered councils to enact bylaws over a range of local matters subject to approval by the Governor in Council. These changes to First Nations' political institutions were likely implemented to ensure that the location ticket system, unlike earlier regimes, was grounded in local political support but still subject to control by federal politicians and bureaucrats. The political institutions established by the *Gradual Enfranchisement Act* and later adopted in the *Indian Act* continue to have important implications for Indigenous land rights today, a point I return to in Chapter 3.

The location ticket system would eventually be integrated into the first federal *Indian Act* in 1876. That regime of limited possessory rights, now called Certificates of Possession (CPs), provides for the main form of private entitlements available in reserve lands today.[83] CPs can be granted to individual community members as evidence of their lawful possession of reserve lands,[84] and they entitle the holder to exclusive possessory rights over both the land itself and any improvements made to that land.[85] Underlying title to these lands, however, remains vested in the Crown and is not subject to seizure by legal process or to charge or mortgage.[86] As with the location ticket system, CP holders enjoy limited rights of alienability in their lands, but these rights remain closely tied to community membership. At the core of this regime is the requirement that CP holders must relinquish their land rights if they cease to be members of the band.[87] Consistent with this foundation, CP holders may transfer their possessory rights only to another community member with approval from the responsible federal minister.[88] Leasehold interests may be granted by individual CP holders to non-members, but this process is also subject to ministerial approval and, in practice, often requires supporting consent of the band council.[89]

This narrow form of alienability in privately allotted reserve lands is mediated to some degree by other provisions in the *Indian Act* that permit grants of long-term leaseholds to non-community members through a special designation procedure.[90] Designations involve a complex process, requiring the assent of a majority of electors of the band voting in a referendum and acceptance by the minister.[91] A final exception to the inalienability of reserve lands occurs when a First Nation elects to surrender a parcel of land to the federal Crown in a modern form of the preemption mechanism. Surrendered lands can then be granted by the Crown in fee simple to private parties, regardless of their membership status in the community.[92] As with the designation process, land surrenders require a vote of the band's membership – although the threshold for surrender is higher, requiring consent by a majority of the band membership as a whole.[93] Perhaps because the regime of CP rights and surrenders under the *Indian Act* carries high transaction costs or because it is in tension with Indigenous legal orders or informal norms, it has been implemented inconsistently across different First Nations.[94]

Title, Treaties, and Self-Government

Indigenous communities in Canada have encountered a growing set of legal options over the past few decades to gain recognition and support for self-governance of their lands in different forms. Community choices about whether and how to achieve greater scope for lands self-governance are, unsurprisingly, complex – making it difficult to distill the determinants of those choices down to a few variables. But focusing on the degree to which different First Nations undertaking land tenure change have sustained inalienable land rights in their communities, we see that a diverging set of institutional arrangements appears to be emerging. On the one hand, some First Nations have pursued new land markets, providing for freer alienability of land rights either through sale – where, for example, land claims agreements allow – or through long-term leasing arrangements under the *Indian Act* or other legislative frameworks. On the other, communities have resisted land market liberalization and maintained or reinvented regimes of inalienable rights even as they have undertaken other land reforms. These are the contrasting choices that I seek to understand in the remainder of this book. Here, I briefly canvas the different land tenure options currently available to Indigenous communities in Canada, highlighting their relevant features in terms of alienable rights.

Aboriginal Title and Treaties

Aboriginal and treaty rights in Canada were constitutionally recognized and affirmed in section 35(1) of the *Constitution Act, 1982*.[95] Among those rights, Aboriginal title marks Anglo-Canadian law's recognition of First Nations' collective entitlements in their "unceded" territorial lands. Title lands remain subject to a strong common law inalienability rule.

For First Nations with potential claims to Aboriginal title, litigating those claims has become an increasingly viable – if resource-intensive – means of asserting lands self-governance and expanding land-based jurisdictions beyond smaller reserves. While the Supreme Court of Canada began to articulate a modern legal framework for Aboriginal title in *Delgamuukw v British Columbia* in the mid-1990s,[96] it was not until the court's recent decision in *Tsilhqot'in Nation v British Columbia* – almost two decades later – that a claim to Aboriginal title was successfully made out.[97]

Much of contemporary courts' openness to title claims has coincided with changes in a conceptual understanding of Aboriginal title's unique or *sui generis* nature. As described above, the predominant frame within which inalienable reserve land rights developed over the course of the nineteenth and twentieth centuries was one of legal "possession" rather than "ownership."[98] This same frame of possessory rights also encompassed the British and Canadian courts' early development of common law Aboriginal title. It was not until the "breakthrough era" of title jurisprudence,[99] marked by the Supreme Court's *Calder* decision in 1973,[100] that Canadian courts would eventually reject the idea of Aboriginal title as a "personal and usufructory" right and reinstate its proprietary status. This shift was further cemented when, during the period of constitutional reform in the 1980s, Aboriginal title gained recognition and affirmation as a protected constitutional right.

But even as the courts have ultimately rejected "possession" as the basis on which Indigenous land rights had been constructed, they have gone to considerable lengths to maintain the inalienability of Aboriginal title. Accepting broad interpretive authority to define Aboriginal title after the constitutional reforms of the 1980s, the Supreme Court in *Delgamuukw* was definitive in finding that "lands held pursuant to aboriginal title cannot be transferred, sold or surrendered to anyone other than the Crown and, as a result, is inalienable to third parties."[101] The court paired this strong rule against transfer with an "inherent limit" on the uses to which title lands can be put. While not restricted to "uses which are elements of a practice, custom or tradition integral to the distinctive culture of the aboriginal group claiming the right" (as with other Aboriginal rights), Aboriginal title "cannot be used in a manner that is irreconcilable with the nature of the claimants' attachment to those lands."[102] Although the court declined to elaborate on the full scope of this constraint, it was clear that the inherent limit served to reinforce the inalienability of Aboriginal title lands.

In *Tsilhqot'in,* the Supreme Court clarified the reasoning on which the inalienability of Aboriginal title lands rested – that "group title cannot be alienated in a way that deprives future generations of the control and benefit of the land."[103] This attention to the rights of future generations broke, in part, with past justifications for the inalienability of Indigenous land rights based on settler encroachment. By emphasizing the preservation of Indigenous lands for future generations, the court placed the rationale for inalienability squarely on the costs and benefits to communities themselves even while continuing to allocate control to the Crown via the option to surrender title lands in order to make them available for economic development.

Rather than litigate for recognition of Aboriginal title, some Indigenous communities in Canada have negotiated modern land claims agreements directly with the federal and provincial governments. Following *Calder,* the federal government gradually moved away from its earlier resistance to negotiating such claims. At this time, a number of First Nations entered negotiations in hopes of delineating their treaty rights on a nation-to-nation basis, though many of these negotiations had stalled by the late 1990s.

While the ultimate goals of modern treaty negotiations remain contested, to date these treaties have addressed First Nations' unresolved claims to lands and resources, as well as some questions about the scope of rights to self-governance and about fiscal and jurisdictional relationships with other governments in Canada. Treaty lands generally cover territories subject to claims of Aboriginal title and extend beyond designated reserve areas.[104] In addition to defining the nature and extent of Indigenous land rights in their treaty territories, modern treaties may also delineate a community's lawmaking powers and frameworks for its political institutions. Generally included within a modern treaty First Nation's authorities are powers to legislate the community's own property regime. The Nisga'a Nation, introduced in Chapter 1, is one example of a modern treaty First Nation that has elected to create limited alienable entitlements in its lands, along with an associated regime for lands self-governance. Other First Nations have reached land claims settlements but have retained the inalienability of their lands to varying degrees.

Self-Government and Sectoral Governance Agreements

Another route to a form of lands self-governance is for First Nations to negotiate nation-by-nation self-governance agreements covering specific subject areas such as land and resource management, taxation, and environmental protection. This pathway achieves some of the objectives of self-governance but tends to avoid more contentious issues such as the settlement of unresolved land claims. While existing self-governance agreements do not purport to vest ownership of Indigenous lands directly in the First Nation, they do tend to delineate a broader range of legal interests and governance tools compared to those available under the *Indian Act*. Several of these tools enable freer alienability of reserve lands as well as greater scope to craft customized proprietary interests and regimes of land regulation.

Distinct from negotiated self-governance agreements, sectoral governance initiatives – principally those established under the *Framework Agreement on First Nation Land Management* – offer a pathway for communities to engage in targeted land tenure change by providing a specific process for opting out from the lands-related provisions of the *Indian Act*.[105] That process requires each participating community to develop its own land code – a localized property and land regulatory regime that affords First Nations a certain degree of flexibility to tailor their own land laws and decision-making institutions. The *Framework Agreement* and its implementing legislation, however, maintains the central restrictions on inalienability found in the *Indian Act,* although it provides greater access to some limited forms of leasehold transfer.[106] Several communities now have operational land codes under this framework, and some have developed subsidiary land laws delineating the form and allocation of property interests as well as related regulatory matters.[107]

From a bird's-eye view of the different land regimes canvassed above, a distinction appears to be emerging between those communities who are pursuing the freer alienability of their land rights and those who have worked to sustain inalienability. The following chapters explore these contrasting sets of community-level decisions. As we have seen, interest-group theories go some distance toward explaining the persistence of inalienable land rights before the modern era of land reform, but the different legal options described here, as well as changing economic and political conditions, suggest that new approaches are needed to better understand institutional dynamics in contemporary contexts of Indigenous land tenure change.

3

Leaders and Land Reform

In this chapter, I focus on how prominent community leaders and political structures interact to generate new institutional pathways. While I take up the idea from interest-group accounts that land rights are produced through political-economic processes, the theory developed in the remainder of this book takes its main inspiration from the process of *team production* in an organization. Drawing principally from the fields of organizational theory and information economics, my approach interprets land reform in Indigenous communities as more closely resembling the dynamics and challenges of organizational teamwork than the contested terrain of electoral politics. In the case studies I explore in later chapters, each community sought to establish a basic level of economic security and took it as given that Canadian law and politics posed significant barriers to establishing lands self-governance toward this end. To the extent that conflicting interests surfaced around these broad goals, they appeared to centre on how best to restructure property regimes and which values – implicit in such institutional changes – should guide or go along with economic change. This account diverges from most political analyses of land reform as a process of exchange between elected politicians and an electorate that makes demands contingent on the costs and benefits of reform.[1] The reality of land reform in some First Nations today challenges this stark division between market and state actors. In the cases studied in this book, community members appeared to be heavily involved in collective decisions about land reform and development and closely connected to the processes of planning, designing, implementing, and utilizing new regimes as they emerged.

As I explain using the formal model below, this shift in frame from political interest groups to team production describes a set of institutional dynamics that may more accurately reflect decision making around inalienability in some self-governing Indigenous communities in Canada. Several key insights follow.

First, the fundamental problem confronted by communities undertaking land reform could be as much about dealing with *uncertainty* as it is about resolving community members' conflicting interests and incentives. Existing models of land reform tend to underestimate the challenges associated with imperfect information about the conditions of economic development and about the long-term consequences of institutional transition for community economic security and resilience.

Second, these concerns about uncertainty provide the entry point for describing the central role played by individual leaders in shaping their communities' relationships to land markets. In short, some leaders are highly valued because they enjoy privileged access to information that – when communicated accurately – helps their communities to coordinate their collective efforts and maximize the gains from institutional change.

Third, because a leader's information is valuable, they may be able to demand something in return for conveying that information accurately. But because individual leaders have different preferences and commitments, these demands will differ between communities – and potentially lead those communities down dramatically different institutional pathways. The special position of leaders, in other words, gives their preferences and commitments outsized effects. As the cases in later chapters show, some leaders acting at pivotal moments in a new property regime hold demonstrable commitments to sustaining control over community lands. Other leaders prioritize the economic gains predicted to flow from liberalization of land markets. Differences in these commitments and beliefs translate directly into different institutional outcomes.

And fourth, the different forms of compensation, or "rents," demanded by different leaders can have surprising consequences for community political institutions over time. Some types of rents are easy to identify and agree on, affording leaders considerable autonomy and generating more centralized structures for decision making. Other forms of leadership rent are open-ended and themselves uncertain, requiring leaders to structure and participate in more inclusive and transparent decisions. These different political institutions, in turn, can have lasting consequences for future decisions around institutional design and implementation.

Approaching land reform from the perspective of team production rather than contested politics therefore helps to unlock the puzzle, described in Chapter 1, of how communities continue to sustain regimes of inalienable land rights by emphasizing the interaction between prominent individual leaders and changing political institutions. To formalize this new perspective, I turn to a game-theoretic model initially developed by the economist Benjamin Hermalin,[2] and more recently extended by John Ahlquist and Margaret Levi to study the group production of industrial bargaining power by dockside labour unions.[3] Ahlquist and Levi address the question of why some unions have historically retained a core focus on the economic interests of their membership, while other unions have led and participated in public protests, work stoppages, and other global-scale political actions that are mainly designed to benefit others outside the union – that is, how some unions have successfully developed an expanded "community of fate" that extends beyond the interests of the union's immediate membership. Their answer to this question turns on the proposition that such communities of fate are shaped by leaders with specific personal commitments to social justice, who enshrine "organizational governance arrangements" – substantive aspirational principles and procedural rules and norms – that sustain those commitments over time.

While Ahlquist and Levi develop their theory in a setting that seems quite remote from the context of Indigenous land rights in Canada, their study of dockside labour unions can be seen as part of a more general project to understand how a group that organizes "to collectively generate some public or club good through time ... endogenously expands its scope of action to include projects that may not directly benefit [its] members."[4] If we take the puzzle of inalienability from Chapter 1 to be another form of this general problem – one in which community land reforms raise fundamental trade-offs between present and future generations – then Ahlquist and Levi's model might be usefully adapted to study the role of Indigenous leaders and community political institutions in sustaining inalienable land rights. I argue based on comparative case studies that, where Indigenous communities in Canada have both undertaken the process of land reform and sustained inalienability rules, they have relied on leaders who prioritized the preservation of community lands and their central significance to the welfare of future generations, and on an evolving set of political institutions that work to enshrine those commitments and to extend them beyond the founding leadership cohort.

Because the role of leaders has only recently emerged as a significant theme for scholars of institutional change, I begin this chapter with a brief overview of the different approaches taken to explain why leadership "matters" for institutional and economic change. The remainder of the chapter develops the formal model and describes the main predictions tested against my case studies in Chapters 4 and 5.

On Leadership, Law, and Development

Over the past half-century, a burgeoning field of research in the field of law and development has tried to work out the institutional conditions that lead to "good development" – whether defined in terms of economic growth, human flourishing, capabilities, or other measures. There appears to be some agreement among law and development scholars that such reforms should be sensitive to context but should also aspire to a core set of reform objectives such as adherence to the rule of law and the creation of clearly defined and publicized legal entitlements. More difficult to achieve has been a clear understanding of how existing institutions can be changed over time.[5] There appear to be many circumstances where good reforms seem obvious in theory but extremely difficult to achieve in practice. While much of law and development research has focused on the Global South, many of the field's core insights are potentially adaptable to Indigenous communities in Canada. These contexts frequently share important links, such as colonial histories and the consequences of those histories for the strength of local institutions.

In trying to understand the process of institutional change for development, primary attention has been given to "structural" accounts that mirror the Demsetzian and interest-group theories described in Chapter 2. These accounts take structural variables, such as resource or political endowments, as the primary determinants of change. Recently, however, a small number of researchers have started to explore in more depth how individual leaders' aims and attributes influence growth and other development outcomes through the medium of institutional reform.[6]

Some of the most prominent studies in this vein have made broad claims that prominent leaders are in fact *the* key determinants of good development. Lee Alston – who, along with his co-authors, studies leadership in a recent book on Brazilian development[7] – has mused that it is time for development theory to move "beyond institutions."[8] Benjamin Jones and Benjamin Olken observe that "if institutions have explanatory power, it is then perhaps a natural next step to ask whether national leaders, who may partly control or substitute for formal institutions, exert personal influences on growth."[9] Likewise, in explaining the successes of good governance and rule-of-law reforms in Singapore, Botswana, and elsewhere, Robert Rotberg argues that strong leaders with sufficient "political will" ultimately matter more for development than institutions, although institutional reforms remain the primary means through which leaders appear to achieve their individual aims.[10]

While other writers have been more cautious about describing the relationship between leadership, institutional change, and development,[11] each new study in this vein contributes to a mounting critique of law and development scholarship for ignoring the important role of individual actors in its accounts of change[12] – a critique that echoes recurring claims from cognate fields that "the broad repertoire of scholarly explanations [of social change] has left very little room for human agency in general, or for leadership in particular."[13]

How Leaders Change Institutions

Leaders in this emerging literature on law and development play a host of different functional roles. One way that leaders can shift institutions is by changing the law when they are sufficiently powerful to do so. That strong leaders can produce legal reform by fiat will strike some as a fairly intuitive – if largely trite – observation. Equating leadership with political authority has a relatively long pedigree in the field of law and development, in particular with earlier theories of the "developmental state" through which autocratic leaders figured prominently in attempts to "bring the state back in" to accounts of development.[14]

In addition to the political power that enables leaders to implement their preferred changes, much has been said about their exercise of "political will" for the public good. Rotberg's study of leadership suggests that this exercise is based not on leaders' own "moral scruples" but on an instrumental calculus to promote growth and development and to protect or reinforce their own legitimacy over time.[15] What this argument fails to explain, of course, is how some leaders come to possess this foresight and political will while so many other authoritarian leaders eschew the same calculus when faced with clear opportunities for reform.

A second way that leaders can change institutions flows from their capacity to manipulate the procedural levers of lawmaking in a manner that forges connections among networks of elites and gets "others in power to go along."[16] This is a leader's capacity to set the agenda for collective decision making – what some have described as itself a "structural" theory of leadership.[17] Contrary to Rotberg's account, Adrian Leftwich argues that political and economic "settlements" – in which leaders negotiate coalitions between the private sector, labour, and other political elites – have been crucial to developmental state successes.[18] This vision of leaders as coalition builders and masters of strategic manipulation also pervades Alston and colleagues' recent volume on Brazil's institutional reforms since the mid-1990s.[19]

If Rotberg's account of leadership by fiat leaves individuals unconstrained to pursue institutional changes, the view that leaders are artful manipulators of procedure and elite coalitions is burdened by its dependence on the pre-existing political institutions that set the terms for coordinative action. As Ledger Helms has noted, these "perspectives in political leadership research could be said to focus more on the institutional context in which leaders operate and less on the phenomenon of leadership itself."[20] Like Rotberg's account, such a structural theory leaves us wondering exactly what it is that leaders themselves actually "do" to produce change.

A third set of studies has predicted that leaders can influence institutions more gradually over time by engaging in public activities that set an example for others to follow.[21] In this model, individual leaders seed a new set of practices that eventually grow into informal norms and ultimately become codified as formal rules. When leaders act "disruptively" – that is, outside the bounds of expected practices and norms – their salience among other political actors and the general public makes these actions especially influential in shifting public expectations. Leaders, in other words, use their special position of influence to set in motion gradual changes in informal institutions that – after a period of dissonance with status quo rules – may become formalized, supplanting old rules with new ones or fulfilling the objectives of the old rules by ensuring that they are faithfully observed and enforced. Here, norms – or "slow-moving institutions" – can frequently precede formal rules as the driver of change.[22]

More so than leading by fiat or coalition, the theory of "leading by doing" brings us closer to an account of what leaders themselves do to transform institutions. This account focuses attention on leaders' salience to their followers as a crucial aspect of leadership, and suggests that leaders' influence on law reform can be much more subtle – and less immediate – than simply mandating change. It does not, of course, attempt to explain why leaders might choose to engage in disruptive actions that can themselves be personally costly. Moreover, the leading-by-doing theory may be more relevant to some types of institutional reform, such as anti-corruption measures and political reform, than others, such as land reform – though the interaction between changing norms and formal laws can produce powerful consequences in the latter as well.[23] Finally, it is not always clear that even a simple action by leaders or others will always be understood and applied across a population of followers, as interpretive complexity tends to increase along with the dissemination of information across individuals and groups.[24]

Finally, there has been a growing interest in the relationship between ideas, leadership, and institutions. Work in this area characterizes leaders as actors who influence public beliefs to create the conditions conducive to reform. This perspective on leadership is linked closely to a renewed emphasis on the role of ideas and beliefs in political economy and to a new body of work that challenges predominant public choice theories of vested or elite interests as the primary determinants of policy and institutional changes. Dani Rodrik, for example, has critiqued "the notion that there is a well-defined mapping from 'interests' to 'outcomes'" in the dynamics of change, arguing that the beliefs of relevant actors shape their own preferences for reform, affect how they respond to existing institutional constraints, and determine how they understand the available choices and how those choices relate to or cause outcomes.[25] Because they impact each stage in the mapping from interests to outcomes, individuals' ideas and beliefs about the world are key targets for prominent leaders to exert influences in ways that differ significantly from the strategic moves available to coalition builders. Because of both their general salience and their control over ideational as well as material resources,[26] leaders can have a heavy impact on shared ideas about whether status quo institutions are working or not, or about the set of available options for reform.

Rodrik and others have drawn on Edward López and Wayne Leighton's concept of leaders as "political" or "institutional" entrepreneurs who "notice loose spots in the structure of ideas, institutions, and incentives and then find ways of implementing these new ideas into society's shared institutions."[27] Likewise, some have pointed out that "development entrepreneurs are leaders who commit to making social organizations work for the greater good by creating the circumstances that lead to the adoption of better institutions," including by bringing institutional alternatives "to the public consciousness."[28] Recognizing that institutional path dependence is a powerful force resisting change, López and Leighton argue that "when the right elements come together at the right time and place and overwhelm the status quo, it is because special people make it happen."[29] In their view, political entrepreneurs are not necessarily leaders who themselves develop and articulate new ideas or ideologies. Instead, leaders as entrepreneurs are individuals who are uniquely situated to identify existing or impending points of disequilibrium in the existing set of institutions, which they successfully translate into "opportunities for profitable arbitrage."[30] That is, leaders under this theory do not affect change by simply imposing their own ideas or beliefs on others; rather they perceive and articulate latent beliefs and work to foreground those beliefs in the public view.[31] Rodrik draws a useful analogy here to theories of technological innovation – just as new technologies relax production constraints on physical resources, new ideas promoted by political entrepreneurs relax certain political constraints to allow more room for institutional changes within existing structures of decision making and control.[32]

Like leading by doing, the theory of ideational entrepreneurship emphasizes leaders' general salience to their followers, but may also clarify a more direct route through which leaders use their resources to influence law reforms. Moreover, existing work has not yet grappled with the question of how pre-existing institutional structures shape information flow and interpretation and thus constrain a leader's ability to further impact institutional changes.

Organizational Theory

As in the field of law and development more generally, leaders have also not played a very prominent role in studies of property regime change. To the extent that leadership has attracted any attention in the political economy of property, leaders have generally occupied structural positions of authority consistent with the leading-by-fiat and leading-by-coalition theories discussed above. For example, we might say that colonial governments that controlled the transfer of Indigenous land rights in British North America included individuals who made decisions about the allocation of land resources and presumably held influence over the broader direction of colonial land policy. But leadership in this frame is largely coextensive with the state and its coercive authority to enforce new regimes of property.[33] Those who exercise authority in the name of the state necessarily form part of the political leadership. But when paired with the assumption that political leaders themselves seek to satisfy their own interests, "leadership" largely becomes a component of interest-group theory, where the preferences of those in leadership positions are the medium of exchange through which elites achieve or purchase their desired distribution of resources.

A richer concept of leadership in settings of property transitions – and one that can respond to some of the challenges raised above – requires us to look beyond the conventional sources that lawyers and economists have used to describe the political economy of institutional change. In this respect, theoretical work on institutional change within organizational settings offers a particularly promising source for new perspectives.

Organizational theory has long been an incubator for research on leadership in settings distinct from the context of electoral politics and the state – settings that have important consequences for defining the relationship between leaders and institutional change because they lack the element of coercive authority that is so often assumed in political contexts and that tends to drive the view that leaders act relatively freely to implement change. More so than political leaders, the corporate managers, union officials, and others who lead organizations generally have limited ability to coerce their members into complying with their objectives, and instead rely heavily on their ability to persuade others to follow their lead. Much of organizational theory has therefore been devoted to understanding what Max Weber called "charismatic" leadership.[34] The most fundamental question here is: How do leaders achieve their organizational goals by getting others within the organization to go along? An answer to this question helps to explain why people choose to follow the sometimes idiosyncratic aims and aspirations of their leaders, how leaders coordinate group activities, and how they acquire the ongoing consent of group members, including consent to endure the costs of institutional reforms and other aspects of organizational change, especially when these costs are uncertain from the outset.

One recent line of work in this vein argues that leaders are valuable to their followers because they have access to and control over valuable information about broader economic conditions, policies, political dynamics, or world affairs.[35] This information is valuable to followers because it enables them to coordinate their productive activities, and it enables leaders to strike a bargain in order to gain compliance with at least some of the leaders' costly organizational goals. From this perspective, individual leaders drive institutional change by forging a type of contract with their followers – one that is itself subject to implementing certain institutional constraints that facilitate coordination and ensure credible commitments over the long term.

This "informational" perspective on leadership finds its roots in the contractarian tradition motivated by Ronald Coase's early work on the nature of the firm. Coase sought to explain why firms exist as an organizational form – that is, why factors of production within the firm are arranged hierarchically and under the centralized management of leading "entrepreneurs," while factors outside the firm tend to be allocated by price mechanisms in the market.[36] His answer proposed that firms make it possible to economize on the high contracting costs that typically characterize arm's-length transactions. By standardizing and streamlining inputs such as labour contracts to allocate workers among particular tasks, firms offer distinctive advantages over market mechanisms of decentralized allocation. However, as Armen Alchian and Harold Demsetz would later recognize, a firm's managers are in no better position to achieve these efficiencies by fiat or authoritative control than are market actors.[37] Alchian and Demsetz argued that the unique and defining feature of the firm is its leader, or "centralized contractual agent in a team production process."[38] This reframing of the leader-follower relationship within an organization as fundamentally contractual in turn led to a set of questions about how firm managers contract with or otherwise induce team members to coordinate inputs, given that individual contributions to group effort are generally difficult or impossible to observe directly and therefore cannot serve as the basis for a binding contract a priori – a problem that would become widely known as "moral hazard in teams."[39]

Attempts to resolve the moral hazard problem have given rise to a view of leadership that links institutional theory with the economics of incomplete information.[40] Following Herbert Simon's study of bounded rationality,[41] the individuals who comprise organizations are no longer assumed to have complete information about the actions of others or about the broader economic, social, and political conditions that link their own actions to collective outcomes. For example, individuals may have limited knowledge about the general state of the economy or about national politics – knowledge that they need in order to decide how much of their own effort to contribute in concert with others toward the organization's collective mission. Leaders who have privileged access to this information can therefore demand support for their own goals and corresponding institutional changes as a kind of quid pro quo for continuing to deliver effective leadership.

I now turn to a formal model – one developed by Hermalin and adapted by Ahlquist and Levi – in order to illustrate these ideas in application.

Team Production of Institutional Change

Consider a community of N members working to improve local economic conditions by establishing a self-governing property regime. Assume that each member of the community chooses to contribute costly effort, e_i, to this project and can do so by various means – for example, by taking on bureaucratic tasks, by participating in planning and consultation, or through taxes or other monetary payments. Each member gains net benefit, V_i, from the collective effort of the group. A state variable, θ, captures exogenous conditions – such as the performance of the regional economy or whether the political climate is conducive to greater economic independence – that influence returns from group members' collective efforts. For simplicity, assume that θ takes on one of two values depending on whether the state of the world is "better" (θ_H) or "worse" (θ_L) for pursuing the group project.

Define each member i's net benefit from participation as:

$$V_i = \frac{\theta}{N}(e_i + \sum_{J \neq i}^{N} e_J) - \frac{e_i^2}{2}, \quad \text{where} \quad \theta \in \{\theta_L, \theta_H\},\ 0 > \theta_L > \theta_H \qquad (1.1)$$

This setup assumes that the new regime is a club good (that is, a good exclusive of non-members and non-rivalrous), the benefits from which are divided equally among all members of the group.[42] In this context, researchers have long defined the central dilemma of property transitions as a classic free-rider problem. They have taken it largely on faith that "establishing and enforcing any new system of property rights requires someone to spend time and labor, but the system itself appears to be a public good, the benefits of which will flow to everyone in a given place, even those who refused to help with the organizational work."[43] Because each member i shares in the collective output of the group, and assuming that individual contributions cannot be monitored cost-effectively, each is assumed to confront private incentives that minimize individual contributions to creating the new regime in the first place.

The model here suggests that this emphasis on the free-rider problem in property transitions may be misplaced. A key feature of equation 1.1 is that for any given contribution of effort, e_i, the value of the state variable θ will determine whether or not individual and social payoffs actually cause free riding in the result. To illustrate, assume $e \in \{0,1\}$ in a two-player, single-shot non-cooperative setting. Equation 1.1 for player 1 then becomes:

$$V_1 = \frac{\theta}{2}(e_1 + e_2) - \frac{e_1^2}{2},$$

producing a free-rider problem only for a limited subset of two-player games where θ is common knowledge and $0.5 < \theta < 1$.[44] For example:

	Contribute ($e_1 = 1$)	Don't contribute ($e_1 = 0$)
Contribute ($e_2 = 1$)	0.25 / 0.25	0.375 / −0.125
Don't contribute ($e_2 = 0$)	−0.125 / 0.375	0 / 0

FIGURE 3.1 An example of the free-rider problem ($\theta = 0.75$).

In Figure 3.1, social benefit, $\theta(e_i + \sum_{j \neq 1}^{N} e_j)$, is highest when both players contribute because the magnitude of θ yields group benefits that are large relative to effort. But the game produces a classic prisoners' dilemma: the dominant strategy for both players in equilibrium is to contribute nothing. In the two-player setting, this result holds for all $0.5 < \theta < 1$.

But at other values of θ, i.e., $0 < \theta < 0.5$ and $\theta > 1$, no free-rider problem exists. For example:

	Contribute ($e_1 = 1$)	Don't contribute ($e_1 = 0$)
Contribute ($e_2 = 1$)	1.5 1.5	1 0.5
Don't contribute ($e_2 = 0$)	0.5 1	0 0

FIGURE 3.2 An example of cooperative team production ($\theta = 2$).

In the game in Figure 3.2, social and private benefits are aligned because the relative cost of effort is low: the only equilibrium is one in which both players choose to contribute. Likewise, where $0 < \theta < 0.5$, players observe that relative returns to private effort are low and choose not to contribute, again achieving the social optimum because exogenous conditions are such that participation is simply not worthwhile.

Clearly, the value of θ matters a great deal to the players in making their choices about individual contributions of effort. If we make the further assumption that players have imperfect information – that is, the true state of the world, θ, is unknown to group members when they decide whether or not to contribute – then this structure creates the basic rationale for a leader, defined here as an individual member of the group who has special access to the true value of θ. If a leader can be depended upon to accurately reveal the true value of θ to the group before group members choose their level of effort, then members can be efficiently induced to contribute when the world is in the "better" state (θ_H) and not to contribute when the world is in the "worse" state (θ_L) – notwithstanding those situations, $0.5 < \theta < 1$, when free riding is a potential barrier to collective action.

All else being equal, as the number of players grows, the size of the set containing free-riding equilibria will likewise increase. At a minimum, however, the two-player example under imperfect information serves to illustrate why free riding may not be the main problem that groups need to overcome – at least for those that are smaller in size.

The problem in this setting is that leaders who enjoy privileged access to information face their own incentives to deceive their followers about the true value of θ. This is because the leaders' return is always increasing in their followers' levels of effort. Suppose that a leader announces $\hat{\theta}$ as the public value of θ, which other members of the group use to decide their contributions of effort. The leader's utility is:

$$V_{LDR}(e_{LDR},\hat{\theta}) = \frac{\theta}{N}\left(e_{LDR} + \sum_{J \neq LRD}^{N} e_j(\hat{\theta})\right) - \frac{e_{LRD^2}}{2}$$

Here, the leader's best strategy is to maximize $e(\hat{\theta})$, meaning that the leader always has reason to announce θ_H, even when the true value is θ_L. This result is illustrated in the Leadership Game matrix in Figure 3.3.[45]

Nature		Follower: Contribute a lot	Follower: Contribute a little
	Better state (θ_H)	5, 5	2, 3
	Worse state (θ_H)	2, 0	1, 1

FIGURE 3.3 A leadership game (left-handed payoffs are the leader's).

The Leadership Game in Figure 3.3 reveals how leaders can take advantage of their privileged information to induce community members to contribute even in the bad state of the world. It is in a leader's interest to lie about the true value of θ whenever the bad state occurs, thereby inducing their followers to contribute more. As one author has noted, this "is the free rider problem in reverse – the leader wants everyone else to think the ... [value of θ] is higher than it really is so that they will give even more ... from which the leader will benefit."[46] The leader's followers, of course, understand this danger and will rationally disbelieve any public announcement about the value of θ made by the leader. Without any mechanism to ensure that the leader reliably tells the truth, this problem renders the leader's privileged information – and thus the role of leadership itself – largely worthless to the group.

Leadership Rents

The central dilemma in this model with imperfect information is therefore about how a leader's followers can induce the leader to truthfully reveal privileged knowledge of θ. An endogenous solution requires some mechanism that makes it sufficiently valuable for the leader to reliably tell the truth. Ahlquist and Levi's answer to the problem yields their key insight from studying leadership in dockside trade unions: leaders can be induced to tell the truth about the value of θ if they have an opportunity to develop a reputation for honesty over time and if they are adequately compensated by their followers for maintaining that good reputation, in the form of "leadership rents." In this context, leadership rents represent any monetary or non-monetary payment to the leader in excess of the costs of leadership. Crucially, these rents might take one of several forms, whose value to the leader will vary depending on leaders' individual preferences. While some leaders may demand certain "perks" of office – such as higher pay, alternative material rewards, or prestige – others may seek community members' contributions toward broader political or ideological goals. For Ahlquist and Levi, the goals of interest are those held by activist union leaders who use their positions of leadership to pursue global issues of economic and social justice. Some union leaders pursuing these ends have demonstrated considerable success in convincing their membership to make additional sacrifices beyond the standard work stoppages and union dues normally associated with union membership, all in the interests of others who are not themselves members of the union. In this respect, activist union leaders differ markedly from leaders of "business unions" who maintain a focus on the economic interests of their immediate membership. Instead of demanding payments in the form of political activism, successful business union leaders tend to collect leadership rents mainly in the form of higher pay or other benefits associated with holding office.

I aim to show how this model can usefully be adapted and extended to explain why some First Nations in Canada – despite facing economic and political pressures for liberalized land markets – have nevertheless sustained regimes of inalienable land rights. In the context of land reform, inalienability rules – especially those that preserve community ownership or control over their lands for future generations – serve as a kind of intergenerational redistribution from current to future community members. At least in the early stages of land reform, in order to persuade community members to forgo some present private gains from liberalization in order for others to achieve future benefits, leaders can demand these self-sacrifices in return for the leader's honest disclosure of θ to the community's membership. For any given community, these demands are based purely on the leader's combination of non-material and material preferences. Where leaders demonstrate strong preferences for inalienability, the model predicts that community members may be willing to satisfy those preferences as part of the quid pro quo for access to valuable information that benefits the economic performance of the community as a whole. Likewise, where leaders demand rents in the form of monetary payments, favourable land deals, or other sources, the model predicts a greater liberalization of land markets and the freer alienability of land rights. In other words, leadership rents in this model, as the expression of a leader's commitments to preserving the community's land base for the future, serve as the basis for variation in inalienability observed across different communities.

To be clear, this baseline model is premised on the strong assumptions that community members always (1) uniformly prefer land market liberalization, and (2) do so based on full knowledge of its private benefits and costs relative to those of inalienability. These assumptions require leaders who favour inalienability to demand their preferred institutional trajectory as a form of leadership rent. Leaders who favour alienable land rights, by contrast, are comparatively free to demand other forms of compensation.

These assumptions are "strong" in the sense that they clearly abstract from the real-world diversity of preferences and knowledge among community members in any given setting. Why not assume that community members uniformly *resist* liberalization based on, for example, community norms, overriding concerns about land loss and community fragmentation, or the community's own legal principles and traditions? I begin to address this question by relaxing the assumptions of uniform and determinate preferences among members in Chapter 5. As a starting point for the baseline model, however, these assumptions serve as useful generalizations in contexts where the immediate benefits of alienability are especially high – such as urban or peri-urban communities facing rising land and housing prices. This explanation underpins the selection of my comparative case studies to test the baseline model in Chapter 4. Moreover, from an analytical perspective, these assumptions provide a good starting point because they represent the most challenging set of conditions under which to sustain inalienability. The case in which community members mostly prefer liberalization but nevertheless agree to sustain inalienability is, in other words, the hardest one to explain.

Following Ahlquist and Levi, introducing rents, r_{it}, the value of rents to leader, γ_1, and the fixed cost of leadership, ξ, into Equation 1.1

yields the following utility functions for leader ($i = 1$) and followers ($\forall i > 1$), respectively:

$$U_{1t} = \frac{\theta_t}{N}(e_{1t} + \sum_{J=2}^{N} e_{Jt}) - \frac{e_{1t}^2}{2} + \gamma_1 \sum_{J=2}^{N} r_{jt} - \xi \tag{1.2}$$

$$U_{it} = \frac{\theta_t}{N}(e_{it} + \sum_{J=2}^{N} e_{Jt}) - \frac{e_{it}^2}{2} - \frac{r_{it}^2}{2}, \forall i > 1 \tag{1.3}$$

Based on Equations 1.2 and 1.3, the complete model is defined by a stage game, Γ, and the repeated, non-cooperative game, Γ_δ, in which δ is the probability of continuing to the next round. The stage game unfolds as follows:

1. The leader learns the true value of θ_t.
2. Members of the community pay total leadership rents, R_t, to which each member contributes equally, $r_{ij} = \frac{R_t}{N-1}$.
3. The leader announces the value $\hat{\theta}_t$ (not necessarily equal to θ_t).
4. Members of the group choose $\tilde{\theta}_{it}$ (their beliefs about the value of θ_t) and non-cooperatively contribute costly effort, e_{it}.
5. The leader reveals the true value of θ_t and players realize outputs and their payoffs.

Assuming that the leader has an infinite lifespan with a discount factor equal to δ, Ahlquist and Levi show that the existence of leadership rents produces a trigger strategy equilibrium in which members of the group revert to playing $\tilde{\theta}_{t+1} = \bar{\theta}_{t+1} \equiv E[\theta_{t+1}] = p\theta_H + (1-p)\theta_L$ (i.e., ignoring the leader's announcement) in the next round, *t*+1, should the leader lie at time *t*. In essence, the availability of valuable leadership rents expands the set of the leader's discount factors, δ, that will produce truthful leadership in equilibrium.[47] Group members therefore have good reason to pay leadership rents – up to the value of the leader's knowledge to each member – that induce the leader to accurately convey the privileged information.

This baseline model yields three central predictions that are evaluated in the empirical case studies in Chapter 4. First, differences in the degree to which a community's lands are alienable should reflect differences in the preferences and commitments of founding leaders during formative periods of land tenure change. In those communities that have successfully sustained regimes of strong inalienability, the model predicts that founding leaders will have demonstrated clear commitments to the preservation of control over the community's land base for future members. We should expect that these leaders worked to convey their commitments so that they were well known to community members, including by making public arguments about the value of the community's land base and the importance of maintaining those lands in community ownership for the future. Conversely, in those communities that moved to regimes of freer alienability, the model predicts that leadership rents such as better salaries, in-kind payments, or prestige will be demanded by formative leaders. These leaders are predicted to eschew commitments to preserving control over the community's land base in favour of a focus on economic growth in the immediate term.

Second, recall that the game modelled above is repeated over time, with the probability of the leader's telling the truth and moving to the next round equal to δ. This repeated game structure not only provides an explanation for why leadership rents are effective but also explains how leaders come to offer a credible deal to their followers – honest information for rents – in the first place. As Ahlquist and Levi point out, "it seems hard to imagine that a well-informed individual simply appears on the scene, claims special knowledge, and the rank and file coordinate on an effective trigger strategy."[48] To address this point, they offer an extension of the Hermalin model that provides for electoral competition between potential leaders, showing that as long as incumbent leaders maintain their reputation by telling the truth, they are not likely to be replaced by challengers who, by definition, group members know less about in terms of the type and level of rents they will demand.[49] While I do not elaborate further on the details of this extension here, I adopt its basic prediction that leaders' demands for rents will not emerge until they can establish an initial track record of good economic performance and can link this result to the success of their leadership. Community members will be unwilling to forgo the potential gains from greater alienability and market access unless they have confidence that the payment of costly leadership rents will produce results. This feature of the model predicts that an explicit and public commitment to inalienability will emerge only after some period of time during which formative leaders prove their truthfulness and demonstrate their ability to produce at least some degree of improved economic growth. Further issues related to how leaders and followers select and commit to a given type and level of rents are addressed in the next section.

Third, the model predicts that, at some level of leadership rents, these payments may come into tension with the fundamental economic goals of land reform. Community members will be willing to endure the self-sacrifices entailed by inalienability rules only insofar as those rules do not undermine the community's ultimate potential for economic success. In other words, there is some threshold value of aggregate leadership rents, $R_{max} \geq R_i$, over which members will be unwilling to contribute because those rents have simply become too costly.[50] This feature of the model does not require that members themselves will always prefer material economic gains to other goals, but it does assume that economic development goals are the principal reason for undertaking land reforms – at least for the communities studied in this book. Two related hypotheses flow from this constraint. One is that leaders will likely attempt to reconcile inalienability with economic development in ways consistent with their political goals for preserving control over the community's land base. This might, for example, cause leaders to advocate for policies or development models that encourage outside investment on community lands without the need to grant secure title. A second hypothesis is that we should expect to see leaders who support inalienability making public claims that such rules actually facilitate economic growth or support the community's goals for economic development in other ways.[51]

Political Institutions

The baseline model developed above provides a central rationale for leadership in addressing the most significant collective action problems associated with land reform, and offers a means for community members to enlarge the set of equilibria in which leaders tell the truth by agreeing to endure the costs of inalienability up to some threshold. But a pair of challenges remain in using this model to explain how leaders ensure that inalienability rules endure over the long term.

One problem concerns equilibrium selection. Because there are multiple truth-telling equilibria, each associated with different forms and levels of leadership rents, a group requires some means by which members and leaders can actually select between them.[52] One way to think about this problem is to ask: How do leaders actually articulate their demands on group members once they have established a reputation for truthfulness, and how do members come to agree?

A second and more significant challenge concerns the problem of credible commitment and incomplete contracting as leaders and followers seek to establish, monitor, and evaluate the scope of rents that leaders demand. As described in Chapter 1, inalienability exists along a spectrum of constraints on the marketability of community lands – from outright prohibitions on transfer to more fine-grained adjustments to land uses and the requirements of ownership. In light of this complexity, we would expect the content of inalienability rules to be evaluated and renegotiated by the community over time based on economic conditions and on the political aims of the leadership. But this same feature of inalienability makes it unlikely that leaders and their followers can ever form a complete contract – that is, that they can fully pre-commit to the form and level of leadership rents in any given period of the repeated game.[53] Likewise, the fluid nature of inalienability makes it difficult to define and measure when community members try to calibrate the acceptable level of rents going forward – especially, as the case studies below show, when gradual changes in norms and practices precede changes in formal rules.

To address these two problems, Ahlquist and Levi turn to "organizational governance," defined as "the formal rules and informal norms that delineate how decisions are taken, how the organization will respond to future events, and how and on what basis organizational members should evaluate the actions of the leaders."[54] At one level, organizational governance is simply a public statement of principles that delineate leadership rents and therefore respond to the problem of equilibrium selection by explicitly defining and communicating the expectations of both leaders and their followers. Principles such as an organizational commitment to racial equity are both straightforward enough to be communicated easily, but also sufficiently substantive to establish what kinds of political projects activist unions are likely to undertake in pursuit of that goal. At another level, organizational governance comprises a set of collective choice institutions that address the contracting problem. Specifically, more inclusive or participatory decision-making processes – such as those that support direct democracy among union members and greater transparency – are theorized to mitigate the uncertainty of incomplete contracts because they provide ongoing opportunities for members to provide their input and to challenge leaders' decisions when they disagree. Ahlquist and Levi's findings show that inclusive decision making is more prevalent in activist unions than in those focused on members' narrow business interests. Group members who are actively involved in decisions about political actions are therefore more likely to accept higher levels of political activism as a form of leadership rent. This line of argument draws some inspiration from principal-agent research showing that more responsive political controls can, counterintuitively, give politician-agents more freedom of action by strengthening their overall legitimacy in the eyes of their principals.[55]

Until this point, I have closely analogized my stylized model of land reform to that employed by Ahlquist and Levi to study political activism among labour unions. But it is here that the distinctive context of inalienability may contribute the most toward a broader theory of leadership and institutional change. Ahlquist and Levi's emphasis on "organizational governance" is a relatively vague concept, and one that tends to oversimplify the challenges of addressing equilibrium selection and incomplete contracting, recalling earlier critiques of Gary Libecap's social contracting theory of property transitions described in Chapter 2. There are several ways in which I aim to refine and extend the idea of organizational governance to better reflect the land reform context.

First, while formally stated principles – whether in an organization's charter or in a community plan – may go some way toward helping a group select an equilibrium point for leadership rents, such principles, on their own, seem too vague or insubstantial to provide a foundation on which a group can base their expectations and to which leaders can credibly commit. The setting of Indigenous land rights in Canada suggests that legal actions asserting such rights – especially high-profile public interest litigation – are an alternative or perhaps additional means through which leaders signal the form and scope of rents. In the cases I study in Chapters 4 and 5, leaders pursuing strong inalienability are simultaneously engaged in nationally significant court battles to define common law Aboriginal title and treaty rights over their traditional territories – cases that assert, and ultimately establish, basic jurisprudential recognition for and commitments to territorial integrity and the historic relationship of Indigenous communities to their lands and resources. While none of these cases has concerned issues of alienability directly, the broader legal principles on which they were argued, and sometimes decided, served as a signal to community membership that defined leaders' political commitments to preserving the community's land base – and did so in ways that required significant commitments of time, money, and other resources. Leaders' use of legal action in this way relates partly to what Amy Kapczynski has referred to as the "gravitational pull of law" in framing certain social issues and movements. Kapczynski argues that "legal frames are more constrained – more weighty, if you like – than many because they are imbued with doctrine and history, and tethered to institutions that are authorized to define and implement the law."[56] This does not suggest that such national legal battles over Indigenous land rights were waged by community leaders purely or even primarily for reasons instrumental to local economic development. But leaders in these settings appeared to recognize that widely publicized legal disputes could provide the basis for asserting political commitments that served their ends apart from the particular issues being litigated in the courtroom. Likewise, an emphasis on a community's own laws, legal principles, and legal traditions might reinforce the substantive commitments of some leaders to preserving community lands and to the well-being of future generations, providing another focal point for land reforms in those communities with stricter constraints on alienation.

Second, as Ahlquist and Levi suggest, one way to address the problem of incomplete contracting is to make ongoing decisions about the content of inalienability rules and norms more inclusive of group members, such that rules can be legitimately adapted as conditions change. But as Giandomenico Majone has observed, other collective choice institutions can also serve as substitutes for participatory decision making to address problems of time inconsistency[57] – for example, delegating decisions to non-majoritarian bodies such as independent agencies or corporate entities. We should therefore expect communities who sustain inalienability rules to select from among a range of responses to the incomplete contracting problem, or perhaps to employ multiple responses when they are commensurate. But we can also expect that these responses may sometimes be in tension with one another – when, for example, delegation to arm's-length agencies makes it more rather than less difficult for community members to provide their input on decisions.

A third issue, related to the second, is that more inclusive collective choice institutions may also emerge in communities with liberalized land markets – not because they address incomplete contracting around leadership rents, but because they respond to the growing demands of non-members who become community residents by purchasing title or possessory rights. Inevitably, when a community increases the marketability of its lands, especially for residential housing development, new outsiders will take up residence and, eventually, may represent an economically powerful constituency that demands greater participation in community decisions about land rights and regulation that affect their interests. We can therefore expect that some communities who start out with relatively centralized and controlled collective choice institutions will gradually expand their inclusiveness over time to accommodate the demands of non-members for greater participation. This implies that inclusive decision-making processes may not be confined to communities with strong inalienability, though it suggests that such processes will occur in communities with liberalized land markets only after those markets have attracted a substantial proportion of non-member residents or other investment interests.

Finally, the problem of credible commitments concerns not only the participation of community members and non-member residents but also the involvement of third-party entities outside the community. Powerful third parties might seek to influence leaders in several ways, such as by paying competing rents or imposing constraints on leaders through legal or financial controls. For Indigenous communities in Canada, the most significant version of this dynamic may be the relationship between the federal bureaucracy and community leaders, though it has also likely included influence from corporate and other private actors. Leaders in communities with strong inalienability rules might therefore be expected to actively distance themselves from third-party influence as part of a strategy to improve their responsiveness and to be seen by their membership as independent and impartial.

A Summary

The model developed in this chapter confronts the puzzle of inalienability from Chapter 1 on the assumption that sustaining a regime of inalienable land rights poses a net cost to individuals because it demands that they forgo at least some immediate benefits of market exchange. In doing so, the model also identifies a reason why individuals are willing to bear at least some of these costs some of the time – because they represent a form of "leadership rent" that is valuable to beneficial leaders. By paying these leadership rents, community members can induce their leaders to truthfully disclose their privileged knowledge about the state of the world, thereby enabling members to coordinate their efforts around land reform and their participation in economic activity and community development. Next, in Chapter 4, I show that this model's predictions are consistent with a set of comparative case studies exploring how the choices and actions of actual leaders influence the trajectories of institutional change in their communities.

4

Save or Sell?

THE MODEL DEVELOPED in the previous chapter generated several testable predictions about the land reform trajectories, leadership goals, and political institutions that we should expect to find in those First Nations pursing alienable land rights compared with those that have worked to sustain inalienability. This chapter aims to test those predictions against two comparative case studies. The Westbank First Nation, near the city of Kelowna in British Columbia, has experienced rapid economic and population growth since the mid-1980s, primarily due to the large influx of new business and non-member residents purchasing long-term leasehold interests in the community's reserve lands. The community has taken an aggressive approach to creating new land markets, with a majority of the community's two primary reserves allocated to private interests and nearly as much currently subject to leasing agreements. The Membertou First Nation, near the city of Sydney in Nova Scotia, has also built an impressive record of economic development while preserving community control over its land base and sustaining the inalienability of its reserve lands – despite holding valuable tracts that are now within the city's urban core. While pursuing different models of land tenure, governance, and development, both of these communities have attracted national recognition for their dramatic gains in community development and well-being.

These cases therefore provide an ideal comparison to evaluate the theoretical model's predictions about the role of leaders and political institutions in shifting or sustaining legal rules about inalienability.

An important challenge in identifying useful comparators in this context is the great diversity of First Nations across Canada in terms of their geography, institutional settings, cultural traditions and histories, resource endowments, economies, demographics, and relationships to provincial and federal governments. A number of empirical studies examining Indigenous land reform have attempted to address this complexity by using large-sample data sets to isolate variables that best correlate with transitions between property regimes of various kinds.[1] These studies have yet to generate a comprehensive picture of the key drivers of reform, and none have explored the crucial role played by the leaders or political institutions, which are the focus of this study. Existing studies have also explored land reform at a more general level than my focus here on the question of inalienability. One common theme that emerges from these data, however, is the impact of location and geography on the form and pace of land regime change. This work lends support to the assumption that First Nations located close to urban centres experience stronger pressures for some type of land reform compared with more remote communities, likely as the result of greater population growth, higher land values, and the links between these over time.[2] Urban and remote communities are also likely to confront different resource endowments and opportunities for land development that will influence the dynamics of institutional change.

This chapter compares the Westbank and Membertou First Nations as two communities that are located in close proximity to sizeable urban areas. I assume that urban proximity generates strong land development pressures – especially as the neighbouring cities grow – and that in both cases the First Nations have faced significant incentives to create and support alienable land rights. The two communities also share other important commonalities. Both are relatively small, and local economic development in both has been primarily focused on business development, tourism, and other sectors that capitalize on their proximity to regional growth centres. Neither community has significant natural resource endowments on its reserve or former reserve lands suitable for development, although Westbank currently holds and manages a forestry licence on its traditional territory.[3] Finally, while both First Nations governed their lands under the provisions of the federal *Indian Act* for much of the period under study, both have now either implemented or are currently in the process of implementing formal institutional changes to move away from the *Indian Act* land regime. Nevertheless, neither community has had or currently has the recognized authority to create property interests that are fully alienable to non-members, often working within the constraints of existing legislative regimes to realize their objectives.

A number of key differences also distinguish the two cases. The two communities clearly have different cultural contexts and histories. While reserve lands fall mainly within federal jurisdiction, there are also important regional and provincial differences across Canada that affect regime change – such as the very different modern treaty processes in British Columbia and in Atlantic Canada that govern recognition of Aboriginal title and treaty rights on traditional lands. And while both communities have pursued land regime changes on their reserve lands, these regimes themselves take different forms. None of these differences are expected to significantly affect the analysis, but where confounding factors exist I have addressed these below. In the next chapter, I shift context to test the model in two remote First Nations that have also taken divergent paths to land reform.

The model in Chapter 3 predicts that prominent leaders are instrumental in coordinating communities' projects for land regime change and development, and in both cases strong leadership is evident as a driving force. Moreover, the model predicts that leaders will need to demonstrate their capacity to deliver on successful development initiatives before demanding leadership "rents," either in the form of material gains or in the pursuit of non-material goals. Once leaders feel confident in delineating "rents" in return for their continued successful leadership, however, we should expect that their personal goals for land reform will play a prominent part in determining the future trajectory of inalienability and the types of political institutions needed to support those changes. In First Nations like Westbank that have embraced alienable rights, we would expect to find leadership that emphasized the immediate demands of economic growth and commercial development, and we would expect to identify at least some instances of leaders obtaining material gains from the emergence of more alienable rights. By contrast, in First Nations like Membertou that have maintained inalienability, the model predicts that leaders will articulate objectives around preserving the community's land base and maintaining control over those lands, especially in the interests of future generations.

The model in Chapter 3 also has implications for community governance. Because material rents in the form of monetary compensation or preferential land transactions are – to a degree – easier to establish and monitor, political institutions in Westbank are predicted to be more centralized and to offer fewer opportunities for community participation. By contrast, because non-material rents are more difficult to define and monitor on an ongoing basis, we would expect to find in Membertou clear mechanisms that articulate and define the scope of leaders' commitments to inalienability, as well as a set of political institutions that openly engage community members and work to reinforce the credibility of leaders' commitments in the face of changing circumstances over time.

Westbank

The traditional territory of the Syilx people spans the Okanagan Valley in the southern interior of British Columbia and northern Washington state. The valley's shrub-steppe grasslands run between the Fraser and Columbia River watersheds, where they sustain a remarkably diverse ecology adapted to the semi-arid climate.[4] A series of lakes throughout the Okanagan – the largest of which is Okanagan Lake at the southern end of the Okanagan River – produce a rare proximity between wetlands and arid grasslands.[5] Prior to contact with Europeans, the Syilx defined their territory over the whole of the valley, but in 1846 the Oregon Treaty divided existing communities along the forty-ninth parallel. Today, the Okanagan Nation Alliance – a transboundary alliance of eight member communities – includes the Okanagan Indian Band, Osoyoos Indian Band, Penticton Indian Band, Upper Nicola Band, Upper and Lower Similkameen Indian Bands, and Westbank First Nation, as well as the Colville Confederated Tribes in Washington state.

In the mid-1800s, the area near the present-day city of Kelowna was settled by Europeans who pursued mainly agricultural production in those areas with sufficient access to water for irrigation.[6] The reserve lands of the Okanagan Indian Band – of which the Westbank First Nation was originally a part – were first established by Indian Reserve Commissioner Peter O'Reilly in 1888. The two primary Westbank reserves, Tsinstikeptum 9 and 10, were described by a Royal Commission in 1913 as farmland that was "at present of no practical value, but under [a] water system would be worth" a total value of $571,600 – a finding that the commission used to justify reducing the community's total reserve land area by over 1,700 acres.[7] While Westbank's lands were designated as farmland, they were not especially well suited to agriculture due to their location and low fertility – a familiar story across Canada in which reserves were often located on marginal lands, while better quality soils were allocated for European settlement.[8]

In the early 1960s, members of the Okanagan Indian Band residing on the Tsinstikeptum 9 and 10 reserves separated to form their own autonomous band. When the Westbank Indian Band was created, the residents of Tsinstikeptum 9 and 10 consisted of a few hundred people. Today, Westbank's residential population numbers over nine thousand, less than 10 percent of whom are members of the First Nation.[9] The Tsinstikeptum 9 and 10 reserves, which continue to form the main residential and commercial centres of the community, sit adjacent to the municipality of West Kelowna and immediately across Okanagan Lake from the city of Kelowna, a sizeable urban centre with a population of roughly 125,000.

Located in one of the country's fastest-growing regions, Westbank has been lauded as an example of successful community development.[10] Over the past decade, the First Nation has more than quadrupled its economic output and achieved high levels of business investment and employment.[11] Average total income among Westbank members in 2011 was over $29,000 and the community had an unemployment rate of 12 percent.[12] As former chief Robert Louie has described it, "we have a strong entrepreneurial spirit in our community, and we are a very business-oriented group overall."[13] Westbank has focused its on-reserve economic activity on commercial real estate development, including a number of residential and retirement communities that account for the large increase in the number of non-member residents on the community's reserve lands over the past few decades.

Beginning after its separation from the Okanagan Indian Band in the mid-1960s, Westbank gradually moved toward a regime of increasingly alienable land rights. Private allotments to band members gradually increased over time, and community leadership actively supported individual lease agreements in ways that helped to streamline onerous federal approval processes. While these leaseholds were less secure than fee ownership, they became sufficiently standardized to ground private markets that saw non-member lessees readily purchase and trade their interests and investment in land development. The Westbank government also participated directly in these new markets by leasing unallotted community lands to third parties.

Until the end of the twentieth century, Westbank First Nation's active use of land allotments and long-term leases appeared to create a de facto regime of alienable land rights in its reserve lands, largely without modifying the formal rules restraining transfers in the federal *Indian Act*. In 1996, Westbank became one of fourteen original signatories to the *Framework Agreement on First Nation Land Management,* and by 2000 had negotiated the *Westbank First Nation Self-Governance Agreement* with Canada.[14] That *Self-Governance*

Agreement – along with the *Westbank First Nation Constitution* and Land Code – was eventually voted by community members and the agreement was given effect through federal law in the *Westbank First Nation Self-Government Act* on April 1, 2005.[15]

The *Westbank First Nation Self-Government Agreement* recognizes and defines the community's authority to make and enforce its own laws with respect to lands, natural resources, environment, culture and language, education, health services, business licensing, transportation, public safety, and law enforcement.[16] While the agreement is more limited in scope than the modern land claims settlements examined in the next chapter, it nevertheless implements some aspects of Westbank's inherent rights to self-government.[17] The agreement did not alter the state of title in Westbank reserve lands, which remains in the hands of the federal Crown for the use and benefit of the community.[18] But through Westbank's new constitution and a suite of subsidiary land laws passed pursuant to the agreement, formal rules pertaining to the granting and exchange of possessory interests – especially long-term leaseholds – were liberalized. Likewise, the land regulatory environment was standardized to reflect the type of land use plans and zoning laws familiar off reserve, with a clear priority to "create certainty of land use."[19]

While land allotments remain available only to Westbank members under the agreement,[20] the processes for granting these interests was streamlined and no longer requires ministerial approval.[21] Likewise, the agreement eliminates the complex designation and surrender processes dictated by the *Indian Act* and Westbank now makes its own internal decisions for granting long-term leases to non-members. Leaseholds of fifteen years or less can be granted directly by the council through resolution, leaseholds between sixteen and forty-nine years in term require a majority vote of community electors at a special meeting, and leaseholds longer than forty-nine years require a community-wide referendum.[22] But perhaps the biggest change under the agreement is the removal of any constraints on the creation and transfer of leasehold interests by individual allottees. Westbank members are now free to grant and transfer leaseholds and other interests to members and non-members alike, without restriction as to the term and without a requirement for approval by the council.[23] Westbank's constitution also makes limited provision for community members to grant mortgages in their allotment lands.[24]

Early Barriers to Development

The theoretical model in Chapter 3 predicts that community leaders were an important influence on the emergence of alienable land rights in the Westbank First Nation. In this case, formative leaders are expected to favour market-oriented economic growth and commercial development. But because – by assumption, under conditions explained above – leaders' preferences for alienability align with those of their members, they should have greater scope to demand material rents as compensation for effective leadership (compared with leaders who prefer inalienability). The model also predicts that these leadership goals will be reinforced by a relatively closed set of political institutions that centralize control and decision making in the hands of the leadership. While there may be mechanisms available for leaders to hear community members' concerns or disagreements, formative leaders are not expected to be especially responsive to dissent given that the "terms" of contracting – leadership's privileged information in exchange for material benefits – are relatively well defined.

In the late 1950s, Norman Lindley, who would become the first chief of the Westbank Indian Band, and a small group of prominent community members came together to champion the idea of residents from the Okanagan Band's Tsinstikeptum 9 and 10 reserves forming their own band using a formal process for secession established by the *Indian Act*.[25] In 1957, the group petitioned the Indian Agent at the Department of Indian Affairs (DIA) office in Vernon, British Columbia, for the authorizations they needed to initiate the process. The petitioners offered several reasons for their desire to form their own community, not the least of which was a feeling that the leadership of the Okanagan Indian Band was not sufficiently attentive to their interests. At the heart of their grievances appeared to be the desire by residents of Tsinstikeptum 9 and 10 to capitalize on their close proximity to the growing city of Kelowna by leasing some of their lands to city businesses for commercial development. Driven by the construction of a new bridge connecting Kelowna directly with Tsinstikeptum 10 over the Okanagan River, several development opportunities had presented themselves to the residents, including a significant proposal to construct a new college campus on the reserve lands. Other members of the Okanagan Indian Band, however – many of whom were primarily engaged in agricultural enterprises at the northern end of Okanagan Lake – resisted calls to commit to long-term leasing arrangements and, the Westbank residents charged, had little interest in including the minority residents of Tsinstikeptum 9 and 10 in their decision making.[26] These problems were exacerbated by the physical distance between the different factions in the Okanagan community, with the Westbank members having to travel long distances to council meetings. Residents of Tsinstikeptum 9 and 10 also lacked any elected representation on the Okanagan council.[27]

Motivated by these concerns, in 1963 Westbank residents put their proposal for division to a vote of the Okanagan Indian Band membership and were defeated by a narrow majority. Nevertheless, the DIA overruled the results of the referendum and proceeded to designate the Westbank Indian Band as a separate entity with approximately 165 members, roughly 20 percent of the Okanagan Indian Band membership at the time. The newly established community took control over three reserves totalling 2,318 acres.[28] Lindley was appointed chief by acclamation, a position that he held for five years before being voted out of office in the mid-1970s.

During the first decade after the secession of Westbank, economic development was slow and the pace of land transactions appeared well below the initial expectations of those supporting secession.[29] Two main challenges prevented the community from achieving its aspirations. First, federal policy concerning Indigenous peoples in Canada was highly unstable in the postwar era, leading to shifting relationships between local communities and the federal bureaucracy. During the immediate reconstruction period in the 1950s and 1960s, Indigenous communities, individuals, and organizations were increasingly vocal in asserting their claims to self-government and self-determination, and increasingly willing to raise issues surrounding land claims and entitlements to other natural resources. Indigenous peoples gained the right to vote federally in 1960, and in 1961 compulsory enfranchisement was no longer mandated by the *Indian Act*.[30] With support from key allies in the academy, the frame of federal politics gradually appeared to shift from "assimilation" to one of "integration," and eventually – with the report of the Hawthorn Commission in 1967 – to a form of recognition of the cultural, political, and legal distinctiveness of Indigenous peoples under the so-called federal citizens plus policy.[31]

Led by anthropologist Harry Hawthorn, the commission recommended that First Nations governments be afforded greater autonomy, including control over revenues generated from leasing and development of reserve lands.[32] These recommendations both contributed to and tracked a shifting set of expectations and practices by Indigenous leaders working to assert community autonomy, though many communities lacked the resources and infrastructure to take on these roles to build capacity quickly. But the release of the federal government's infamous White Paper in 1969 – with its continued emphasis on the assimilation of Indigenous peoples into Euro-Canadian society and the firm denial of Aboriginal title and resource rights – threw this evolving agenda into turmoil.[33] The White Paper also demonstrated the degree to which the federal bureaucracy remained wedded to a particular set of goals and procedures that would pose substantial challenges to Westbank in pursuing its development objectives.[34]

The second set of challenges facing Westbank during this period concerned the surrounding economic conditions for land development. The Westbank leadership struggled to balance the cost advantages to outside developers of developing reserve lands against the regulatory uncertainty created by what was, to many outsiders, an unfamiliar legal and political environment.[35] Proximity of the Westbank community to Kelowna was not the only attractive feature for would-be developers and investors; there were also key advantages flowing from low or non-existent property tax rates,[36] the lower land costs associated with long-term leasing compared with outright purchase, and the general lack of land-use regulations on reserve. At the same time, some developers were unsure about securing returns on investments in permanent infrastructure on leased lands, and the complex processes of federal approvals threatened to significantly increase the costs of these transactions.[37] One means to navigate this second set of tensions was for the Westbank leadership to promote the development of mobile home parks, which reduced the capital costs of investment and were more amenable to settings with less regulatory oversight.[38]

In the spirit of exercising greater autonomy over development of their reserve lands, Westbank members voted in favour of the prospective surrender of both Tsinstikeptum 9 and 10 for leasing – the latter in 1965 and the former two years later. The surrender of Tsinstikeptum 10 included an ambitious plan for a private developer to develop the entire reserve, but the proposal was closely scrutinized and ultimately rejected by DIA officials, who argued that the project terms did not yield a fair return to the community. A subsequent proposal on similar terms was also rejected by the department, and without any significant developments during the surrender period the land was returned to reserve status in 1972.[39]

The failure of these initial attempts at increasing the alienability of Westbank's reserve lands overlapped with Lindley's replacement by Noll Derricksan as chief in 1968 and, ultimately, with Derricksan's replacement by his younger brother, Ron Derrickson, in 1974.[40] Consistent with the theoretical model's predictions, there is no evidence that either Lindley or the elder Derricksan was able to demand substantial leadership rents during this period, given their inability to generate real economic gains for the community as a whole. Instead, the early leadership in Westbank proved unsuccessful at building a reputation for delivering on community goals.

Nevertheless, as one official at Indian and Northern Affairs Canada (INAC, the successor agency to the DIA) noted in reporting on this early period of development in Westbank, the community leadership had, since the formation of the new band, worked to set out a clear set of principles or terms to guide community coordination around the path of economic development. These included priorities that "Band lands should be used as the base to establish a viable economic and social environment for the community" and "land development by both Band and locatee interests would be encouraged."[41] By the early 1970s, this work of defining priorities for land development and a strategy to implement them took on a renewed emphasis through the creation of a comprehensive community land use plan and the formation of a new Westbank Indian Band Development Company.[42] The plan served as an important focal point for clarifying and articulating the business-oriented economic and social development objectives that had been emerging over the previous ten years and that would guide community development for at least the next two decades. Observers from the federal government noted at the time that "since the plan has been adopted and implemented by the Band there has been an easing of concerns among the Band membership over the significant change that is taking place on their reserves."[43] In other words, the plan provided a focal point for community members to identify and find mutual agreement on leaders' vision for community development – a vision that placed the liberalization of reserve land markets at its centre.

It was not until the tenure of Chief Ron Derrickson, who led Westbank from 1974 to 1986, that the community finally began to realize an increase in land transactions that would lead to economic gains. Derrickson continued to build on the approach of his two predecessors, focusing on land transactions to draw outside investment and developers into the community. In the early years after separation from the Okanagan Band, Derrickson, who was ambitious about the community's development plans and anxious to see them implemented, clashed at times with the more cautious style of Chief Lindley. Despite these differences, however, the two appeared to be in general agreement on the direction of community development.[44] But Derrickson also demonstrated a unique capacity and willingness to work closely with INAC officials during this difficult period of Indigenous-federal relations, breaking through some of the barriers that had impeded development before his tenure – though not without generating considerable controversy both within and outside the community.

Derrickson, whose parents were inaugural councillors of the Westbank Indian Band after its secession in the mid-1960s, was involved with community politics from a young age.[45] Before his tenure as chief, he was an active business owner with a remarkable breadth of interests, including enterprises in cattle ranching, a mining company, a farm machinery business, and a drive-in theatre.[46] When he took over as chief in 1976, Derrickson inherited not only a strained relationship with INAC but also the community's history of unsuccessful land surrenders and development proposals, as well as a number of projects that had been undertaken by individuals and by the community and were under considerable financial stress. Under Derrickson's leadership, Westbank's embrace of land markets would finally begin to yield returns. By 1980, the community's annual revenue from reserve land leases reached $830,000, up dramatically from $22,000 in 1971. Likewise, annual revenues to Certificate of Possession (CP) holders rose over the same period from $15,000 to $466,000.[47] The number of business enterprises on Westbank's lands also increased from 1971 to 1982: community-owned businesses from one to nine, individual member-owned business from four to nine, and non-member businesses from four to twenty-two. By this point, First Nation–owned businesses in the community encompassed real estate development, vineyard operations, cement production, utility management, and the operation of mobile home parks.[48] These changes also coincided with a dramatic increase (over 60 percent from 1971 to 1982) in the on-reserve population.[49]

Land Deals and Leadership Rents

Westbank's leadership cohort during its formative period of economic growth and transition to alienable land rights illustrates a complicated dynamic surrounding the payment of "leadership rents," though one that remains consistent with predictions from the model developed in Chapter 3. Once leaders were successful at achieving a substantial level of economic growth, they began to demand material rents that resulted in what appeared to be considerable personal financial gains. These rents generally came in the form of favourable land acquisitions and financing arrangements for commercial land developments that were owned by or personally beneficial to leaders and their families. In 1986, a Royal Commission was formally established by the federal government to investigate several of these deals, giving particular scrutiny to those in which lands were acquired by Chief Ron Derrickson. In its Final Report, the commission observed that

> during the years that Ron Derrickson was Chief of the Westbank Indian Band, he was allotted parcels of land situate on both Reserves 9 and 10. Some of those lands are quite valuable and it appears that the consideration received by the Band was quite modest. It did not appear that the Band adopted the practice of putting the question of these allotments before a Band meeting.[50]

After he was elected, for example, Derrickson received a land allotment of two valuable waterfront lots located on Tsinstikeptum 9, along the shores of Okanagan Lake and adjoining a third lot already allotted to Derrickson. He subsequently leased all three lots for a ninety-eight-year term to a private development company with plans to construct a resort hotel. Rental income and inducements associated with the deal were estimated to total nearly $3 million. Although the transfer was approved by federal bureaucrats at INAC, it appeared that the deal was never put to a vote by the band council, though this characterization was later challenged by the band executive. Derrickson himself would claim that the transfers were based on informal claims he previously held in the lands, although the Royal Commission found no evidence that these claims were registered.[51] Other examples would follow in which Derrickson or his family members acquired valuable interests in Westbank's reserve lands with little or no direct financial benefit accruing to the band.[52]

The most prominent example of such rents involved a tract of land on Tsinstikeptum 9 allotted to Noll Derriksan and subsequently leased to a company that Derriksan incorporated under the name Toussowasket Enterprises Ltd. Under a plan to construct a mobile home park, Derriksan leased the lands to Toussowasket for a thirty-year term and began development with considerable financial support from INAC through the Indian Economic Development Fund and the Federal Business Development Bank. The development was partially completed in 1976, but by that point it became embroiled in financial difficulties associated with a downturn in the mobile home rental market. In the face of Toussowasket's mounting debt, the band, under Ron Derrickson's leadership, eventually acquired a 50 percent share in the company in exchange for assuming a substantial portion of its liabilities, and INAC contributed an additional $300,000 to keep the project solvent.[53]

After details of this episode became public knowledge, allegations began to surface that Westbank leaders were appropriating band funds for personal gain, abetted by favouritism on the part of INAC officials. It was this series of accusations that, after several internal investigations by INAC, caused Parliament in 1986 to appoint John Hall, a prominent British Columbian lawyer, to lead a federal commission of inquiry (the Hall Inquiry) into the financial affairs of Westbank and the activities of its leadership.

At least during the period of rapid economic growth in Westbank prior to the Hall Inquiry, the rents demanded by formative leaders were apparently tolerated, to a degree, by community members as compensation for leaders' successes in coordinating community activities to increase land transactions and access for outside investors. In part, these rents may have been accepted by the community as a fair return to successful leadership in circumstances where First Nations chiefs and councillors faced tremendous challenges and received little pay. In line with the reality for many First Nations, Westbank encountered acute funding shortages from the federal government in ways that likely made it difficult not only to retain qualified leadership but also to meet the bare minimum administrative costs of running the community's government. Evidence from the Hall Inquiry demonstrates that, after the Westbank Indian Band was established, wages for the chief and two councillors were very low, on the order of $250 to $700 per month.[54] Consistent with the theoretical model, Westbank community members may have assessed the level of leadership rents relative to other sources of leaders' compensation and the costs to individuals who took on leadership roles in what were doubtless very difficult circumstances.

Moreover, while the individual land transactions with leaders detailed by the Hall Inquiry may have produced few direct benefits for the community, there is little question that the formative leadership cohort was ultimately successful in pursuing community economic development and at least some of the benefits of this activity appear to have been distributed among community members. The band continued to be involved in several land development ventures generating increased public revenues, on-reserve employment and housing had improved, and the outflow of migration had been reversed to attract a growing number of members back to the community.[55] Leaders also invested in community infrastructure, including a commercial office complex, a community hall, a recreation centre, an intermediate care facility, and a targeted housing program for the elderly.[56] Significantly, because leaders appeared to collect their rents mainly in the form of real estate interests in reserve lands whose value increased in part as a result of spillovers from growth in the local economy, they also had incentive to continue driving that growth along with the benefits it brought to the community as a whole.

Finally, the Hall Inquiry heard some evidence that, even in light of the events leading up to the commission's investigation, Chief

Derrickson continued to enjoy strong support among some community members, who regarded him as "a capable administrator and skilled businessman."[57]

Nevertheless, even if Westbank leaders sustained community support for a time during an early period of growth, leaders' material gains may eventually have exceeded the threshold level of rents that community members were willing to tolerate, causing a backlash against the leadership. In spite of some community support for Derrickson, the Hall Inquiry also noted that "others, both within and outside of the Band, viewed him as a petty tyrant who could bend the Department to his will to the advantage of himself and his family."[58] The inquiry itself was motivated in part by pressure from Westbank members who began to view the series of lucrative land allotments to members of the Derrickson family as extravagant, resulting in "resentment, jealousy and suspicion" as to the legitimacy of these rents.[59] Some community members, it should be noted, protested not only the level of rents but also "the direction the Band Council was taking in its land use planning ... [where] Chief Ron Derrickson represented the pro-development faction," who "viewed the reserve land as a valuable economic development base."[60]

On the other hand, the inquiry records and other documents show that at least some of the backlash, and the attendant characterization of the leaders' rents as illegitimate, was driven by non-community members who owned long-term leases on Westbank lands and who resisted the upward adjustment of land rents on the Westbank reserve lands. Public outcry was also motivated to a certain extent by Members of Parliament in Ottawa who were only too willing to stereotype Indigenous leaders as corrupt officials generating exorbitant personal gains at the expense of their own communities and of the Canadian public more broadly. In this light, it is impossible to overlook the broader context – as suggested by one INAC official reporting on economic changes in Westbank in the early 1980s – in which non-Indigenous politicians and others were unwilling to accept and support a First Nations community's right to self-government, especially through a period of rapid economic and social change.[61]

Although not specifically discussed by the inquiry, it is also possible that community support for the Westbank leadership was eroding because leaders were showing a broader pattern of mismanagement that directly had an adverse effect on their ability to continue supplying the economic benefits of leadership. The band's dealings with Toussowasket Enterprises, which ultimately led to the inquiry, represented a very public business failure that would surely have reflected poorly on leaders' reputations as good business managers and successful land developers.

In any case, the events surrounding the Hall Inquiry strongly suggest that the Westbank leadership eventually did surpass the threshold level of rents that community members were willing to tolerate. Certainly, even in context, the absolute benefits attached to some land transactions favourable to the leadership appeared to be very high – in the millions of dollars in some cases. Under these circumstances, and consistent with the model's predictions on this point, excessive demands by leadership will disrupt the equilibrium in which leaders who successfully deliver on economic gains continue to be awarded material rents. It was in part this disequilibrium that Westbank's governance reforms in the late 1990s and early 2000s would seek to address.

Centralization and Political Control

In addition to the issue of leadership rents, the theoretical model also predicts early political institutions in Westbank that were relatively centralized, making it easier for the leadership cohort to control decision making about lands and development. This prediction is borne out to a degree, at least until Westbank implemented the final recommendations of the Hall Inquiry beginning in the early 1990s.

By the time of the inquiry, considerable dissent appeared to be emerging within the community around leaders' vision for community development. That dissent was well documented by the Hall Inquiry as a "schism between pro- and anti-development factions within the Band."[62] In particular, some individuals were becoming skeptical of how new markets for Westbank's reserve lands and the influx of non-member residents through mobile home and residential community developments would impact the community's ability to govern itself and maintain its cultural fabric. There were also vocal concerns about how the collective wealth generated from individual land allotments would be distributed. As the Hall Inquiry report noted:[63]

> On numerous occasions during the course of this Inquiry, it was suggested that there is a basic division among the Westbank Band members between those who favoured development and those who did not. While there are obviously differences of opinion among Band members over the issue of development of Reserve lands, it did not appear to be simply a dispute between those in favour of development and those opposed. Rather, there was and is a division of opinion as to how development is to take place, including what type of development and when and where it is to occur. There is no agreement in place to equitably distribute the proceeds from developments on locatee lands. Without such an agreement, a situation could arise where the landowner who has a golf course, for example, could receive far less than one who has a resort hotel, even though one development complements the other and the comprehensive plan may be viewed as one for the common good and prosperity of all Band members.

Complicating these challenges, by the end of the 1980s Westbank's lands were occupied by approximately 3,500 residents who were not members of the band. Despite the growing population of non-members, there existed no formal mechanism under the *Indian Act* for these individuals to participate in community decision making. Non-members held no rights, for example, to vote in elections for chief and council or to participate in community referenda. As the population of non-member residents grew, these individuals increasingly pressed for greater participation – not for formal voting rights per se, but for some kind of established channels through which their perspectives and interests might make their way to the leadership. Larger land developers and other powerful economic interests, however, no doubt had their own means of exerting such influence.

There is no evidence available from this period to show that the Westbank leadership took action to address these various pressures for greater community and non-member participation. Nor did leaders appear to entertain dissenting opinions from community members who disagreed with their plans for alienating reserve lands to create rapid community economic development. Certainly, the Westbank leadership did make efforts at certain points to consult with community members. Weekly council meetings and quarterly community-wide meetings were open to all members and provided a limited forum in which individuals could acquire information about community governance. Beginning in 1980, the executive also piloted a program in which community members were awarded cash allotments on the basis of their participation in community affairs.[64] It is not clear, however, that input from these limited forms of participation was ever integrated into the leadership's decisions. Dissenting voices that eventually emerged within the community did not appear to affect the leadership's commitment to liberalizing reserve land markets overall, and development during this period proceeded apace despite some opposition.

The degree to which political institutions were constrained and decision making centralized within the Westbank leadership was also illustrated by leaders' close oversight of land transactions and development projects, especially as the pace of economic change accelerated. Leaders were personally involved in most aspects of these transactions, including negotiating the terms of land leases, adjusting rental terms, and implementing financing and regulatory measures.[65] This oversight was formalized to a degree when Chief Derrickson sought delegated authority under the *Indian Act* for greater control and management over reserve lands, allowing community leaders to approve certain transactions without federal oversight.[66] Another important tool in achieving this end was the Westbank Indian Band Development Company (WIBDC), established in the mid-1970s. The community's early attempts in the 1960s to lease its reserve lands for development were based on a model in which outside commercial investors took the lead on large development projects, negotiating with the First Nation to pay dividends or other returns to the community, in addition to any rental income returned to individual allottees. As noted above, these negotiated deals were largely rejected by INAC as yielding insufficient return to the band. By the mid-1970s, the Westbank leadership changed tactics and, through the WIBDC, sought to take a much more active role as a direct partner in such large-scale projects.

Finally, the closed political structures established by the Westbank leadership during this period appeared to suffer from a general lack of openness and transparency about band affairs. One of the Hall Inquiry's most prominent findings was that Westbank lacked robust rules to ensure transparency, especially concerning financial reporting and publicizing of decisions about land transactions.[67] INAC produced a set of general guidelines at the time that applied to leasing reserve lands and to conflicts of interest, but the inquiry found that those guidelines appeared not to have been effectively adopted or enforced.[68] By comparison, leaders built close relationships with INAC officials, and these channels of communication may have been more open than those between the leadership and their members.

Membertou

The Membertou First Nation has pursued a path to community development that contrasts sharply with Westbank's embrace of private land allotments and transferable rights. According to the federal Indian Lands Registry System, Membertou has registered only two land leases to third parties on its main reserve since these transactions were first recorded in the 1950s – one to the federal government for operation of a gas pipeline, and the other to the city of Sydney for construction of a new municipal playground (both have long since expired).[69] Likewise, in a community with over nine hundred members living on reserve,[70] Membertou has allotted less than fifty tracts to individual members, leaving the majority of its reserve lands in the collective possession of the First Nation as a whole.

Membertou presents an intriguing contrast with Westbank as a community with urban reserve lands that, to date, has sustained a regime of strong inalienability, despite the rapid pace of economic growth within the community over the past few decades. The band faced a $1 million annual deficit and had only $4 million in annual revenues in the mid-1990s, but by 1999 the deficit had been nearly eliminated and band revenues had grown to over $9 million annually.[71] By 2016, annual revenues – principally from band-owned and operated businesses – had grown to nearly $45 million.[72] Despite having what is undoubtedly a valuable urban land base attractive to outside investors, Membertou has almost entirely rejected the kind of liberalization in land rights that saw much of Westbank's lands allotted to private interests and a large influx of non-member residents purchasing long-term leasehold interests. Instead, it has pursued a collective corporate-type development model that retains the community's close control over reserve lands and governance. As one member noted to the media, Membertou "is like a corporation that we all own."[73]

As in Westbank, community leadership appeared to play a pivotal role in determining outcomes for Membertou's property regime. Membertou's leaders demonstrated a commitment to resisting any loss of community ownership in or control over reserve lands, sustaining the *Indian Act*'s default restraints on alienation even while pursuing alternative legal structures to generate economic growth. This section describes how Membertou's leaders secured members' consent to sustain this inalienability regime as a form of leadership rent, requiring members to forgo private gains from individual land allotments and transfers, and in effect redistributing some of those potential gains to future generations. This does not imply, of course, that leaders required community members to sacrifice all private gains from community development; indeed, leaders appeared attentive to the need for redistributive mechanisms, such as paying annual dividends from band-owned businesses, in order to ensure that members enjoyed collective benefits from growth. The model does assume, however, that sustained restraints on alienation are costly to individual community members – costs that members are willing to bear only insofar as their leaders continue to provide value in coordinating group efforts to generate collective gains.

Displacement and Development

While I argue that leaders have been pivotal in determining Membertou's property regime, it is likely no coincidence that the historical threat of dispossession from their lands has loomed especially large for Membertou's leaders and community members alike. The community's original reserve lands comprised approximately two acres designated in 1847 as the Kings Road Reserve, known to the Mi'kmaq as Kun'tewiktuk ("the rock"), in the heart of the city of Sydney. By the final decades of the nineteenth century, urban growth in Sydney had started to generate substantial pressures for new lands, and not only did the Kings Road Reserve occupy relatively valuable harbourfront property but it was also situated along an increasingly busy transportation artery into the city. Along with rising land values, the Mi'kmaw community's visibility fuelled animosity and a pervasive racism on the part of non-Indigenous residents and city officials who regarded the community as "a clog in the development of that part of the city" and who would subsequently pursue several avenues to force the community's relocation.[74]

Beginning the late 1800s, these efforts on the part of local business elites and city officials were staunchly resisted by community leaders, who were supported by some federal bureaucrats worried that relocation would contribute to the rapid collapse of the community's economic and social fabric. Early on, advocates of relocation had few legal options to force the community to move, but amendments to the *Indian Act* in 1912 eliminated the prior requirement for community consent to a surrender of reserve lands and, on this basis, the question of relocation was referred to the Exchequer

Court for judicial resolution. In 1916, the court ruled in favour of relocating the community of approximately 120 individuals then residing at Kings Road to a site of approximately sixty-five acres on the city outskirts, issuing an order for $5,000 in collective compensation for the removal.[75] It was not until a decade later that the displacement was finally initiated, after which all individuals who continued to reside at Kings Road were relocated.

Despite the predictions of INAC officials, the community would survive its dispossession to the new location at Membertou but oppressive economic and social conditions persisted there for much of the twentieth century. Until the 1990s, Membertou relied primarily on federal transfers to sustain itself and – with few operative businesses and high unemployment – was almost entirely dependent on federal oversight. By the mid-1990s, however, under the influence of Chief Terrance Paul and a carefully assembled executive cohort, the community began to experience a dramatic shift in economic development by building a suite of commercial enterprises owned and operated through the Membertou Development Corporation (MDC). The range of businesses now operated by the MDC includes an insurance brokerage, a data centre, a geomatics services company, a trade and convention centre, a commercial realty business, a seafood company, and extensive on-reserve gaming operations. Unlike Westbank, Membertou has not pursued these initiatives by leveraging its land base through long-term leases, but instead acts as the primary business owner and operator. Likely as a consequence of this path, Membertou has not seen extensive non-member residential development on its reserve lands.

In this case, the price of successful leadership and its attendant economic gains did not appear to come in the form of material gains for leaders,[76] but from members' agreement to go along with – if not always active support for – leaders' vision for a community that would generate economic growth while sustaining collective relationships with its lands. Those private costs were likely not insignificant, as community members gave up individual gains from land allotments and new land markets and, at least initially, endured strict austerity measures as the community reoriented its finances and dug itself out from a deep fiscal deficit.

Before these leaders and their supporting political institutions are described in more detail, two alternative explanations for Membertou's apparent commitment to inalienability during its formative period of economic development deserve attention. First, the small size of Membertou's reserve lands relative to its population – perhaps coupled with its history of land loss and dislocation from the Kings Road Reserve – may have raised the relative costs of land transactions for the community and caused members to prioritize inalienability over shorter-term gains from liberalized land markets. Without large tracts of surplus land to lease to outside developers, Membertou would likely have confronted different investment opportunities than communities such as Westbank, whose relative reserve land base is at least an order of magnitude larger. Scale effects – such as the increasing returns associated with larger land developments like new residential subdivisions – may also have played a role in making alienability a less attractive option. Certainly, an important component of Membertou's development plan has been to purchase non-reserve lands for band-owned projects, often in strategic locations in other parts of Sydney. Yet if land scarcity were the predominant explanation for Membertou's trajectory, we would expect to observe a shortage of available residential or commercial lots on reserve, whereas there appears to have been an ample supply of lands for new business projects and to meet the housing needs of existing residents. That is not to suggest that the community's historical experience of dispossession may not have exerted a powerful influence over the values and perspectives of the Membertou leadership and at least some members of the community. This dynamic, however, is consistent with the model, providing a possible background explanation for how leaders ultimately came to adopt their commitments to sustaining a regime of inalienable land rights.

Second, on the demand side, the city of Sydney experienced its own economic downturn from the late 1960s, precipitated by closures in its primary steel and coal mining industries.[77] These closures dealt a strong blow to the local economy from which it has yet to recover. From this perspective, Membertou may not have faced Westbank's level of rapid regional population growth, outside demand for affordable housing – especially in the form of mobile home parks – or expanding markets for other commercial developments. While Membertou's surrounding region in Cape Breton does have a viable tourism economy, this too is relatively weak compared with the rapidly growing demand for vacation and retirement properties in the more temperate Okanagan Valley. But we might expect that poorer regional economic conditions, at best, only partially explain the different trajectories of Westbank and Membertou. While these conditions could reasonably depress the demand for Membertou lands, it would be surprising if that demand were eliminated entirely. The near-complete rejection of liberalized land markets and lack of any long-term leases on the Membertou reserve suggest some broader commitment to sustaining inalienability rules over the long term.

Leaders' Commitments

Chief Terrance Paul has been Membertou's leading figure during its formative period of economic development, elected in the mid-1980s and re-elected to the position continuously for over thirty years. Paul was born in Membertou in 1951, where he grew up in conditions of deep poverty.[78] By his early twenties, he had joined the exodus of young Mi'kmaq leaving the province in search of employment.[79] Paul eventually settled in Boston, where the urban Indigenous population of 4,000–5,000 were majority Mi'kmaq and Wolastoqiyik from Nova Scotia and New Brunswick seeking to escape poor social conditions and high unemployment in their home communities.[80]

In Boston, Paul found work as a job placement officer with the Boston Indian Council (BIC, now the North American Indian Center of Boston), a federally funded Indigenous organization founded in 1968 with a broad mandate to help resettle newcomers in the Boston area, assist them in finding temporary job placements, and support new skills and training for long-term employment, as well as provide limited legal support for immigration and other issues.[81] The BIC was equally involved in providing cultural supports and teaching Indigenous traditions through skills and language courses and public art projects.[82] The organization was also active in federal advocacy efforts around tax policies and income supplements. Shortly after joining the BIC, Paul was promoted to director of finance and eventually became its president for a period, after which, in 1978, he left Boston to return home to Membertou. Paul's experiences through the BIC working with Indigenous diasporas living in a large urban centre may have influenced his later commitments around land and development at home. During his time at the BIC, the organization also partnered with the Harvard Business School, a relationship that would, according to Paul, have an impact on his commitment to open and transparent business practices during his political career.[83]

Paul was first elected chief of Membertou in 1984, but it was not until the mid-1990s that his leadership began to yield tangible economic gains for the community. One of Paul's key strategic decisions during this early period was to attract back to Membertou highly skilled community members who had moved away for other educational or employment opportunities.[84] These recruits formed a core executive team that would succeed in eventually eliminating the community's deficit and balancing its budget, though not without imposing a period of strict fiscal austerity on the band.[85] These individuals were primarily businesspeople and corporate lawyers who envisioned Membertou's new governance model as itself a kind of corporate entity, often blurring the lines between the community's political and corporate development arms.[86] At the centre of this approach was a dual commitment to band-led development – often through partnerships with outside businesses – and strict community control over on-reserve land rights. Membertou's leaders made it "quite clear ... that property ownership on the reserve is not available to either outside companies or band members for commercial purposes."[87] Consistent with this corporate model, community leaders signalled their emphasis on band-led commercial partnerships and the generation of collective wealth in the MDC's Statement of Principles:[88]

- To create wealth and development for the Membertou First Nation community;
- To disseminate Membertou's corporate vision and strategy to its community and to the corporate world;
- To define and develop relationships with potential partners in the corporate sector;
- To promote efficiency and profitability within Membertou's current businesses;
- To establish investment protocols for all profits created by the corporate strategy to the maximum benefit of the Membertou Band and its community;
- To create partnerships with other Mi'kmaq First Nations to ensure that those communities share in Membertou's intellectual properties and corporate success; and
- To develop a strategy that ensures that all of Membertou's corporate entities are operated in a fashion that conveys our commitment to excellence.

From this perspective, band-led corporate development served as a kind of direct substitute for a regime of alienable private land rights that members might otherwise have used to develop reserve lands individually or to initiate transfers to outside investors. While leaders' choice of a corporate model has no doubt produced robust growth for the community and improved members' economic well-being, this path would nevertheless have required members' active compliance to forgo any expected private gains associated with a liberalized land regime of the type pursued in Westbank. These private opportunity costs, rather than material payments in the form of higher salaries or favourable land deals, represent the "rents" demanded by Membertou's leadership in exchange for their instrumental value in coordinating the community's efforts for improved development.

Political Institutions

Given the nature of these leadership rents, the model in Chapter 3 raises two significant challenges. First, it is not clear how leaders and community members in Membertou agreed on the level of rents when such payments are not made in easily quantifiable terms of land or money. While formal restraints on alienating the fee in reserve lands under the federal *Indian Act* are clear, the legislation provides for other mechanisms – especially land allotments and long-term leases – that can support a range of more or less liberalized land markets. Decisions about the degree to which these mechanisms are employed in turn can influence future rule changes during more formal processes of land reform. There are, in other words, multiple possible equilibria available along the spectrum of inalienability and it is not immediately clear from the theoretical model what kind of mechanism might serve to select between these equilibria in practice. Second, given its inherent uncertainty, the scope of members' support for leaders' non-material goals are subject to change over time. Although material leadership rents can be set with relative precision *ex ante,* it is nearly impossible for leaders to demand – and for members to agree to supply – a fixed level of non-material rents as the basis for a complete contract.[89] Membertou's leaders are therefore expected to have established some way to deal with the incomplete contracting problem in order to successfully sustain the community's consent to a regime of inalienable land rights over time.

With respect to the problem of equilibrium selection, well-publicized principles conveyed by the leadership go some way toward defining how strictly alienability will be restrained in fact – for example, in the face of particular development projects or opportunities requiring a long-term land lease or surrender. Such principles specific to land were only indirectly introduced through the MDC's Statement of Principles above, and appear to have been largely absent in local channels of communication with community members, such as other public statements by leaders, regular newsletters or local media, a community land use plan, or a community constitution. Instead, Membertou's leadership appeared to turn to an unexpected alternative – a set of high-profile legal actions of national significance for Indigenous land rights, which leaders used to publicize and make concrete their commitments to preserve historical relationships with their lands and to balance economic growth with other social and cultural objectives.

Membertou leaders were especially active in supporting legal claims that asserted both substantive and procedural rights concerning the community's traditional lands and waters during Membertou's formative period of development. While it is not unusual that Membertou, like several other First Nations in Canada, pursued litigation to ensure legal recognition for these rights, the timing of these cases, the form in which they were litigated, and the degree to which they were supported by the leadership are all consistent with the claim that the court actions expressed and reinforced leaders' commitments to territorial integrity and the historical relationship of the community to its lands. While neither of the cases I highlight below concerned Membertou's reserve lands, the public legal claims on which they stood lent clarity and a certain degree of legitimacy to the commitments of leaders attempting to resist pressures to liberalize reserve land markets. This picture not only helps explain how Membertou's leaders addressed the problem of equilibrium selection but also illuminates the complex interplay between what are sometimes treated as separate and distinct legal regimes – one dealing with reserve lands, governed by federal statute, and the other dealing with claims to Aboriginal title and treaty rights.

Second, Membertou's leaders constructed a set of new, inclusive political institutions that addressed the incomplete contracting and credible commitment problems. First and foremost, the leadership institutionalized means for community members to provide their input on key economic development decisions, especially when these had the potential to affect community control over its land base. Specific mechanisms such as community-wide referenda also appeared linked to the development of an active political culture in which members felt free to challenge or contest leaders' proposals. Likewise, and in line with its corporate-type governance model, Membertou leaders created new systems of accountability that encouraged open and transparent monitoring of leaders' decisions about land and development. In this way, community members could more easily track the degree to which leaders were adhering to actions that fell within the scope of their claimed rents. Finally, the Membertou leadership established a strict separation from the federal bureaucracy responsible for oversight of reserve land governance, thereby signalling to community members that leaders were acting with relative autonomy, as well as potentially making leaders more responsive to their members without the sometimes countervailing pressures of accounting for their actions to bureaucrats at the federal level.

Equilibrium Selection

The 1990s were a decade of rapid judicial development in the area of Indigenous resource and land rights in Canada, spurred on by a significant shift in federal policy in the early 1970s and the addition of section 35 to the *Constitution Act, 1982,* in which "the existing aboriginal and treaty rights of the aboriginal peoples of Canada are hereby recognized and affirmed."[90] Beginning with *R v Sparrow,*[91] the Supreme Court of Canada issued a series of decisions that mapped the content of Indigenous natural resource rights under section 35, as well as its decision on Aboriginal title in *Delgamuukw v British Columbia.*[92] These developments also preceded the Supreme Court's efforts a decade later to expand the procedural rights of Indigenous peoples who were in the process of asserting their entitlements to protected lands and resources.[93]

Much of this early litigation occurred in Western Canada over lands where historical treaties were never completed. In 1999, the focus shifted to Atlantic Canada with the Supreme Court's decision in *R v Marshall.*[94] In 1993, Donald Marshall Jr., a prominent member of the Membertou First Nation, was arrested and prosecuted under the federal *Fisheries Act* for eel fishing off the coast of Pomquet Harbour and selling his catch without a licence.[95] Marshall argued that the "Trade Clause" of a 1760 treaty with the

British continued to protect his right to harvest and trade fish without external regulation. The Supreme Court's decision in *Marshall* recognized the right of the Mi'kmaq to fish for a "moderate livelihood" and gave this right priority over other commercial demands on Atlantic fish stocks, setting off a national backlash from politicians in Ottawa and from other commercial fishers in the region that was "frequently threatening and occasionally violent."[96]

By the time the *Marshall* case was litigated in the early 1990s, Donald Marshall Jr. was already a well-known figure in Atlantic Canada and nationally for his arrest and wrongful conviction for murder in 1971, his subsequent acquittal by the Nova Scotia Court of Appeal in 1983, and an ensuing Royal Commission that criticized the prosecution of Marshall's case and located its failures in the systemic racism of the criminal justice system.[97] The *Marshall* fisheries case built on a long history of Mi'kmaq engagement with Canadian courts to protect and gain recognition for their resource rights.[98] While it is not clear that Marshall's *Fisheries Act* charge was elicited specifically to generate a test case on Mi'kmaq fishing rights,[98] he appears to have been actively encouraged by the Membertou leadership to continue asserting his fishing rights in the face of federal orders to desist. According to Chief Paul's own public statement:[100]

> So of course we had our lawyer involved in this and he certainly understood the treaties and the rights that we have. And after a very short discussion about what was going on, we were advised to tell [Donald Marshall] Jr. to keep fishing. So Jr. had called me about three or four times and that was my answer, "Keep fishing." So finally the government took us to court. This is what everybody wanted to do anyway. We certainly wanted to do it because we believed that we had that right and the treaty gave us that right.

Marshall's profile as a prominent national figure undoubtedly contributed to the case's suitability as test litigation.[101] Membertou's leaders also contributed directly to funding for the defence in *Marshall* – which at trial alone amounted to forty days of hearing time – through two regional organizations representing the thirteen Mi'kmaq communities in Nova Scotia, the Union of Nova Scotia Indians and the Confederacy of Mainland Mi'kmaq.[102]

The legal question litigated in *Marshall* concerned the scope of Mi'kmaq treaty rights to fish and was therefore distinct from any legal issues concerning Membertou's reserve lands, but the case gave public expression to two fundamental ideas that signalled and clarified the scope of Membertou's leaders' commitments in the latter context: (1) individuals and communities would fight vigorously to protect legal entitlements to lands, waters, and resources, which were seen as central to Mi'kmaq culture and societies; and (2) these entitlements had an important functional role to play in sustaining and growing modern Mi'kmaq livelihoods and economies.

With respect to the first of these principles, the Supreme Court affirmed in *Marshall* that the Trade Clause of the 1760 treaty did in fact create an enforceable treaty right "to continue to obtain necessaries through hunting and fishing by trading the products of those traditional activities," rather than a kind of time-limited covenant that subjected the Mi'kmaq to a temporary trade regulatory regime.[103] That is, the case was a success for the litigants insofar as it established judicial recognition that the 1760 and other Peace and Friendship Treaties signed during this era grounded a set of persistent entitlements supported by a reading of the texts as "a shared understanding of and commitment to a normative framework for cross-cultural relationships."[104] On the functional role of these treaty rights, the litigants would argue that the Trade Clause established a general right of the Mi'kmaq to fish commercially and not merely for subsistence needs. The Supreme Court agreed, though only in part, finding that the treaty language of "necessaries" translated into a right to fish for a "moderate livelihood" rather than a right to "trade generally for economic gain."[105]

In the same year that the Supreme Court's *Marshall* decision was released, Membertou leaders – again through the Union of Nova Scotia Indians – also challenged a decision of the National Energy

Board approving the $3 billion Sable Island natural gas pipeline project and finding that the project proponents had complied with requirements to consult and coordinate with Indigenous communities affected by the project.[106] The Mi'kmaq claimants were successful at the Federal Court of Appeal in overturning the board's decision on the ground that it had breached the requirements of procedural fairness by failing to provide the claimants with a fair hearing. By temporarily putting a stop to the project, the Court of Appeal's ruling provided the claimants with sufficient leverage to force the project proponents to negotiate. While Membertou leaders were insistent on their rights to participate in decisions about the pipeline affecting their community, they were also pragmatic about its economic potential, ultimately using their successes in the courts to negotiate for greater inclusion of community members in employment related to the project and a broader role for the community as a whole in regulatory oversight.

These successes in court no doubt benefited Membertou by giving outside business interests incentives to recognize land and resource rights and to collaborate with community leaders on proposed resource development projects,[107] but the leaders' dedication to pursuing these cases also had the effect of signalling their commitments to their members internally. The lengthy public legal proceedings, particularly in *Marshall,* defined the scope of those commitments more robustly than would have been possible through mere statements of principle in corporate charters, during band elections, or in the normal course of community affairs.[108] Whatever else these cases achieved – and each one had significant accomplishments in its own right – they provided an effective means for Membertou's leaders to define the scope and level of their leadership rents in pursuit of local economic development on reserve lands, signalling to community members that the preservation of the community's lands for future generations would remain a priority while demonstrating that leaders were attentive to the community's pressing economic needs and would not use inalienability rules as an absolute bar to development.[109]

Credible Commitments

Even as these legal actions helped to define the form and level of leadership rents, it would still be implausible to assume that the admittedly broad background principles above constituted the basis of a complete contract to which leaders could credibly commit. The nature of inalienability rules and the changing environment of local economic development are such that non-material rents of this type inevitably require change and redefinition over time. In order for leaders to sustain an equilibrium supported by the compliance of their members, the model predicts more robust political institutions than those needed in cases where only monetary or other material rents are under consideration.

Inclusive Institutions

As in Westbank, the formal rules governing the participation of Membertou's members in land transactions, including approval of long-term leases and land surrenders, are set out in the federal *Indian Act,* though, as we have seen, these procedures can be used to centralize control in a single leader or small executive. The *Indian Act* also establishes relevant rules for election of the band chief and council. Membertou's leadership went well beyond the *Indian Act* regime to implement a more robust set of political institutions that provided for community input at pivotal moments in local land development, especially on land issues seen as directly impacting individual members. In constructing these political institutions, leaders also appeared to draw to a degree on traditional Mi'kmaw decision-making institutions.[110] The theoretical model predicts that these more inclusive arrangements were crucial in sustaining the community's consent to preserve the inalienability of Membertou lands over time.

Of particular importance was the frequent use of a community referendum mechanism developed by the leadership to get input directly from members on key decisions that included the potential for the transfer of property interests in reserve lands to third parties. In the mid-1990s, the Nova Scotia provincial government began to permit gaming operations on reserve lands and signalled its willingness to negotiate revenue-sharing agreements as a means of supporting community economic development. The construction of gambling venues with video gaming terminals in particular offered a lucrative business opportunity to build from tourism markets already established through a nearby casino operated by the city of Sydney. When confronted with such a development opportunity, however, Membertou's chief and council took the decision to a community vote, where it was defeated on the basis that benefits from the development would be too concentrated in the hands of a few developers and inadequately shared by the community as a whole.[111] The proposal was, in one observer's terms, built on a "private entrepreneur model."[112] A redesigned plan was then formulated in which the band itself, through its development corporation, would build and operate the gaming facilities. This reworked proposal also included a plan to pay annual dividends from the development to each community member, providing a means for direct redistribution of gains from the project. The latter proposal was adopted by the community in a subsequent referendum with 87 percent support.[113] By 2003, annual band revenues – of which about one-third were related to gaming – had grown to $21 million.[114] In a more recent example, Membertou's leadership has opened an online referendum to community members on legislative reforms concerning the division of matrimonial property on reserve.[115]

Over time, Membertou also developed other participatory governance mechanisms, some of which appeared to borrow heavily from its corporate shareholder model and were designed to build members' confidence in the leadership. These included more formalized processes for members' participation in regular band council meetings, as well as the appointment of divisional managers as points of first contact to receive members' complaints or feedback.[116]

Transparent and Accountable Governance

As a representative for Chief Paul testified before the House of Commons Standing Committee on Aboriginal Affairs and Northern

Development in 2012, "accountability, transparency, and disclosure of information to our people is very important to our leadership and all members in the community, whether it be elders, youth, young mothers, or children."[117] In theory, inclusive collective choice institutions that enable *ex ante* participation in decision making can go only so far toward addressing the problem of credible commitment. Community members must also be able to monitor and evaluate their leaders' performance *ex post* in order to determine whether or not they have upheld their side of the bargain.[118] Consistent with this theory, Membertou developed a set of robust – and in some instances unique – mechanisms that have attracted national recognition as a model of good governance. Some of these mechanisms were relatively straightforward, though no less effective in bringing community members along. For example, Chief Paul implemented a set of requirements for disseminating the band's annual audited financial statements directly to all members, as well as posting them publicly – a system that preceded what are now federal requirements for such disclosures under the *First Nations Financial Transparency Act,* passed in 2013.[119] While these public disclosures no doubt increased the confidence of Membertou's partners in joint commercial ventures, their dissemination directly to members also indicates that leaders viewed the procedures as playing a significant role in providing the community with the means to participate in ongoing monitoring of leaders' decisions and activities.

Other initiatives involved more extensive governance reforms. Foremost among these was the community's successful effort to gain ISO 9000 certification. This process required Membertou to meet a set of voluntary international standards administered by the International Standards Organization and normally sought by corporations to increase customer and investor confidence and to signal management and production quality. When Membertou acquired its certification in 2005, it was the only First Nation in Canada to have done so[220] – what management researcher Jacquelyn Scott characterized as a "watershed decision for changes in operational management practices" in the community, one that served in part "as a signal of Band credibility" and had "significant impacts on band governance."[121] As with financial disclosures, the ISO certification process was only partly oriented outward to business partners and customers; it also "required an extensive transformation of the Band's relationship with its community members."[122] More surprisingly, leaders testified to the opportunities for using the process to articulate and translate traditional Mi'kmaw governance practices already in use in the community into those that were recognized in the standards program, perhaps generating further support from a diverse constituency of community members.[123]

Distance from the Federal Bureaucracy

Finally, a significant component of the leadership cohort's approach to creating space for membership input and direction in Membertou was to rely on a set of land use practices and property rights that circumvented the formal requirements of the *Indian Act* and thus the federal bureaucracy in Ottawa. While on the surface these mechanisms appeared to work against the rigorous accountability processes established by the leadership, they may well have been instrumental in addressing the incomplete-contracting problem by distancing leaders from the perception that they were too closely aligned with federal bureaucrats and thus insufficiently responsive to the membership. This is in stark contrast with Westbank, where a frequently repeated accusation in the course of the Hall Inquiry was that community leaders were too closely aligned with INAC officials and too disconnected from local demands.

One distancing mechanism in Membertou was the use of so-called buckshee leases to rent commercial premises on reserve to non-member businesses. These buckshee leases were informal rental arrangements used to avoid the onerous federal approval processes required even for non-land leases. They were unenforceable in the courts, and thus "rooted in a high degree of goodwill with significant reliance on Membertou's good name."[124] Nevertheless, they were a useful business practice that minimized transaction costs while also evading one of Ottawa's key levers of control.

A second strategy pursued by Membertou was simply to purchase fee simple lands adjacent to the reserve on which to undertake larger development projects.[125] Although these projects were ineligible for the favourable tax treatment they would have enjoyed if constructed within the reserve, Membertou could undertake development on these lands free from federal oversight.

Conclusions

The comparative case studies in this chapter are largely consistent with the theoretical model's predictions from Chapter 3. In both cases, prominent leaders were pivotal in determining how their communities responded to the long history of restraints on the alienation of Indigenous lands as they confronted new contexts and challenges of self-governance. Guided by different objectives and commitments, these leaders established durable political institutions to sustain a kind of social contract with their membership that would distribute the benefits from local economic development.

It is worth emphasizing here that the theoretical model sought to describe how inalienability was sustained or not, but generated no predictions about whether alienable or inalienable land rights were optimal in these particular cases. Both Westbank and Membertou have, each in its own way, grown their local economies and made considerable strides in building new systems of lands self-governance.

What the comparison between these cases reveals is the important influence of community leaders on institutional change and the surprising connection between inalienability and political institutions. Communities that resist the liberalization of land rights are sometimes characterized as insular and plagued by graft, but the case studies in this chapter call this assumption into question. To the extent that inalienability represents a net cost to individual group members, leaders committed to sustaining such regimes may actually be more likely to forgo personal material gains. And as Membertou's experience illustrates, leaders who wish to maintain these commitments to inalienability face an imperative to develop open and accountable political institutions that involve community members directly in decision making, offer opportunities for monitoring, and establish the leadership's autonomy from outside influence.

A second issue that has gained increasing attention in law and development contexts concerns the sequencing of institutional reforms – namely, that more open and accountable political institutions must be established first, before economic institutions such as regimes for property and contractual rights can be implemented.[126] The case studies in this chapter complicate this view by demonstrating that political reforms might sometimes be "led" by property reforms and other institutional changes, at least insofar as the latter are closely bound up with the objectives and preferences of influential leaders. This is an insight that I explore further in Chapter 6.

The next chapter builds on these and other lessons by investigating another set of comparative cases that are located in more remote geographies and concern communities that have undergone more extensive land and governance reforms through modern treaty agreements. These additional cases provide a different context in which to test and revise the theoretical model.

5
Ideas and Interests in Uncertain Times

The dynamics of property regime change during formative periods in the Westbank and Membertou First Nations were largely consistent with the predictions of the theoretical model developed in Chapter 3. In that model, community members who collectively contribute their effort toward local land reforms comply with leaders' goals not because those goals are necessarily shared by the membership but because it is generally in their interests to go along. Moreover, when leaders craft political institutions that reinforce the contingent bargain they strike with community members, the equilibria supported by those political institutions can be relatively stable in practice. For leaders committed to sustaining regimes of inalienable rights, these findings may come as something of a surprise. Going along with leaders' goals necessarily has its limits, but the model implies that leaders may not need to expend additional effort or other resources to convince their followers about the merits of a particular course of action for institutional change, as long as the leaders continue to make good on the expected benefits of their leadership.

This instrumental view on leadership in institutional change is at odds, however, with the "charismatic" role so often ascribed to prominent leaders in other areas of the organizational and managerial literature. Here, leaders "by the force of their personal abilities are capable of having profound and extraordinary effects on followers," acting as "revolutionary social forces ... responsible for significant societal transformations."[1] In other words, a causal role is frequently ascribed to leaders' ideas, aspirations, and preferences based on how they shape public debate and persuade others to redefine and reinterpret their own interests – a role that seems impossible to overlook amid the contested politics of Indigenous land rights in Canada, especially given the historical context described in Chapter 2 and the high stakes of reform for communities working toward lands self-governance and economic security.

In formal terms, this chapter explores the "charismatic" influence of leaders on property transitions by relaxing two key assumptions from the baseline model above: first, that community members have a uniform set of private incentives favouring greater alienability irrespective of the leader's own goals, and second, that community members' preferences are well defined. I examine the new predictions generated by the theoretical model when members' preferences for or against alienable land rights are both heterogeneous and uncertain from the outset.

In order to test the implications of revising these two assumptions, I develop two additional case studies based on land regime changes by the James Bay Cree Nation in northern Quebec and the Nisga'a Nation in northwestern British Columbia. These cases differ from the Westbank and Membertou First Nations in two principal respects. First, both First Nations studied in this chapter comprise several remote communities in northern environments located hundreds or thousands of kilometres from the nearest major urban centres in Montreal and Vancouver. In these settings, natural resource development and traditional modes of production, including hunting and trapping, fishing, and forestry, form important components of the Cree and Nisga'a economies. Second, whereas Westbank and Membertou undertook more incremental land reforms – initially under the *Indian Act* and later using legislative tools such as self-governance agreements and new land management regimes – both the James Bay Cree and the Nisga'a belong to a small number of First Nations in Canada who have entered into modern treaty agreements through extensive negotiations with federal and provincial governments.[2] These modern treaties encompass large tracts of land and delineate the division of legal authorities over several dimensions of community governance, some of which go well beyond issues of land rights. Compared with the smaller areas of reserve land and the narrower focus on sectoral reform defining land rights and management authorities in Westbank and Membertou, the Cree and Nisga'a cases cover reforms that are both less incremental and considerably more complex along the spectrum of potential alienability rules, making the outcomes of institutional change more difficult for all parties involved to predict.

These geographic and institutional features of the Nisga'a and James Bay Cree regimes are consistent with the new assumptions I make in this chapter about community members' heterogeneous and uncertain preferences for land reform, explained in greater detail below. Based on these new assumptions, the extension of my theoretical model seeks to explain the diversity in both alienability and political institutions between these cases by also accounting for leaders' substantive ideas and the discursive practices they undertook to develop and convey those ideas. I argue that, in the face of uncertain preferences on the part of community members, both Nisga'a and Cree leaders had incentives to invest early in efforts to align community preferences for land reform with their own. Moreover, the ideas held by leaders had causal effects on political institutions in each community.

I start by developing the theoretical extensions to my baseline model before testing the new set of resulting predictions against the Nisga'a and James Bay Cree case studies.

Integrating Ideas

In Chapter 3, the baseline model assumed that individual community members faced private incentives to develop a regime of alienable land rights, such that any restraints on alienation were taken as a private cost in the form of forgone gains from trade, which members paid as non-material leadership rents in exchange for leaders' honest disclosure of their privileged information. In urban settings with growing populations that generate strong demand for marketable land, this structure of private incentives may be a plausible generalization across the community as a whole. So while individuals in Membertou were willing to comply with leaders' demands to sustain restraints on alienation that worked against their private incentives, they did so not necessarily because they preferred a regime of inalienability on its own terms but because they recognized that it was in their interests to go along. The power of this approach was that it explained how some inalienability regimes are sustained even when community members do not share their leader's own commitments to preserving control over the land.

The assumption that community members hold homogeneous preferences for land reform is relaxed here to acknowledge that in other settings, demands for individuated alienable land rights over private tracts of land are likely to be greatly attenuated. At the same time, First Nations in remote settings are more likely to face pressures for natural resource development over much larger areas of their collectively held lands and waters. Undoubtedly, these development pressures and possibilities have generated monetary, employment, and other benefits for some communities in return for the alienation or the negotiated cession of community land rights. But they have also raised the potential costs of alienability – in terms of both the scale of transfers and the threat of future negative externalities from forestry, hydroelectric development, and other projects, particularly in their effects on hunting, fishing, and other forms of traditional livelihood. As a result, these conditions likely increase the probability that community members hold heterogeneous preferences for or against alienable land rights. While some may favour legal reforms to liberalize land markets and pave the way for natural resource development or as a means to collateralize smaller tracts of land, others may prefer to sustain strict regimes of inalienability in the face of immediate threats related to the negative socio-economic, cultural, and environmental impacts of reform.

The lack of strong private incentives for liberalized land markets also makes it plausible that, prior to fundamental changes such as the implementation of a new treaty regime, many community members in the settings explored in this chapter did not form well-defined preferences regarding land market liberalization, for at least two reasons. First, even while reserve land regimes under the *Indian Act* provided for limited forms of transferable entitlements, the lack of demand for such entitlements meant that community members might have been only infrequently, if ever, confronted with questions about their preferences for or against alienable rights. Second, the new land regimes negotiated under modern treaty agreements present more complex and uncertain choices around inalienability. It is generally difficult, if not impossible, to determine from the outset both the content and consequences of the forms of property that will emerge when a new treaty is initially negotiated.[3]

A renewed emphasis on ideas and beliefs in theories of institutional change has drawn new attention to the central role of uncertainty in how individual preferences and interests come to be defined and interpreted. In her study about the formation of corporate interests in the context of liberalizing global services trade, Cornelia Woll points to a growing divergence in how the concept of uncertainty has come to be defined in relation to economic rationality.[4] While neoclassical theory generally defines uncertainty as a lack of knowledge about expected costs and benefits, economic sociologists have argued that uncertainty is best understood as a "lack of knowledge about relationships between means and ends"[5] – a distinction first popularized by the economist Frank Knight in the early twentieth century, who defined the former concept as "risk" to distinguish it from the concept of uncertainty as the lack of "a well-defined mapping from 'interests' to 'outcomes.'"[6] Over time, this definition of Knightian uncertainty was gradually conflated with, and ultimately supplanted by, the concept of risk in neoclassical economics, leaving little room to connect situations of complex decision making with the formation of actors' interests over time.

Uncertainty and Heterogeneity

To extend the theory, I return to John Ahlquist and Margaret Levi's study of dockside trade unions, which served as the basis for the model described in Chapter 3. Ahlquist and Levi acknowledge the possibility of heterogeneous and uncertain preferences for or against leaders' political projects and explore how union leaders managed heterogeneity after they had established their basic instrumental value to the union membership. Recall that, in the setting of team production, each member of the team contributes effort (e_i) and leadership rents (r_i), yielding utility that is subject to an unknown productivity factor, θ:

$$U_{it} = \frac{\theta_t}{N}(e_{it} + \sum_{J=2}^{N} e_{Jt}) - \frac{e_{it}^2}{2} - \frac{r_{it}^2}{2}, \forall i > 1 \qquad (1.3)$$

In this model, group members are agnostic about the substance of total rents, $R = (N - 1)r_i$, paid to the leader in exchange for effective group leadership. That is, members uniformly express no preference for or against the objectives of the leader and are instrumentally supportive of those objectives only insofar as they induce the leader to truthfully reveal the value of θ. As Ahlquist and Levi observe, introducing the assumption of heterogeneous preferences implies that group members can and sometimes do hold private valuations of leaders' rents, represented by a parameter, γ_i, such that:[7]

$$U_{it} = \frac{\theta_t}{N}(e_{it} + \sum_{J=2}^{N} e_{Jt})_t - \frac{e_{it}^2}{2} + \gamma_{it} R - \frac{r_{it}^2}{2}, \forall i > 1 \qquad (6.1)$$

In this revised model, γ_i indicates the degree to which an individual's preferences for land reform are aligned or not with those of the leader. Group members with $\gamma_i < 0$ will be opposed to the leader's goals and experience leadership rents as a pure cost, while those with $\gamma_i > 0$ will derive additional utility from pursuing the leader's goals, independent of the benefits they derive from truthful leadership. Because γ_i is specific to each individual within the group, the distribution of γ_i describes whether and to what extent the leader enjoys community support, in the aggregate, for the leader's preferred direction of reform.

Extending the model in this way opens up the possibility that leaders may invest resources not only to deliver the benefits of good leadership to members by furthering local economic development but also to persuade members that it is in their own interests to follow the leader's preferred path of institutional change. In Membertou and Westbank – two urban reserves in which private incentives to create and participate in liberalized land markets were assumed to be high – there was little evidence that community leaders communicated with their membership in ways that were intended to persuade them that the leaders' aims were valid. Members' compliance with sustaining inalienability in Membertou was mainly explained by the instrumental benefits that leaders offered rather than by any success leaders might have had in persuading members to go along. In the Nisga'a and James Bay Cree cases, I describe below how leaders were more heavily invested in communicating with and persuading their members in ways apparently designed to change their beliefs and to convince them of the benefits of the proposed reforms.

For Ahlquist and Levi, the introduction of heterogeneous and initially uncertain preferences among union members underpins a process of what they call "preference provocation," whereby individuals first follow their leaders for instrumental reasons but gradually have their values of γ_i revealed after participating in union activities.[8] This process generates an emergent heterogeneity among members' preferences to which leaders must respond, often through some of the very political institutions that leaders themselves construct to deal with equilibrium selection and commitment problems. To the extent that leaders can "manage" such heterogeneity after it emerges, they have a better chance of remaining in office and continuing to enjoy leadership rents.

The Nisga'a and James Bay Cree cases suggest that a different process may be taking place in the context of land tenure reforms. In both cases, community leaders were willing to expend considerable effort to persuade their members from the outset about how future land reforms would serve their interests – well before those leaders demonstrated their effectiveness or made concrete demands on the group to undertake institutional changes. Rather than responding to divergent preferences as they emerged, leaders proactively invested in persuasive efforts and political campaigns to bring their members' beliefs and preferences into alignment with their own – presumably in anticipation that this would allow leaders to demand higher rents in the future once community members were asked to implement decisions about treaties and subsequent reforms. Just as the model in Chapter 3 predicted that leaders need to demonstrate some measure of success in local economic development as a means of building credibility before demanding leadership rents, this extension predicts that early investments in political persuasion expand the potential scope of those rents once leaders are in a position to realize them.

Revisiting Rents

The revised model also has important consequences for explaining the political institutions that Nisga'a and Cree leaders established to support their goals for land reform. Perhaps the greatest challenge for introducing heterogeneous and uncertain preferences into the model is that these new assumptions muddy the clear distinction from Chapter 3 between the two different types of rents that leaders might demand from their followers in exchange for continuing to supply the benefits of good leadership. In essence, these new assumptions reduce the explanatory power afforded to different rental "types" in the baseline model. Westbank leaders who supported land market liberalization and sought to collect well-defined material rents enjoyed centralized control over community decision making. By contrast, Membertou leaders who wished to sustain regimes of inalienable land rights confronted equilibrium selection and incomplete contracting problems that forced them to define and signal their public commitments and to design more open and inclusive political institutions that supported member participation and feedback over time. But if leaders cannot expect that community members are uniformly for or against land market liberalization and if individuals are generally uncertain about the causal link between alienability and community outcomes, then leaders' own preferences either for or against alienability are equally likely to be experienced as "ideological," or otherwise non-material, rents.

Consistent with this result, in neither of the two cases studied below is there evidence that leaders demanded or received substantial material rents. Nevertheless, Nisga'a leaders pursued a regime of marketable fee-simple-like rights, while Cree leaders demonstrated a commitment to sustaining constraints on the alienability of their lands. Because in both cases there was considerable disagreement and uncertainty about these goals among community members, leaders were forced to forgo the material rents that might have been available had their followers' preferences been well defined and more uniformly aligned. Instead, leaders in both cases were forced, at least initially, to demand rents in the form of members' willingness to go along with non-material goals.

Given that Nisga'a and Cree leaders pursued political goals that were different in their substantive commitments to alienability but nevertheless the same in type, the baseline model predicts little variation in the political institutions that evolved within each community. But while I identify a few signs of convergence, there is tentative evidence that the political institutions developed and employed by the Nisga'a are more centralized than those in James Bay. The theory therefore needs to be further extended to explain these differences. In the next section, I argue that rather than being driven by the form of leadership rents, political institutions in each case may have been shaped by the processes through which leaders' own substantive ideas about land reform and inalienability were negotiated and defined.

Discursive Institutional Analysis

Institutional analysis has increasingly sought to integrate the causal role of ideas into theories of institutional change. The revised model above suggests that leaders' ideas may play a dual role in the context of Indigenous land reform. First, because leaders have reason to invest up front in persuading community members to align their emergent preferences, leaders' ideas about land market liberalization have a more direct and substantive link to the outcomes of land reform. A deeper understanding of what those ideas are and how they came to be established, communicated, and interpreted can therefore help to explain how leaders successfully sustained their preferred pathways of reform over time by directly shaping their followers' interests. Second, the revised model raises the question of whether leaders' ideas and the process by which those ideas are formed can explain variation in the political institutions that leaders establish during formative periods to entrench their goals for reform.

In order to better understand the role played by leaders' ideas in this context, I draw on an emerging branch of institutionalist research that embraces "the explanatory power of ideas and discourse" to "show how they exert a causal influence in political reality and, thereby, engender institutional change (or continuity)." Vivien Schmidt has termed this emerging field "discursive institutionalism."[9] Less a coherent theory of change than a constellation of theoretical approaches to studying the role of ideas, discursive institutionalism nevertheless offers a set of conceptual classifications that at least begin to clarify the causal role of leaders' ideas in the Indigenous land reform context.

First, discursive institutionalists distinguish between three different levels at which ideas operate.[10] At the most concrete level, ideas are solutions offered by entrepreneurial leaders or others to respond to or resolve specific, predefined problems. Here, "alienability" and "inalienability" capture specific legal forms but also ideational solutions to a set of assumed problems confronting First Nations and in pursuit of a set of assumed objectives held by each community. But while an "idea provides the means for solving the problem and accomplishing those objectives," it is generally true that "problems and objectives are not pre-established."[11] At a higher level, ideas therefore take the form of "problem definitions" that articulate and circumscribe both the domain of lawmaking and the scope and nature of the problems to which legal solutions are addressed. Clearly, leaders not only put forward and advocate for their preferred solutions along the spectrum of possible alienability rules but also invest considerable effort in defining the broader problems to which land reforms seek to respond. Once set, these problem definitions in turn define the range and type of solutions available and influence which solutions are regarded as better or worse. Finally, ideas can operate at the level of "public philosophies" or "worldviews" that span particular problem-solution sets and speak to the whole range of underlying assumptions "that undergird the policies and programs with organizing ideas, values, and principles of knowledge and society."[12]

Notice that, at each level, ideas might address one or both concepts of uncertainty described above, either by establishing the costs and benefits of a particular reform (neoclassical uncertainty) or by providing a "mental map" of how the world works according to a set of assumed causal relationships (Knightian uncertainty).[13]

These different categories of ideas offer a way to map the persuasive effort that leaders expend to shape their followers' interests. As Schmidt points out, however, it is not enough simply to identify the ideas that leaders put forward – any plausible theory of institutional change must also describe the mechanism by which ideas are shared and contested between the different actors who interpret them. These, in their broadest sense, are the "discourses" in discursive institutionalism that encompass "both a set of ideas about public life and a process of interaction among public actors and with society at large focused on generating and legitimizing those ideas."[14] This sets the stage for a second conceptual classification offered by discursive institutionalists between the "coordinative discourses" that occur between leaders and other political elites and the "communicative discourses" by which leaders engage the public in debate and disseminate their ideas. The theory recognizes that "although polities always contain both coordinative and communicative discourses, in most circumstances one or the other predominates."[15] It appears that this trade-off between coordinative and communicative discourses may have had direct implications for the form of political institutions observed in the Nisga'a and James Bay Cree cases below.

Further Cases

For many observers of land claims negotiations in Canada, the Nisga'a and James Bay Cree Nations mark opposite ends on the spectrum of possible regimes in the modern treaty context. No stranger to the national spotlight after years of public conflict over its treaty negotiations in the 1990s, the Nisga'a Nation again captured attention when it created a regime of "Nisga'a fee simple" rights in its treaty lands. By making some Nisga'a lands available for private ownership by members and by allowing these entitlements to be traded to non-members in some cases, the Nisga'a Nation created a legal framework that would, its supporters hoped, replicate the benefits of investment certainty and credit access enjoyed by landowners elsewhere in Canada. These reforms were matched by an active pursuit of economic and business development by Nisga'a leaders, who viewed outside investment and private initiative as important conduits through which the Nisga'a would achieve resource development, self-sufficiency, and economic independence from the Canadian state.

For their part, the James Bay Cree have been engaged in an extended struggle to confront, adapt to, and at points resist the tremendous economic and political pressures driving hydroelectric development in northern Quebec. Having signed the first modern treaty regime between a First Nation and the Canadian state in 1975 after a relatively rapid period of litigation and negotiation, the Cree have since forged several new agreements through which they fought to maintain control over their lands and to protect their hunting and fishing economies and ways of life by "reproducing and transforming land tenure in a distinctly non-market form."[16] At the same time, the James Bay Cree have worked to generate new opportunities for community economic development and to capture some of the benefits from natural resource developments within their territories.[17]

But while these two First Nations have pursued different paths of institutional change, their modern legal histories have also been closely intertwined. Both nations were at the forefront of dramatic changes in Aboriginal title jurisprudence in the early 1970s and both belong the small group of First Nations in Canada with modern treaties through which the Canadian state has, with varying degrees of commitment, recognized First Nations' authorities to govern their lands and other aspects of national life. Finally, both nations have had to grapple with contentious internal debates and disagreements about the content and scope of their treaty regimes and about their implementation over time. I elaborate on each of these similarities and differences below.

Negotiating the Nisga'a Final Agreement

The *Nisga'a Final Agreement* (NFA) between the Nisga'a Nation, the Province of British Columbia, and Canada came into effect in May 2000, marking the culmination of a struggle for recognition of Nisga'a land rights spanning more than a century of colonial settlement in British Columbia.[18] At least as early as the 1880s, Nisga'a leaders were formally asserting their land rights in the face of British encroachment and displacement. Against early attempts by the colonial government to unilaterally define reserve sites for the Nisga'a throughout their traditional territories in the Nass River Valley, a delegation of Nisga'a chiefs travelled to Victoria in 1887 to issue a formal protest and invite the British to negotiate.[19] These overtures were largely ignored, however, and in that same year a Royal Commission established several small reserves for the Nisga'a, despite holding several community hearings in which the Nisga'a expressed their opposition. Soon after, in 1907, the Nisga'a formed a Land Committee as a vehicle for political and legal advocacy around the "Land Question."[20] In 1913, the Land Committee sent a petition to the Judicial Committee of the Privy Council in London, complaining of the province's unwillingness to recognize their territorial claims but again failing to achieve any meaningful changes in colonial policy.[21] Despite these setbacks, the Nisga'a Land Committee and other Indigenous organizations in British Columbia continued to pursue recognition of their land rights, though sometimes in alignment with the dominant policy themes of "integration" promoted by Canadian governments at the time.[22]

Other efforts followed, but with the enactment of amendments to the federal *Indian Act* in 1927 making it a criminal offence for First Nations and Indigenous individuals to retain a lawyer or to fundraise in support of litigation against the Crown,[23] Nisga'a advocacy around the "Land Question" was largely stalled until the provision was repealed in 1951.

The fight for recognition of Nisga'a land rights found new footing when Frank Calder was elected as a representative of the Co-operative Commonwealth Federation party in the British Columbia legislature in 1949. Only thirty-four years old at the time of his election, Calder – a hereditary chief of the Nisga'a – was the first Indigenous member of a representative government in Canadian history.[24] For the next thirty years, he exerted a powerful influence over provincial and federal politics and, as president of the Nisga'a Tribal Council, the successor to the Nisga'a Land Committee, he went on to litigate *Calder*,[25] the Supreme Court of Canada's decision that was a distinct break from past refusals by Canadian governments to recognize Aboriginal title and ushered in the modern era of land claims negotiation in Canada. While the Nisga'a were ultimately unsuccessful in proving their claims in *Calder*, the case laid the groundwork for the federal Liberals to establish a comprehensive claims process through which First Nations in British Columbia could negotiate modern land claims settlements to define and gain recognition for their land rights.[26] Just three years after the *Calder* decision, the Nisga'a began negotiations with Ottawa, though it was not until 1990 that British Columbia joined the negotiating table.

Frank Calder was replaced as president of the Nisga'a Tribal Council by another prominent Nisga'a leader, James Gosnell, in 1974. But it was Gosnell's younger brother Joseph, first elected as president of the Tribal Council in 1990, who led the main treaty negotiations through the remainder of that decade.[27] Joseph Gosnell eventually emerged as the public face of the Nisga'a treaty and, once significant public attention was devoted to the negotiations in their final stage, he became a national figure. Gosnell also proved to be a talented orator tasked with the principal job of persuading the Nisga'a people to ratify the treaty. Sometimes in tension with this role, he also oversaw a tightly controlled process of negotiations between the Nisga'a leadership, Canada, and British Columbia – one that was at times criticized by some Nisga'a citizens as an elite process that had "little contact with people in the Nass villages."[28]

Two decades after treaty negotiations began, the Nisga'a, Canada, and British Columbia signed an agreement in principle in February 1996,[29] and the agreement was ratified by the Nisga'a almost three years later, in November 1998. Particularly in the later years after 1990, once the province entered as a significant party, negotiations were difficult and the process generated considerable controversy in British Columbia.[30] The treaty was also criticized by other First Nations and Indigenous advocacy organizations because of the limited scope of the rights it defined and because it infringed on the territorial claims of other communities.[31]

The *Nisga'a Final Agreement* was also contentious within the Nisga'a Nation based on concerns about which lands would be included in the final settlement – with some families losing claims to their territories – as well as the centralization of Nisga'a national governance according to a new set of institutions that took power away from village governments and hereditary chiefs. Nisga'a citizens also raised concerns about the closed process of negotiations. As a consequence, the results of the ratification vote were highly variable, with strong support in the community of New Aiyansh, the centre of Nisga'a political activities through the Nisga'a Tribal Council and Gosnell's home community, and thinner margins in the other four Nisga'a villages.[32] Nor did internal opposition to the treaty cease after it entered into force. In 2007, a group of Nisga'a citizens challenged the constitutionality of the NFA in the courts, arguing that the treaty created a third order of government in Canada inconsistent with the federal division of powers.[33]

The Nisga'a Land Regime

The *Nisga'a Final Agreement* was the first modern treaty in Canada to define both Indigenous land rights and powers of self-government.[34]

As I describe in the next section, an overarching objective of Nisga'a leaders and a central theme of the NFA was to create a high level of certainty in delineating Nisga'a land rights and governance powers under the agreement. From the perspectives of the provincial and federal governments, this objective included the final settlement of any future claims by the Nisga'a to lands within their traditional territories. This objective is clearly set out in paragraph 23 of the NFA:

> This Agreement exhaustively sets out Nisga'a section 35 rights, the geographic extent of those rights, and the limitations to those rights, to which the Parties have agreed.[35]

The legal expression of this goal was to transform Nisga'a claims to common law Aboriginal title – i.e., those at issue in *Calder* – into a type of fee simple estate held directly by the Nisga'a Nation. Overall, the NFA covers over two thousand square kilometres of land in the Nass River Valley, roughly 8 percent of the territory initially claimed by the Nisga'a. The majority of these lands are now governed by paragraph 25 of the NFA, which provides that:

> For greater certainty, the aboriginal title of the Nisga'a Nation anywhere that it existed in Canada before the effective date is modified and continues as the estates in fee simple to those areas identified in this Agreement.[36]

The precise contours of Nisga'a property rights and the alienability of those rights are further defined at two levels. Within the NFA itself, the treaty provides that "the Nisga'a Nation owns Nisga'a Lands in fee simple, being the largest estate known in law."[37] The agreement goes on to say that the Nisga'a Nation may dispose the whole of its estate or any lesser interest in any parcel of Nisga'a lands to "any person" without the consent of Canada or British Columbia.[38]

Within this framework, the Nisga'a have utilized their powers of self-government to further define property rights in Nisga'a lands. A private land entitlement consisting of possessory rights may be granted to Nisga'a citizens directly by the Nisga'a Nation Executive or by one of the four Nisga'a village governments.[39] These original possessory entitlements – not unlike Certificates of Possession under the *Indian Act* – can be transferred only to other Nisga'a citizens or Nisga'a government entities and cannot be owned by outsiders.[40] In 2012, however, the Nisga'a passed new legislation, the *Nisga'a Landholding Transition Act,* that provided the option for possessory entitlement holders to request, and a Nisga'a village government to authorize, the vesting of the full fee simple interest in their entitlement lands.[41] Such entitlements are subject to strict conditions – namely, that the parcel is less than 0.2 hectare in size, is zoned for residential use, and is not subject to mortgage.[42] Nisga'a citizens who successfully apply for a fee simple interest are now free to transfer that interest to any person, including those who are not members of the Nisga'a Nation.

Nisga'a Leadership

Much of the popular and academic attention to the NFA negotiations and subsequent legal changes by the Nisga'a government has focused on debates about the costs and benefits of land cession and alienable land rights in the register of evaluating legal and policy solutions. But Nisga'a leaders well before this period directed their attention primarily to the task of problem definition, framing the central challenges facing their communities around the pervasive barriers of discrimination and dependency erected by the federal *Indian Act* and manifest in the unequal status of Nisga'a individuals, who lacked the full rights of citizenship and landownership afforded to other Canadians.

This perspective on the problems at the heart of the Nisga'a "Land Question" can be traced as least as far back as Frank Calder's political advocacy on behalf of the Nisga'a during his tenure as a sitting member of the provincial legislature. While Calder was no doubt a strong advocate for Indigenous self-determination, he understood that goal through the particular lens of his first campaign platform: "Equal rights for all."[43] For Calder, the greatest threat to the cultural survival of the Nisga'a and other First Nations was the system of dependency entrenched by the federal reserve system and reinforced by the other markers of difference constructed under the *Indian Act*. As a consequence, for Calder, the path to strengthening Indigenous communities lay in legal and policy reforms that promoted individual and collective self-sufficiency and economic independence. Foremost among these reforms were measures to facilitate access to private land ownership for Indigenous individuals. At that time, not only was ownership of reserve lands restricted under the *Indian Act* but provincial law prohibited the ownership of land outside reserves by Status Indians – restrictions that had directly impacted Calder's brother, who was excluded from the land settlement regime established to aid war veterans after he returned from serving in the Second World War.[44] In 1950, soon after his first election to the provincial legislature, Calder introduced a motion for a new bill of rights that among other provisions included a right to "ownership and occupation of property."[45] While this early proposal was rejected by other members of his party, Calder was ultimately successful in shepherding legislative reforms by the Social Credit government to allow off-reserve ownership in 1953.[46]

Calder's most controversial stance on issues of equal rights for Indigenous peoples came with his support of the federal Liberals' White Paper in 1969.[47] That policy, which set out the official support of Pierre Trudeau's government for repealing the *Indian Act,* abolishing the reserve system, eliminating formal Indian status and allocating former reserve lands to individuals in fee simple, met with strong organized resistance from Indigenous organizations and communities across the country who rejected the policy as a renewed attempt to further the cultural displacement of Indigenous peoples and complete their assimilation into Anglo-Canadian society. Breaking with this view, Calder emerged as a supporter of the White Paper and its approach to Crown-Indigenous relations.[48] Though he would dispute the unilateral process by which the White Paper was produced – without consultation with or input from First Nations – Calder was one of the few

Indigenous leaders to support the policy itself. This position put him at odds with other Indigenous leaders and advocacy organizations but was consistent with his past emphasis on equal voting rights, private property ownership, and economic integration.[49]

Though active in provincial and national politics, Calder also played a leading part in establishing and shaping local political institutions within the Nisga'a Nation. While governance in each of the four Nisga'a villages comprised a mix of *Indian Act* chief and council and traditional forms of governance, overarching authority to negotiate land claims was placed in the hands of a small leadership cohort. The Nisga'a Tribal Council was mainly driven by "Calder's politically sophisticated leadership, and under his direction it soon became a strike force for treaty making."[50] Calder was installed as the council's first president at its creation, a position he held until 1974.[51] Treaty negotiations with the province and the federal government in the 1980s and 1990s were largely conducted under the auspices of the Tribal Council by a small number of key Nisga'a leaders.[52]

As these negotiations proceeded, it became increasingly clear that the dual concerns of discrimination and dependency would direct attention toward the solution of creating legal "certainty" in Nisga'a lands. In order for the Nisga'a to achieve economic self-determination, they would need a regime that clearly established the legal status of their lands and moved land rights toward a degree of uniformity with non-Nisga'a rights. As described above, this overarching theme was foregrounded in the final version of the NFA and in subsequent land legislation passed by the Nisga'a Lisims Government. In making these changes to create a new regime of alienable land rights, Nisga'a leaders were careful to link them to ideas about economic prosperity and self-sufficiency. As Nisga'a president Nelson Leeson observed at the enactment of the *Nisga'a Landholding Transition Act,* "it is important for us to be able to find ways of building capacity for our people so that they can stand on their own."[53]

Equally important for the political institutions that emerged were the processes through which such ideas came to be formulated and negotiated. As a provincial and national political figure, Calder had cultivated strong connections to the centres of power in Victoria and Ottawa. In order to build on those connections and negotiate solutions to the problems that Calder and other leaders had articulated, the Nisga'a needed to design political institutions that were well suited to coordinative discourses between elite policy actors. Because typical features of such coordinative processes include closed interactions that are well insulated from community members and the broader public,[54] they are more congruent with highly centralized and largely opaque collective choice mechanisms. By consolidating decision making in the hands of a few high-level political leaders and negotiators, Nisga'a leaders may have found that they could more effectively engage with outside governments and draft a land claims agreement that purported to definitively establish the legal contours of Nisga'a land rights with the high level of certainty they sought to achieve.

An important outstanding question is to what extent these more closed and centralized arrangements for decision making in the process of treaty negotiations may have carried over to those established under the NFA itself – and to what extent they continue to shape the alienability of Nisga'a lands. Under the NFA, a central Nisga'a Lisims Government comprises legislative and executive branches established by the Nisga'a Constitution. The latter consists of an elected president, chairperson, secretary-treasurer, and other officers, and the chairperson of the Council of Elders, as well as the chief councillor of each village government and one representative from each Nisga'a urban local in major urban centres such as Vancouver.[55] Each of these officials, as well as all village councillors, sits in the Wilp Si'ayuukhi Nisga'a, the Nisga'a legislative body responsible for enacting Nisga'a laws.[56] The Council of Elders, composed of hereditary chiefs, is a non-elected advisory body to the Wilp Si'ayuukhi Nisga'a.

While I do not attempt to resolve questions about the nature or impact of Nisga'a political institutions under the NFA here, early research has begun to highlight emerging tensions around these issues. Writing in 2010, Ross Hoffman and Andrew Robinson trace efforts by the Nisga'a Lisims Government to improve communications with the Nisga'a membership, such as establishing a Communications and Intergovernmental Affairs Department "to ensure that people were aware of the complex issues in front of the elected officials, and their struggles to meet the objectives of the Nisga'a Final Agreement for our Nations' membership."[57] At the same time, they identify a "lack of participation of the Nisga'a membership during the Wilp Si'ayuukhi meetings, and in the executive meetings that take place in the Nisga'a Lisims Government building," as well as tensions over the inclusion of Nisga'a political institutions based on the role of hereditary chiefs and the organization of lineal houses.[58] The theory developed in this book suggests that how the Nisga'a navigate such tensions may have significant consequences for the alienability of Nisga'a land rights under the NFA going forward.

The James Bay and Northern Quebec Agreement

Unlike the prolonged legal and political struggles that preceded the *Nisga'a Final Agreement* in the late 1990s, the *James Bay and Northern Quebec Agreement* (JBNQA) between the James Bay Cree, the Province of Quebec, and Canada in 1975 was signed just four years after Quebec premier Robert Bourassa first announced that his government would pursue "the project of the century" – a massive hydroelectric project in northern Quebec encompassing hundreds of thousands of square kilometres of the Cree's traditional territory.[59]

While the James Bay Cree had experienced conflict with outsiders over natural resource development in their territory throughout colonial history – especially around forestry and mining[60] – prior to the 1970s they had remained largely isolated from provincial and federal politics and economic pressures, maintaining traditional hunting, trapping, harvesting, and fishing economies and forms of social organization in which small groups of a few families primarily hunted in the bush during the long winter months, coming together in larger bands only during the summers on the shores of James Bay or on larger inland lakes.[61] Bourassa's announcement in

April 1971 that Quebec would start construction immediately in the eastern James Bay watershed on one of the largest hydroelectric developments in the world left the Cree, who numbered roughly 5,600 people at the time, "astounded."[62] The first phase of the project proposed the construction of several large dams along the La Grande – the largest of the rivers flowing through the Ungava Peninsula into eastern James Bay – and the consequent flooding of large areas of Cree hunting territories and fishing grounds.

In announcing his plans for the La Grande project, Bourassa made no mention of the land rights of the James Bay Cree and it quickly became apparent that Quebec had no intention of recognizing these rights or of seeking consultation with the affected Cree communities. The Cree themselves would learn about Bourassa's aspirations only by way of information trickling into the northern communities via newspaper clippings or by word of mouth.[63] By the summer of 1971, however, concerns over the impending project and its impact on James Bay Cree lands in northern Quebec had convinced a small group of young Cree leaders to organize an early attempt at political resistance that might stop the project or at least slow the pace of development to give the Cree communities time to organize a more comprehensive response.

These young leaders – some of whom would go on to become national and international figures in closely watched legal and political campaigns against hydroelectric development in Quebec – represented a new generation of leadership among the James Bay Cree, one that would ultimately have a transformative impact on community governance. Prior to the introduction of Bourassa's project and the threat it posed to livelihoods in James Bay, "the Cree had never before considered themselves bound together governmentally," and were instead "connected by bonds of friendship and family among hunters."[64] Nor had the governments in Ottawa and Quebec City regarded the James Bay Cree as a cohesive political unit, although each of the nine Cree communities in James Bay formally had band governments under the *Indian Act*.[65] But this context began to shift rapidly as the young Cree leaders – many of whom were raised in James Bay but had also lived and attended university in the south – rallied community support around resistance to Bourassa's proposal and began institutionalizing decision making around Cree land rights as a more cohesive national unit.[66]

As events in James Bay unfolded, Chief Billy Diamond emerged as the most prominent of this new generation of leaders. Diamond's father had been a long-standing *Indian Act* chief in the Cree community of Rupert House, a position that Diamond took over in 1970 at the age of twenty-one.[67] With little experience of either federal politics or local leadership, Diamond quickly adopted a confrontational stance toward the bureaucracy of the Department of Indian Affairs, which he regarded as mostly creating barriers and offering few benefits for his people.[68]

This approach served Diamond well when Bourassa's plans finally made their way to James Bay. Diamond, along with several other young chiefs and prominent community members, and with support from the Indian Association of Quebec, called a meeting of leaders and elders from the Cree communities in the village of Mistassini in June 1971. Observers referred to the gathering as "the beginning of a political process such as the Cree people had never known," or perhaps hyperbolically, "the first meeting ever held by the James Bay Cree in the 5,000 years of their history."[69] After several days of discussion, participants passed a resolution requesting intervention by Jean Chretien, then federal minister of Indian Affairs and Northern Development, as "the trustee of the Indian people."[70] The fraught political context of Quebec separatism, however, in which the Quiet Revolution of the 1960s bred a rising Quebec nationalism and assertions of regional sovereignty and economic autonomy from the rest of Canada – made the federal government extremely reluctant to get involved in the hydroelectric dispute on behalf of the James Bay Cree.[71]

In the vacuum left by federal non-involvement, and with the passing of the *James Bay Regional Development Act* in July 1971 to assert provincial authority over James Bay,[72] Quebec quickly began the first stages of construction on the La Grande project. As it became increasingly clear that Quebec would refuse to acknowledge Cree land rights in the region, the James Bay Cree, led by Diamond and Chief Robert Kanatewat of Fort George, filed an action in the Superior Court of Quebec for an interlocutory injunction against the province, Hydro-Quebec, and the James Bay Development Corporation – the municipal corporation newly established by Quebec to govern the James Bay region – in May 1972 to halt development while the status of the Cree's Aboriginal title could be ascertained.[73]

Even as the Supreme Court of Canada was authoring its judgment in *Calder,* the James Bay Cree presented extensive evidence in the Superior Court of Quebec from Chief Diamond and several Cree elders and trappers, who tried to establish for the court the relationships between the Cree and their lands. Given the status of Canadian law on Aboriginal title before *Calder* was released, the Cree litigants were perhaps not overly optimistic about their chances of success. But in November 1973, Justice Malouf ruled in favour of the Cree, agreeing that they should be able to proceed to make their land claims and issuing an interim injunction to halt the La Grande project. Although the decision was rapidly overturned by the Quebec Court of Appeal and subsequently appealed by the Cree to the Supreme Court of Canada,[74] the trial decision provided the advantage that Diamond and the other leaders needed to negotiate a formal treaty concerning their land rights and to establish compensation for the adverse effects of hydroelectric development in James Bay.[75] Indeed, it was in the shadow of uncertainty before the Supreme Court of Canada released its decision in *Calder* that such negotiations took place.[76]

The Cree Land Regime

Remarkably – and, it seems, intentionally on the part of the Cree leaders – the JBNQA signed with Canada and Quebec in 1975 left much of the uncertainty surrounding common law Aboriginal title and rights at the time unsettled. At a minimum, the treaty established three different categories of lands in which the James Bay Cree had varying degrees of entitlement and over which they exerted varying levels of control. In total, the agreement recognized the rights of the Cree and their Inuit allies to over 900,000 square kilometres of the James Bay region. Just over 1 percent of those lands, however, were designated as Category I lands, on which the more permanent communities were established and in which the Cree and Inuit exercised rights to exclusive use and control. Another 14 percent of the lands surrounding local villages, designated as Category II, were allocated for exclusive hunting, trapping, and fishing activities – though development activities by non-Cree entities were permitted provided that compensation was paid by the province. The remaining 84 percent of the lands covered by the JBNQA were Category III lands, a designation that preserved Cree rights to hunt, trap, and fish, although these activities had to be shared with non-Indigenous Quebecers and development activities over these lands were largely unconstrained.[77]

Crucially, however, the JBNQA left ambiguity surrounding the ultimate status of title in lands covered by the agreement and on the ongoing existence of common law Aboriginal rights in the Cree territories. The agreement also provided for new governance structures and compensation payments from Quebec to the Cree totalling $225 million, guaranteed income support for Cree trappers, and local Cree authority over health and education, but it left much of the detail concerning implementation open-ended.[78] The Cree negotiated two further agreements in later decades: *La Paix des Braves* (the Peace of the Brave) with Quebec in 2002 and the *Cree Nation Governance Agreement* with Canada in 2017.[79] Among other issues, these agreements attempted to clarify the status of Cree lands under the JBNQA, with *La Paix des Braves* transferring responsibility for these lands to the federal government and the most recent agreement providing for lands self-governance under the terms of a new Cree Constitution.

Throughout each of these steps, negotiating the nature of Cree land rights and defining the scope of Cree powers of decision making over those lands, Cree leaders navigated between the constraints of federal and provincial policy still based on the historical doctrine of preemption and the powerful economic forces pressing for greater access to their lands. Just as important, if not more so,

Cree leaders contended with considerable internal opposition and competing viewpoints. As Hans Carlson recounts, these internal debates were reflected in the changing nature of negotiated agreements themselves. For example, in signing *La Paix des Braves,* the Cree allowed further hydroelectric development in their territory but did so against the protests of at least three of the Cree communities. "Many," according to Carlson, "see the development and the promised jobs as the way forward, but a good many see the continued occupation and cultural definition of the land as still being vital to the future of the Cree."[80]

The Influence of Cree Leaders

If Nisga'a leaders developed their approach to alienability, in part, over a relatively long history of linkages to and contention with the Canadian state, the approach of the James Bay Cree leadership was rapidly shaped during the intense period of natural resource politics between Bourassa's announcement of hydroelectric development in northern Quebec in 1971 and the signing of the *James Bay and Northern Quebec Agreement* in 1975. In this context, Chief Billy Diamond and other Cree leaders framed the core problem they faced as one of state encroachment leading to the permanent loss of ecological and cultural integrity within a context of rapidly changing legal, economic, and political parameters – unsurprising given the scale of the proposed development and Quebec's initial position that the Cree held no recognized legal rights over their lands. As Diamond later described it, the staunch and unexpected (by Quebec) resistance from the Cree leaders sprang from a deep sense of astonishment at the changes they suddenly faced:[81]

> When the government of Quebec announced the development of the James Bay territory and, in particular, the James Bay hydroelectric project in the spring of 1971, we were astounded. The subsequent creation of the James Bay Development Corporation to develop all the natural resources of the territory caught us by complete surprise. We were concerned about the devastating impact that this project would have on our way of

> life, and we were convinced that we were not prepared for development. We were also astounded that our rights and claim to our lands could be so blatantly ignored.

In these circumstances, the solution crafted by the James Bay Cree leaders was not simply one of outright resistance to natural resource development in the form of a claim that their land rights were strictly inalienable – a claim that would likely have been untenable in the political environment at the time. Instead, Cree leaders settled on a strategy of embracing the legal uncertainty that existed around the status of Indigenous land rights and the nature of their powers of self-government over their territory. Formally, the JBNQA appeared to mirror the same "cede and release" structure that would later inform the *Nisga'a Final Agreement,* causing the James Bay Cree to surrender all "general claims, rights, titles, and interests, in and to land in Quebec in return for specific and defined rights, privileges, and benefits."[82] In practice, however, Cree leaders understood the agreement to leave open questions about the content of their specific rights – questions that would be answered only through an ongoing process of negotiation with the provincial and federal governments and the formation of subsequent agreements in the register of "an ongoing and dynamic relationship."[83] While this problem-solution set was "envisioned from the outset" by the Cree, it has nevertheless generated ongoing frictions with provincial and federal actors "still clinging to the elusive search for certainty."[84] As Harvey Feit has observed, "confronted by these situated Cree patterns of partial opposition, partial negotiation, and continuing relationships, some analysts have implicitly while others have explicitly called for greater consistency or clarity on the part of Cree leaders."[85] But it was this very lack of clarity that may ultimately have enabled Cree leaders to sustain and to continue sustaining the inalienability of their lands and the traditional economies that are dependent on them – as imperfect and complex as that result has proven to be.

The political institutions forged by the Cree leaders and later established under the JBNQA and modified in subsequent agreements reflect several features of an open and participatory approach to governance that may have been adopted to address the uncertainties inherent in the agreement. The roots of this approach were established not long after the group of young Cree chiefs first organized to resist the hydroelectric developments in northern Quebec. In the lead-up to their court battles and throughout the period before formal negotiations with Ottawa and Quebec, Diamond and others invested considerable effort in advocating for resistance among their own people, especially the influential Cree trappers.[86] In January 1974, the Cree leaders embarked on a tour of all eight Cree villages to discuss an initial offer by Quebec and future options regarding litigation and negotiation.[87] In the negotiations themselves, while Cree leaders initially worked under the umbrella of the Indians of Quebec Association (IQA), they eventually broke away from the IQA as not being sufficiently responsive to the needs of their people and in August 1974 they formed their own political organization, the Grand Council of the Crees (GCC).[88] After an agreement in principle was signed with the provincial and federal governments, Cree leaders continued to engage in extensive consultations with community members.[89]

As with the Nisga'a, these ideas and political institutions were linked to the discursive practices of Cree leaders that influenced how they defined problems and solutions. While Cree leaders were closely involved in an intensive period of negotiation with federal and provincial bureaucrats, the defining feature of their engagement with land rights was – in the language of discursive institutionalists – "communicative," between the leaders and community members, rather than "coordinative." The very circumstances of negotiations may have demanded it: Quebec's approach to hydroelectric development set up a much more oppositional relationship than that between Nisga'a leaders and British Columbia, and the politics of Quebec nationalism created a substantial distance between the Cree leaders and politicians in Ottawa.

Once the parties had signed the JBNQA, the Cree leadership had to reimagine their political institutions "within this new geography and ... had to learn a new way of negotiating power in order to maintain themselves and their relationships to the land."[90] Rather than consolidate decision making within a single body, the Cree created a more decentralized structure consistent with the need to balance ongoing negotiations with provincial and federal governments against responsiveness to community members. On the one hand, the Cree engineered a split between their two primary governance institutions. The Grand Council of the Crees continued as the political arm of regional Cree government, responsible for subsequent negotiations with Ottawa and Quebec, and acted as the public face of the James Bay Cree communities in communicating with broader Canadian and international publics. Internally, the Cree Regional Authority (CRA) was created in 1978 to administer the JBNQA, which included managing financial compensation paid under the treaty and exercising authority over Cree rights in Category II and III lands.[91]

Despite these different roles, membership on both the GCC and CRA is identical and comprises the Grand Chief and Deputy Grand Chief – who are elected by the Cree as a whole – as well as the chief and one additional representative from each of the nine Cree communities.[92] This dual structure may help to insulate Cree governance from an overemphasis on the coordinative processes so central to subsequent treaty negotiations. On the other hand, the JBNQA has strengthened the role of the Cree Trappers' Association as a vehicle for ensuring that the interests of Cree hunters and trappers are given a prominent role in future decisions about the land. Over time, it appears that the association has engaged independently in co-management initiatives and strengthened its place as one of the primary decision-making bodies shaping future negotiations.[93]

Conclusions

In this chapter, I extended the baseline model from earlier in the book by introducing greater complexity along two dimensions: first, by allowing for heterogeneous preferences among community members and thus competing internal perspectives about leaders' objectives; and second, by allowing for initial uncertainty about those preferences and the potential for changing interests over time. Once preferences are assumed to be heterogeneous and dynamic in this way, it is nearly impossible to avoid the potential impact of leaders' ideas on how individuals come to define and interpret their different interests. While leaders continue to play an important instrumental role in getting community members to go along with their preferred direction of reform, the ideas those leaders develop and promote can also have a significant influence on persuading community members and in structuring the political institutions that cause early trajectories to persist.

Nevertheless, as this chapter has shown, the layering of a discursive institutionalist analysis onto models of rational choice is a theoretical project that is still in its infancy – although not one, as some have argued, that necessarily generates fundamental incompatibilities.[94] With that context in mind, I have undertaken a modest extension of the core analysis in Chapters 3 and 4 in order to test the model against the different geographic and institutional settings facing the Nisga'a and the James Bay Cree. At best, this chapter offers the beginnings of a more coherent approach to integrating ideas and discourses into theories of land regime change, and it provides some early evidence consistent with my theoretical model's predictions. Ultimately, however, the model's capacity to account for the increased complexity in the Nisga'a and Cree cases is mixed. While the existence of community members' heterogeneous interests within each case is at least suggested by the available data, more work is needed to show how those interests changed over time and to link these changes to leaders' investments in persuasive effort. Likewise, the connection between leaders' discursive practices and the resulting political institutions in each community is an intriguing one, but raises questions about how leaders have resolved tensions between their own incentives to close off or open up decision making, particularly when outside negotiations may affect the degree to which leaders need to be responsive to their constituents.

Overall, despite the long histories of land rights struggles in both the Nisga'a and Cree cases, it may still be too early to fully evaluate the institutional dynamics at play. Given that, in these cases, formal changes in community land regimes have largely preceded the actual transactions around land that appeared to drive much of the change in Westbank and Membertou, the next stages of legal and economic change for both the Nisga'a and the James Bay Cree may be particularly fruitful periods for further research and analysis. From this perspective, the insights I discuss above are necessarily preliminary and provide a basis for future work in this vein.

6

The Future of Inalienable Property

Consistent with Claire Priest's critique that Demsetzian narratives about "a steady march toward alienability and modernity are inaccurate,"[1] the cases studied in this book foreground the contingencies involved in episodes of land market liberalization. These contingencies depend on the goals of prominent leaders and on the political institutions they build or adapt to achieve their ends, and are linked to the physical environments and exogenous shocks that can shift predefined pathways of institutional change. For Indigenous communities whose land regimes are "entangled" with colonial-state legal systems and economies,[2] strong pressures no doubt often exist to increase access to their lands and resources in line with the Demsetzian narrative. But embracing alienability is by no means an inevitable outcome for communities. For those concerned that current processes of Indigenous land tenure change in Canada pose a threat to legal pluralism and institutional diversity, the findings in this book may offer grounds for some measured optimism.

In this frame, my study yields several insights that help to advance a general theory of transitions between property regimes in Canadian Indigenous communities and comparable contexts. First, the theoretical model and supporting empirical evidence suggest that post-Demsetzian analyses have overemphasized interest group politics and its associated free-rider problems, at least in small group settings. While free riding characterizes one subset of possible equilibria in the process of land reform – a subset that expands as the number of participants increases – the model of group production developed in this book draws greater attention to the information problems that confront group members as they plan their optimal contributions of effort to the collective project of the group in a world of bounded rationality.

From a game-theoretic perspective, these problems of group coordination under uncertainty may well swamp concerns about free riding and give renewed focus to solutions that resolve information asymmetries. In such a world, leaders with access to valuable information about the conditions of "production" offer considerable benefits to their followers. This leads to another key insight of my study: that whatever their other functions, leaders serve an instrumental role in land regime change that is conceptually distinct from the inspirational or motivational roles most often ascribed to them in political contexts.[3] Leaders, like other individuals, are apt to strike bargains to satisfy their interests, whether in the form of material compensation like higher pay or other perks of office, intangible rewards like reputation and prestige, or projects that further the leaders' political, ideological, or cultural commitments by recruiting members' support for and participation in achieving those goals. Recognizing that leaders are no doubt vulnerable to influence by others and constrained by the structures in which they act, their own interests and ideas can have an outsized impact on the trajectory of reform.

Applying lessons from recent research in different organizational settings, my study is consistent with the idea that both the form and content of "rents" demanded by leaders have important consequences for the resulting political institutions that govern community decision making. From a group member's perspective, simply paying one's leader a higher salary has the benefit of being easy to calculate and monitor, but these types of material rents provide little incentive for leaders to be more open with and inclusive of group members when it comes to working out the details of property regime change. In fact, paying leaders material rents may have just the opposite effect, for example, by encouraging them to hide side payments from their membership, an issue I discuss in more detail below. Alternatively, non-material rents appear more likely to encourage the development of inclusive political institutions. This result, in turn, challenges assumptions about groups who sustain inalienable land rights as necessarily being insular and more vulnerable to control by authoritarian regimes.

This book has also shown that the form of leadership rents is not their only feature of interest. As the baseline model predicts, leaders' demands on their followers are almost certainly made as part of an exchange with followers to satisfy each of their respective interests – but those demands are also, in part, attempts to change group members' interests in ways that bring them into closer alignment with the leader's own. At some point, all leadership rents are "ideological" in the sense that they express particular ideas about leaders' worldviews, problems, and solutions that are open to adoption and interpretation by others. It should come as no surprise that the ideas leaders subscribe to and the processes by which those ideas are formulated and adopted can have a direct and lasting impact on property transitions. Institutional analysis has only begun to develop the tools to describe these aspects of change in a way that links leadership, ideas, and institutions together. Robust models of change must take seriously constructivist arguments that interests are not merely analytical priors but are themselves created, contested, and adapted in the process of transition. It is not enough, however, simply to posit that leaders' "ideas matter" for institutional change: there remains a great deal of both theoretical and empirical work to be done to explain how leaders come to hold the beliefs they do and to understand how leaders mobilize their ideas to persuade others.

Finally, the dynamics of group production and the rents available to leaders will themselves be shaped and constrained by exogenous factors and stochastic shocks, underscoring the complex interplay between agency and structure as causal features of institutional change apparent in each of the cases. For the communities studied in this book, the influence of geography – especially proximity to an urban centre – was assumed to be an especially important factor affecting individual preferences for land market liberalization and the uncertainty those individuals face about the consequences of institutional change. That assumption remains to be tested across more cases, and there are no doubt other significant factors still to be uncovered in future research.

Together, these insights not only contribute to a better understanding of institutional dynamics in land reform contexts but also speak to broader attempts by legal scholars to define a modern political economy of property. Dissatisfaction with the "just so" stories of Demsetzian analysis has led several of these scholars to reorient attention to the diverse politics and political structures that generate so much of contemporary property law.[4] For too long, critics charge, property theory has treated political institutions as epiphenomenal to the analysis of transitions between property regimes. Scholars of this new political economy have started to rewrite political actors and institutions into stories about property rights and to reposition a structural account of politics at the heart of explanatory analyses. Nevertheless, a coherent political economy of property remains elusive, its component parts severely disjointed and its useful insights into property transitions fragmented at best. The approach developed in this book provides one example of how that project might improve its coherence and bring political institutions – as well as the leaders and other agents who develop them – into the foreground.

In part, several of the lessons summarized above translate and confirm earlier findings from other settings in which team production models have been used to explain the role of leaders in institutional and organizational change. But this study, drawing on the unique contexts of land reforms in Indigenous communities in Canada, has also extended, adapted, and in some instances challenged these earlier findings to advance the broader theoretical approach. Several open questions and challenges remain, however. In the remainder of this concluding chapter, I elaborate on a few central issues.

Corporate Governance

The Membertou case study in particular suggests that models of corporate governance may play a unique role in navigating the dynamics of inalienability. From one perspective, Membertou's reliance on a model of corporate governance as the means to sustain a regime of inalienable land rights comes as something of a surprise. Not only might First Nations who resist land market liberalization be assumed to be anti-business but the theoretical model itself predicts that leaders who pursue inalienability will invest in open and participatory political institutions as a way of addressing the incomplete contracting problems associated with political rents. Given that corporate structures for governance and collective choice are presumptively hierarchical and tend to be relatively insular compared with democratic political institutions, their creative use by Membertou's leaders to achieve a high level of transparency and accountability to community members is a result that deserves attention in future work.

These findings are even more surprising in light of the fact that "Aboriginal business corporations" have been the subject of pointed criticisms by observers who advocate for the preservation and collective governance of Indigenous lands. As Colin Scott argues:

> Lands and resources could be held by Aboriginal governments on behalf of their constituencies, analogous to the manner in which provincial governments have historically held Crown lands on behalf of their citizenries, or they could be vested as the property of Aboriginal business corporations, whose role would be more narrowly proprietary and entrepreneurial. Reliance on the latter option imposes unacceptable

> risks and liabilities ... Where Aboriginal control of lands and resources hinges solely on the commercial success of development corporations, other Aboriginal and environmental interests are readily compromised, and the land itself may be forfeit. Aboriginal governments, on the other hand, constituted on a regional scale, can engage in strategic and coordinated economic development across multiple sectors, in a way that an Aboriginal business corporation cannot. First Nations governments are also more likely than Aboriginal corporations to be able politically to address and balance the wider spectrum of interest, from traditional to industrial, of their constituencies.[5]

Scott raises a key comparative question about the relative costs and benefits of different political institutions for governing inalienability. What broader lessons might be drawn from the Membertou example? A preliminary insight is that Scott's distinction between corporate and public governance may be an oversimplification. The political institutions actually developed in Membertou, for example, appear to be a hybrid of public-participatory and corporate governance models. In fact, this very mix may have enabled Membertou leaders to balance the inherent tensions between signalling cohesive political commitments to land integrity and inalienability on the one hand and ensuring openness, transparency, and political participation to evaluate and renegotiate those commitments over time on the other. Membertou's unique form of corporate governance has proven to be remarkably flexible in this respect. Leaders pursued economic development initiatives and set the agenda for reform, while making creative use of corporate businesses norms such as ISO certification and audited public financial statements to improve transparency, accountability, and responsiveness to community membership. The added benefits of using corporate governance to attract outside investment and forge joint ventures no doubt reinforced its instrumental value in maintaining equilibrium. In this sense, corporate governance acts not so much as a substitute for public political institutions but as part of a subset of possible hybrid arrangements.

One route to expand on these insights might be built on Simon Deakin's observation that the corporate form can be modelled as a type of "commons" in the sense of "a theory about the conditions under which collective action to preserve and sustain resources of value to society becomes possible."[6] As Deakin points out, "the firm as such cannot be owned, but in the context of the modern business enterprise, there are multiple, overlapping and often conflicting property rights or property-type claims" that must be structured and reconciled.[7] Of particular interest is the emphasis that corporate law has afforded to restraints on alienation in the form of shareholder lock-in and the various corporate arrangements that have emerged to deal with attendant challenges.[8] Deakin's main point is that corporate ownership and governance can usefully be studied using Elinor Ostrom's framework for institutional analysis of the commons,[9] developed in the context of common pool natural resources, with its attention to both operational property rights and higher-order collective choice institutions. Deakin's approach therefore offers a promising route for elaborating on further lessons about the relationship between governance and inalienability by continuing to investigate and draw links to the institutional dynamics of the modern firm.

The link between corporate governance and Indigenous lands has also been relevant in other cases beyond those studied in this book. In the early 1970s, corporate landholding was imposed by the United States Congress on Indigenous peoples in Alaska as part of the *Alaska Native Claims Settlement Act* (ANCSA).[10] The act established 13 regional and 220 village landholding corporations in which eligible individuals became shareholders with rights that were non-transferrable except by bequest.[11] Indigenous peoples in Alaska had long remained relatively insulated from Euro-American settlement, though settlers made increasing demands on natural resources in the region following the sale of Alaska to the United States in 1867. After Alaska joined the union in 1959, and with the discovery of vast crude oil reserves in the early 1960s, the ANCSA settlement was quickly enacted by Congress with support from development interests but apparently little consultation with Indigenous communities themselves.[12] As in Canada, ANCSA's corporate model of landholding was criticized by observers, not only for being unilaterally imposed on Indigenous Alaskans but also for its "business model of modernization," which was seen as antagonistic to community traditions and values.[13] Nevertheless, as Thomas Thornton observes:

> ANCSA corporations did not replace tribal governments or traditional social, economic, and political structures. Rather, the regional and village corporations constituted two additional, dynamic layers on the existing structures. The result has been a fascinating, often conflicting, and perhaps revolutionary mix of the traditional and the modern, the local and the global, the financial and the cultural, the Native and the non-Native.[14]

In this context, Indigenous Alaskans have engaged in struggles that seem to resonate with some of the dynamics in Membertou. Observers have argued that "the single most important task facing Alaska Natives is the continued ownership and control of their corporations" as a means "to preserve their lands and Native heritage."[15] But the opportunities for working within ANCSA corporations to balance economic development with cultural resilience are rarely straightforward. For example, while restraints on the ability to alienate ANCSA shareholders' rights provide a measure of protection to ensure that control remains in the hands of community members, studies of "corporate culture" have shown that corporate ownership and control within the modern firm tend to become separated and more diffuse over time, leading to disengagement on the part of shareholders and a managerial approach to governance that does not appear particularly well suited to the context of Indigenous lands.[16] There is also a question of whether corporate governance models increase the vulnerability of leaders to outside influence, reducing their responsiveness to community members. On the other hand, recent research on Inuit economic development corporations in the Canadian Arctic has suggested that forms of corporate land and resource governance may successfully operate as a precursor to formal self-governance and land claims settlements by acting as "de facto self-government" to build capacity and exercise land rights and governance in practice.[17]

One promising approach for future work in this area might compare the Membertou and Alaskan experiences. Foremost among these are the different historical processes by which community and corporate leaders in the two cases came to form their hybridized governance institutions. In Membertou, the community worked within a set of imposed institutions under the *Indian Act* to integrate aspects of corporate governance, while in Alaska Indigenous communities worked within a set of imposed ANCSA corporations to integrate other forms of political and tribal decision making. We might expect that these very different starting points have had important consequences for addressing inherent tensions around inalienability.

Finally, the lens of corporate governance may offer a window into how leadership rents might best be set to sustain good leadership but also to ensure that the gains from leadership are more equally distributed among members of the group. How leaders spend their rents in practice "varies widely and depends on a combination of personal goals, incentives, and political constraints."[18] Studies in the literature on corporate governance, for example, have developed new models about the relationship between information disclosure, monitoring, and executive compensation that may have implications for calibrating the level of material leadership rents and the form of political institutions in settings of land regime change.[19]

Leadership Rents and Good Governance

It should come as no surprise that, as mechanisms of wealth redistribution, land reform and property regime change raise opportunities for elite capture, rent seeking, and other forms of political corruption. Notably, prior research suggests that concerns about corruption arise in cases where land titling and market liberalization are being actively pursued as well as in cases where strict restraints on alienability are maintained. With respect to the former, a considerable body of research on land title formalization programs has shown that liberalizing land markets "may create conditions for opportunistic behaviour whereby the wealthy and well informed can manipulate the process to their own advantage."[20] Problems here have been linked to the greater material resources available to leaders and other elites to engage in land registrations, purchases, and speculation, as well as their greater access to information about requirements for title registration and to the inner workings of the bureaucracy.[21] Increasingly, attention to global large-scale land transactions in recently liberalized land markets have only added to these concerns.[22] With respect to regimes with strong restrictions on alienability, "closed" societies of this sort have been linked to illiberal regimes and authoritarian political controls.[23] Conversely, polities that opt for more equitable forms of land redistribution can create the conditions for successful good governance reforms.[24]

All this raises the question of whether the "leadership rents" described in this book might themselves be viewed as a form of corruption, or whether they might at least create conditions that can lead to bad incentives on the part of the governing leadership cohort. This question revolves around the perceived legitimacy of political deals between leaders and community members, in which leaders exchange their valuable information about the conditions of production for payments, in whatever form, over and above other costs of leading. From one perspective, the existence and sustainability of leadership rents in the model is simply the direct result of making explicit what too many functional theories of leadership leave unaddressed – that is, what it is that leaders actually "do" and why they are valuable to their followers. Here, leaders provide valuable informational signals to community members, allowing them to better coordinate their collective efforts toward land reform. We might therefore reasonably expect that both organizational and political leaders will seek a certain level of compensation for employing their talents, particularly if those talents could be put to other remunerative uses.[25]

This position aligns to some degree with an existing literature arguing in favour of "political and economic side payments" that can help to overcome barriers to institutional change.[26] While much of this literature focuses on exchanges between leaders and other political elites, many of its arguments could be equally applied to the leadership model developed here in which payments are made from community members directly to leaders. The problem with this analogy is that leaders' demands for rents can sometimes go too far beyond what community members are willing to tolerate, resulting in exorbitant rents and efforts by the community to remove the leader from office. Insofar as leadership rents are susceptible to monitoring and community members have the capacity to do so, simply replacing the offending leader can work to re-establish equilibrium. The more pressing problem, of course, is that leaders in these circumstances will face strong incentives to hide some of the rents they receive. In this respect, communities with leaders who demand political rather than material rents may have an advantage because the more open and inclusive political institutions they develop to resolve their inevitable commitment problems, as well as the "publicness" of the signals they deliver to address equilibrium selection, enable followers to more easily monitor their behaviour. As Margaret Levi and Brad Epperly have observed, rule-of-law institutions are themselves contingent on leaders being able to make credible commitments to freedom from corruption, "even in unforeseen contingencies."[27] For communities that sustain inalienability regimes, a type of virtuous cycle may therefore emerge in which leadership rents and good governance incentives are self-reinforcing.

A further problem is related to "outside" rents that might be paid to community leaders by third parties. It is certainly plausible that some leaders will be vulnerable to payments from powerful outside interests who want to gain access to community lands through liberalized land markets. Not only could this be a problem because such payments might seem inherently less legitimate as a matter of the collective interest, but outside rents are more likely to reduce a leader's responsiveness to the interests of community members.[28]

A key task for future research is to identify governance mechanisms that enable community members to enjoy the benefits of good leadership while mitigating some of the bad incentives that leadership rents can induce. Certainly, robust monitoring is likely to play a role – but even here there are complex dynamics that communities will need to consider. For example, in their study of the link between better monitoring and leadership in development-oriented community organizations, Guy Grossman and W. Walker Hanlon find that stricter monitoring mechanisms to guard against corrupt behaviour may represent a direct trade-off with leadership quality to the extent that there are lucrative alternatives to organizational leadership available elsewhere, especially in the private sector.[29] The overarching problem is that if monitoring or other governance mechanisms impose additional cost on leaders, these will each be factored into the bargain struck with community members and will ultimately affect the equilibrium level of rents. More promising may be to use the logic of the model to explore how these bargains can be made more contingent such that leaders themselves have good reason to establish governance mechanisms that incorporate active participation and oversight by their followers.

Debates over good governance and corruption within Indigenous communities in Canada continue to be fraught with competing narratives and raise significant concerns about reinforcing negative stereotypes around Indigenous self-government – much as they were during the Hall Inquiry of Westbank leadership in the 1980s. Vocal critics of First Nations governments have claimed that "embezzlement, nepotistic hiring practices, conflicts of interest in business dealings and overpayment of office-holders" are both recurrent and structurally embedded.[30] Perhaps accepting the truth of these claims, Canada's federal government in 2013 enacted the *First Nations Financial Transparency Act,* requiring public disclosure of annual financial statements and the compensation paid to elected chiefs and councillors.[31] But claims of corruption in First Nations and their attendant legislative responses have been critiqued and vigorously contested on several grounds, including a lack of rigorous empirical evidence (a point borne out by financial disclosures themselves under the act);[32] the tendency of critics to draw on cultural stereotypes and to blame First Nations for structural problems that are themselves a direct consequence of colonialism;[33] and an increase in administrative costs that have been laid on already overburdened First Nations governments.[34] The analysis of leadership rents modelled above may offer a new perspective on some of these debates, and may ultimately help disentangle legitimate worries about how to achieve and reinforce good governance – worries that First Nations themselves have often expressed and taken a lead in addressing[35] – from problematic and unsubstantiated claims about corruption.

Scale, Polycentricity, and Geography

Given that each case studied in this book is a small community, one crucial question for extending the model to other development contexts is its ability to scale up to larger polities. This issue is especially significant given that many initiatives to liberalize land markets globally have been conceived and implemented at the level of large nation states.[36] As noted in Chapter 3, one theoretical challenge with scaling the model is that the potential for free-riding behaviour increases with the number of players, such that even when leaders accurately reveal their information, other actors face incentives to contribute less than optimal levels of effort. But there are also other challenges with analogizing team production in larger groups, not the least of which is the model's assumption that group members have both the willingness and the capacity to adequately monitor the leaders' activities, raising the question of whether free-rider problems may lurk here as well.

Closely associated with the issue of scale is how the model developed here might be adapted to account for polycentric settings of land regime change and governance. In fact, while some aspects of "multilevel governance" affecting Indigenous communities were explored in the case studies in earlier chapters,[37] each of these cases might be usefully expanded to study linkages between the dynamics of local land reform and changes in other First Nations and at provincial, regional, and federal scales. For example – as several of the case studies suggest – Indigenous communities in Canada frequently collaborate through regional organizations and move in and out of less formal alliances that can be expected to influence land reform at the community level. In other work, I have examined how national Indigenous social movements in Canada have played a key role in responding to federal law reforms that affected the leasing of reserve lands and in shaping broader legal interpretations of Indigenous land rights.[38] Understanding local communities in a more polycentric context may also help elaborate on the source and influence of potential "external" leadership rents where these have potentially significant consequences for leaders' behaviour.

Finally, my study has pointed to the effect that geography is likely to have on the dynamics of the model, especially with respect to a community's location as urban or remote. More empirical work is needed here to test some of the assumptions I have relied on when interpreting my case studies, and future research could usefully expand the inquiry into other exogenous factors such as natural resource endowments and changing resource prices over time. At a minimum, the cases suggest that, while such factors are unlikely to have the oversimplified effects predicted by Harold Demsetz's theory of property transitions, they may still have a significant role to play in shaping the dynamics of leadership and community politics that determine institutional change.

Notes

Chapter 1: Keeping the Land, Making the Market

1 Nisga'a Lisms Government, "K'amliighahlhaahl (the Creator)," https://www.nisgaanation.ca/kamliighahlhaahl-creator.

2 Richard Foot, "Nisga'a Take First, Wary Steps toward Private Land Ownership," *Victoria Times Colonist*, August 15, 2010, A12; Tristin Hopper, "Homes of Their Own: Starting with Three Houses, Nisga'a Nation Realizes Dream of Privatizing Native Land," *National Post*, November 9, 2013, A4; Ian Bailey, "B.C. Nisga'a Allow Members to Purchase Reservation Land," *Globe and Mail,* November 15, 2013, A6.

3 Suzanne Berneshawi, "Resource Management and the Mi'kmaq Nation," *Canadian Journal of Native Studies* 17, 1 (1997): 117; Pamela D. Palmater, "Matnm Tel-Mi'Kmawi: I'm Fighting for My Mi'Kmaw Identity," *Canadian Journal of Native Studies* 33, 1 (2013): 149.

4 *Re Indian Reserve, Sydney (City)*, 1916 CarswellNat 37, 17 Ex CR 517, 42 DLR 314.

5 Tristin Hopper, "B.C. First Nation Leads Historic and Controversial Move toward Aboriginal Private Home Ownership," *National Post,* November 8, 2013, https://nationalpost.com/news/canada/b-c-first-nation-leads-historic-and-controversial-move-toward-aboriginal-private-home-ownership.

6 For an overview of these arguments in the Nisga'a context, see Sari Graben, "Lessons for Indigenous Property Reform: From Membership to Ownership on Nisga'a Lands," *University of British Columbia Law Review* 47, 2 (2014): 409–15.

7 Ibid., 415–30. Further discussions of these concerns related to Indigenous land reform are in Jamie Baxter and Michael Trebilcock, "Formalizing Land Tenure in First Nations: Evaluating the Case for Reserve Tenure Reform," *Indigenous Law Journal* 7, 2 (2009): 107–11;

Mary Eberts, "Still Colonizing after All These Years," *University of New Brunswick Law Journal* 64 (2013): 151–52; Shiri Pasternak, "How Capitalism Will Save Colonialism: The Privatization of Reserve Lands in Canada," *Antipode* 47, 1 (2015).

8 With respect to modern treaties in Canada, Fernando Aragón finds some evidence that treaties have had a positive impact on real income in the treaty nation's local economy. Fernando M. Aragón, "Do Better Property Rights Improve Local Income? Evidence from First Nations' Treaties," *Journal of Development Economics* 116 (2015). While the study may address impacts of the Nisga'a treaty more generally dating back to the early 2000s, it is unlikely to capture the effects of more recent reforms granting alienable property rights to Nisga'a citizens.

9 Stuart Banner, *How the Indians Lost Their Land: Law and Power on the Frontier* (Cambridge, MA: Harvard University Press, 2005).

10 Susan Rose-Ackerman, "Inalienability and the Theory of Property Rights," *Columbia Law Review* 85, 5 (1985); Richard A. Epstein, "Why Restrain Alienation?," *Columbia Law Review* 85, 5 (1985); Margaret Jane Radin, "Market-Inalienability," *Harvard Law Review* 100, 8 (1987); Margaret Jane Radin, *Contested Commodities* (Cambridge, MA: Harvard University Press, 1996); Lee Anne Fennell, "Adjusting Alienability," *Harvard Law Review* 122 (2009). A brief history of these debates in the case of land is sketched in Robert C. Ellickson, "Property in Land," *Yale Law Journal* 102 (1993): 1375–80. For debates in the context of Indigenous peoples' lands in Canada and elsewhere, see Michael A. Heller, "The Boundaries of Private Property," *Yale Law Journal* 108, 6 (1999): 1213–17; Kent McNeil, "Self-Government and the Inalienability of Aboriginal Title," *McGill Law Journal* 47 (2002); Graben, "Lessons for Indigenous Property Reform"; Malcolm Lavoie, "Why Restrain Alienation of Indigenous Lands?," *University of British Columbia Law Review* 49, 3 (2016).

11 One exception related to land regime choice in First Nations is Malcolm Lavoie and Moira Lavoie, "Land Regime Choice in Close-Knit Communities: The Case of the First Nations Land Management Act," *Osgoode Hall Law Journal* 54 (2017). A more general positive theory of inalienable property rights based on financial market dynamics is put forward by David Andolfatto, "A Theory of Inalienable Property Rights," *Journal of Political Economy* 110, 2 (2002).

12 Susan Rose-Ackerman notes that inalienability has always been the "stepchild of law and economics." Rose-Ackerman, "Inalienability and the Theory of Property Rights," 931.

13 Fennell, "Adjusting Alienability," 1405. On the debate between "exclusion" and "governance" theories of property, see Henry E. Smith,

"Exclusion versus Governance: Two Strategies for Delineating Property Rights," *Journal of Legal Studies* 31, S2 (2002); Gregory S. Alexander, "Governance Property," *University of Pennsylvania Law Review* 160, 7 (2012).

14 James Taylor, *Stakes and Kidneys: Why Markets in Human Body Parts Are Morally Imperative* (Burlington, VT: Ashgate, 2005); Mark Cherry, *Kidney for Sale by Owner: Human Organs, Transplantation, and the Market* (Washington, DC: Georgetown University Press, 2016).

15 Michael Abramowicz, "On the Alienability of Legal Claims," *Yale Law Journal* 114 (2005).

16 John Moustakas, "Group Rights in Cultural Property: Justifying Strict Inalienability," *Cornell Law Review* 74 (1989).

17 Tsilly Dagan and Talia Fisher, "Rights for Sale," *Minnesota Law Review* 96 (2012); Richard L. Hasen, "Vote Buying," *California Law Review* 88, 5 (2000).

18 Alison Storella, "It's Selfie-Evident: Spectrums of Alienability and Copyrighted Content on Social Media," *Boston University Law Review* 94 (2014).

19 Stewart Sterk, "Restraints on Alienation of Human Capital," *Virginia Law Review* 79, 2 (1993).

20 Claire Priest, "Creating an American Property Law: Alienability and Its Limits in American History," *Harvard Law Review* 120, 2 (2006): 392.

21 Robert Ellickson, for example, argues that "as a group becomes literate and its lands become more scarce, its standard bundle of private land rights tends to evolve from the time-limited and inalienable usufruct to something like the perpetual and alienable fee simple." Ellickson, "Property in Land," 1376–77, 1398.

22 Rose-Ackerman, "Inalienability and the Theory of Property Rights."

23 On the concept of intergenerational public goods, see William R. Lowry, *Preserving Public Lands for the Future: The Politics of Intergenerational Goods* (Washington, DC: Georgetown University Press, 1998); Todd Sandler, "Intergenerational Public Goods: Transnational Considerations," *Scottish Journal of Political Economy* 56, 3 (2009).

24 Casting the puzzle of inalienability in these terms – as one of rationalist political economy – should not be taken to suggest that Indigenous communities and individuals lack diverse reasons and logics to sustain or eschew inalienable land rights. If my focus here on incentives and strategic action can be justified, I think it is because this perspective challenges the assumption – on terms internal to economic rationalism – that inalienable entitlements are inevitably legal artifacts and approaches inalienability as a serious institutional

option for some self-governing First Nations as they undertake the work of land tenure reform in contexts of local economic change.

25 Rose-Ackerman defines inalienability as "any restriction on the transferability, ownership, or use of an entitlement." Rose-Ackerman, "Inalienability and the Theory of Property Rights," 931.

26 Fennell, "Adjusting Alienability," 1428.

27 Thomas W. Merrill and Henry E. Smith, "Optimal Standardization in the Law of Property: The *Numerus Clausus* Principle," *Yale Law Journal* 110 (2000): 26–34. Henry Smith contrasts "exclusionary" strategies, which minimize information costs, with governance strategies, which tend to raise those costs, and argues that a key function of property institutions is to manage informational complexity. Smith, "Exclusion versus Governance"; Henry E. Smith, "Property as Complex Interaction," *Journal of Institutional Economics* 13, 4 (2017).

28 For a further discussion of the standardization thesis in the context of Indigenous land rights in Canada, see Jamie Baxter, "Property, Information and Institutional Design," *Journal of Aboriginal Economic Development* 8, 2 (2013).

29 Fennell, "Adjusting Alienability," 1408.

30 Graben, "Lessons for Indigenous Property Reform," 424–38.

31 Kent McNeil refers to the inalienability of Aboriginal title as a "central tenet of the common law." McNeil, "Self-Government," 475. The inalienability of reserve lands is premised on the basic structure of the *Indian Act,* in which title to these lands is held in trust by the federal government for the use and benefit of the First Nation for which they are "set apart"; see *Indian Act*, RSC, 1985, c I-5, s 18(1). There is, however, a spectrum of possible inalienability rules with respect to subsidiary interests under the act; see ch. 2.

32 Harold Demsetz, "Toward a Theory of Property Rights," *American Economic Review* 57, 2 (1967).

33 Saul Levmore, "Two Stories about the Evolution of Property Rights," *Journal of Legal Studies* 31, S2 (2002); Stuart Banner, "Transitions between Property Regimes," *Journal of Legal Studies* 31, S2 (2002). In recent years, several variations on these two contrasting approaches to institutional change have emerged in the property literature, including: Daniel Fitzpatrick, "Evolution and Chaos in Property Rights Systems: The Third World Tragedy of Contested Access," *Yale Law Journal* 115, 5 (2006) (focusing on "enforcement costs"); Abraham Bell and Gideon Parchomovsky, "The Evolution of Private and Open Access Property," *Theoretical Inquiries in Law* 10, 1 (2009) (emphasizing the interplay of community size, extent of dominion,

and asset configuration in the oscillation between open access and private rights); and Abraham Bell and Gideon Parchomovsky, "Property Lost in Translation," *University of Chicago Law Review* 80, 2 (2013) (discussing the role of "translation costs" in the changing property regimes among embedded localized communities).

34 John Borrows, *Recovering Canada: The Resurgence of Indigenous Law* (Toronto: University of Toronto Press, 2002); John Borrows, *Canada's Indigenous Constitution* (Toronto: University of Toronto Press, 2010); Val Napoleon, "Thinking about Indigenous Legal Orders," in *Dialogues on Human Rights and Legal Pluralism,* ed. René Provost and Colleen Sheppard, (Berlin: Springer, 2012).

35 On polycentricity, see Vincent Ostrom, Charles Tiebout, and Robert Warren, "The Organization of Government in Metropolitan Areas: A Theoretical Inquiry," *American Political Science Review* 55, 4 (1961): 831; Elinor Ostrom, "Beyond Markets and States: Polycentric Governance of Complex Economic Systems," *American Economic Review* 100 (2010): 643–44; Paul Dragoş Aligică and Peter Boettke, "The Two Social Philosophies of Ostroms' Institutionalism," *Policy Studies Journal* 39, 1 (2011).

36 John Ahlquist and Margaret Levi, *In the Interest of Others: Organizations and Social Activism* (Princeton, NJ: Princeton University Press, 2013), EPUB. For an overview of this emerging literature, see John Ahlquist and Margaret Levi, "Leadership: What It Means, What It Does, and What We Want to Know About It," *Annual Review of Political Science* 14 (2011).

37 Ibid., 53.

38 Robert Bates et al., *Analytical Narratives* (Princeton, NJ: Princeton University Press, 1998). A now classic example of using analytical narratives for institutional analysis is Avner Greif, *Institutions and the Path to the Modern Economy: Lessons from Medieval Trade* (Cambridge: Cambridge University Press, 2006).

Chapter 2: Property Stories

1 Jamie Baxter, "Storytelling, Social Movements, and the 'Evolution' of Indigenous Land Tenure," *Australian Indigenous Law Review* 18, 1 (2014).

2 Demsetz, "Toward a Theory of Property Rights."

3 Priest, "Creating an American Property Law," 393. The accuracy of Demsetz's historical account has been challenged by some anthropologists. For a review of this literature, see Katrina Wyman, "From Fur to Fish: Reconsidering the Evolution of Private Property," *New York University Law Review* 80 (2005): 120–21.

4 Harold Demsetz, "Toward a Theory of Property Rights II: The Competition between Private and Collective Ownership," *Journal of Legal Studies* 31, S2 (2002): S655.

5 Demsetz, "Toward a Theory of Property Rights," 350.

6 David Weimer describes this as a theory of property transitions that result from the "realization of opportunities" that are Pareto-improving. David L. Weimer, *The Political Economy of Property Rights: Institutional Change and Credibility in the Reform of Centrally Planned Economies* (Cambridge: Cambridge University Press, 1997), 10.

7 Levmore, "Two Stories," S423.

8 Thráinn Eggertsson, *Economic Behavior and Institutions: Principles of Neoinstitutional Economics* (Cambridge: Cambridge University Press, 1990), 250.

9 Demsetz, "Toward a Theory of Property Rights," 348.

10 A good overview of this literature is Michael J. Trebilcock and Paul-Erik Veel, "Property Rights and Development: The Contingent Case for Formalization," *University of Pennsylvania Journal of International Law* 30, 2 (2008).

11 See Ellickson, "Property in Land," 1375 (noting both investment and collateral rationales for inalienability).

12 Gershon Feder and David Feeny, "Land Tenure and Property Rights: Theory and Implications for Development Policy," *World Bank Economic Review* 5, 1 (1991): 138 (lack of alienable property rights may adversely affect productivity); Trebilcock and Veel, "Property Rights and Development," 406. More generally, it has been noted that "voluntary exchanges work for the mutual benefit of both sides, and where these are restrained, potential purchasers share in the losses that are held by original owners." Epstein, "Why Restrain Alienation?," 972.

13 Empirical work across several development contexts has provided mixed evidence of both effects. Kevin E. Davis and Michael J. Trebilcock, "Legal Reforms and Development," *Third World Quarterly* 22, 1 (2010): 27.

14 Feder and Feeny, "Land Tenure and Property Rights," 141.

15 Thomas Flanagan, Christopher Alcantara, and André Le Dressay, *Beyond the Indian Act: Restoring Aboriginal Property Rights* (Montreal and Kingston: McGill-Queen's University Press, 2010), 177–78.

16 Rose-Ackerman, "Inalienability and the Theory of Property Rights," 938.

17 Susan Rose-Ackerman, "Inalienability," in *The New Palgrave Dictionary of Economics and the Law,* ed. Peter Newman (London: Macmillan, 1998), 2:269–70.

18 Rose-Ackerman, "Inalienability and the Theory of Property Rights," 270.
19 Graben, "Lessons for Indigenous Property Reform," 415–24.
20 Ibid., 421.
21 Ibid., 422. As observers have noted, these externalities and coordination costs related to alienable property are not merely speculative: there may be important parallels with historical experience, especially in the United States. Jessica A. Shoemaker, "Like Snow in the Spring Time: Allotment, Fractionation, and the Indian Land Tenure Problem," *Wisconsin Law Review* 4 (2003); Jessica A. Shoemaker, "Complexity's Shadow: American Indian Property, Sovereignty, and the Future," *Michigan Law Review* 115, 4 (2016).
22 James Krier characterizes this as "part two" of the tragedy of the commons. James E. Krier, "The Tragedy of the Commons, Part Two," *Harvard Journal of Law and Public Policy* 15 (1992).
23 Carol Rose, "Property as Storytelling: Perspectives from Game Theory, Narrative Theory, Feminist Theory," *Yale Journal of Law and the Humanities* 2 (1990): 52.
24 Douglass C. North and Robert Paul Thomas, *The Rise of the Western World: A New Economic History* (Cambridge: Cambridge University Press, 1973); Oliver Williamson, *The Economic Institutions of Capitalism: Firms, Markets, Relational Contracting* (New York: Free Press, 1985). Gaps in the logic of institutional change in these two works are diagnosed by Daron Acemoglu, Simon Johnson, and James A. Robinson, "Institutions as a Fundamental Cause of Long-Run Growth," in *Handbook of Economic Growth*, vol. 1A, ed. Philippe Aghion and Steven N. Durlauf (Amsterdam: Elsevier, 2005), 422–23.
25 Jules L. Coleman, *The Practice of Principle* (Oxford: Oxford University Press, 2001), 26. Thomas Merrill notes that the Demsetz thesis "can be seen as an anticipation of the idea that the common law evolves toward efficient rules." Thomas W. Merrill, "Introduction: The Demsetz Thesis and the Evolution of Property Rights," *Journal of Legal Studies* 31, S2 (2002): S331.
26 For examples of case studies in which rising resource values accurately predicted transitions to private exclusionary rights, see David E. Ault and Gilbert L. Rutman, "The Development of Individual Rights to Property in Tribal Africa," *Journal of Law and Economics* 22, 1 (1979); Gershon Feder and Raymond Noronha, "Land Rights Systems and Agricultural Development in Sub-Saharan Africa," *World Bank Research Observer* 2, 2 (1987).
27 Jean-Marie Baland and Jean-Philippe Platteau note that the characteristics of "communal ownership" used by Demsetz as a counterfactual

remain largely undefined. Jean-Marie Baland and Jean-Philippe Platteau, "Division of the Commons: A Partial Assessment of the New Institutional Economics of Land Rights," *American Journal of Agricultural Economics* 80, 3 (1998): 646. On the use of "invisible hand" explanations in law generally, see Adrian Vermeule, "The Invisible Hand in Legal and Political Theory," *Virginia Law Review* 96, 6 (2010).

28 Baland and Platteau, ibid., 647.

29 For studies in the former category, see William H. Riker and Itai Sened, "A Political Theory of the Origin of Property Rights: Airport Slots," *American Journal of Political Science* 35, 4 (1991): 953; Shawn Everett Kantor, "Razorbacks, Ticky Cows, and the Closing of the Georgia Open Range: The Dynamics of Institutional Change Uncovered," *Journal of Economic History* 51, 4 (1991); Fitzpatrick, "Evolution and Chaos"; Jonathan Remy Nash, "Economic Efficiency versus Public Choice: The Case of Property Rights in Road Traffic Management," *Boston College Law Review* 49 (2008); Eric A. Coleman and Esther Mwangi, "Conflict, Cooperation, and Institutional Change on the Commons," *American Journal of Political Science* 59, 4 (2015). For studies in the latter category, see Thráinn Eggertsson, "Opportunities and Limits for the Evolution of Property Rights Institutions," in *Property in Land and Other Resources,* ed. Daniel H. Cole and Elinor Ostrom (Cambridge: Lincoln Institute of Land Policy, 2012); Katrina Wyman, "Problematic Private Property: The Case of New York Taxicab Medallions," *Yale Journal on Regulation* 30 (2013).

30 Susan Rose-Ackerman observes that "evolutionary work ... generally lacks a theory of politics." Susan Rose-Ackerman, "Law and Economics: Paradigm, Politics, or Philosophy," in *Law and Economics,* ed. Nicholas Mercuro (Boston: Kluwer Academic Publishers, 1989), 240.

31 Daniel A. Farber, "Public Choice Theory and Legal Institutions," in *The Oxford Handbook of Law and Economics,* ed. Francesco Parisi (Oxford: Oxford University Press, 2017), 181, citing Kenneth Shepsle, *Analyzing Politics: Rationality, Behavior, and Institutions* (New York: W.W. Norton, 2010).

32 Mark Lubell, Richard C. Feiock, and Edgar E. Ramirez de la Cruz, "Local Institutions and the Politics of Urban Growth," *American Journal of Political Science* 53, 3 (2009): 649. A related but distinctive group of theories unpack this assumption about fixed or uniform political institutions by analyzing the causal link between variation in political structures and the pace or direction of transitions between property regimes. Marilyn F. Drees, "Do State Legislatures Have a Role in Resolving the Just Compensation Dilemma? Some Lessons from

Public Choice and Positive Political Theory," *Fordham Law Review* 66 (1997): 810; James E. Alt and Kenneth A. Shepsle, *Perspectives on Positive Political Economy* (Cambridge: Cambridge University Press, 1990), 2.

33 Baland and Platteau, "Division of the Commons," 648.

34 Gary D. Libecap, "Distributional Issues in Contracting for Property Rights," *Journal of Institutional and Theoretical Economics* 145, 1 (1989): 10.

35 Fred S. McChesney, "Rent Extraction and Rent Creation in the Economic Theory of Regulation," *Journal of Legal Studies* 16, 1 (1987).

36 James Buchanan and Gordon Tullock, *The Calculus of Consent: Logical Foundations of Constitutional Democracy* (Ann Arbor: University of Michigan Press, 1962).

37 Terry Moe, "Vested Interests and Political Institutions," *Political Science Quarterly* 130, 2 (2015). On the path dependency sometimes linked to these dynamics, see Brian Arthur, *Increasing Returns and Path Dependence in the Economy* (Ann Arbor: University of Michigan Press, 1994).

38 Moe, "Vested Interests."

39 Examples include Nash, "Economic Efficiency versus Public Choice" (property rights in road traffic management); Thomas W. Hazlett, "Assigning Property Rights to Radio Spectrum Users: Why Did FCC License Auctions Take 67 Years?," *Journal of Law and Economics* 41, S2 (1998) (slow emergence of private rights in radio spectra); Wyman, "Problematic Private Property" (private property in taxi medallions).

40 Joseph William Singer, "The Ownership Society and Takings of Property: Castles, Investments, and Just Obligations," *Harvard Environmental Law Review* 30 (2006): 323.

41 Nestor M. Davidson and Rashmi Dyal-Chand, "Property in Crisis," *Fordham Law Review* 78, 4 (2010).

42 Analogously, Jerry Mashaw notes that "interest group theories of regulation have had great difficulty, for example, accommodating the undeniable political movement toward deregulation." Jerry L. Mashaw, "Public Law and Public Choice: A Critique and Rapprochement," in *Research Handbook on Public Law and Public Choice,* ed. Daniel A. Farber and Anne Joseph O'Connell (Cheltenham: Edward Elgar, 2010), 22.

43 For example, Nash, "Economic Efficiency versus Public Choice."

44 Libecap, "Distributional Issues in Contracting for Property Rights," 7. An extended discussion of this approach can be found in Gary D. Libecap, *Contracting for Property Rights* (Cambridge: Cambridge University Press, 1993). Interest-group theories are not necessarily dependent on the presence or active involvement of the state, and

have been used by economic anthropologists to explain property transitions in decentralized or norm-based settings in which formalized decision-making institutions are largely or wholly absent. Jack Knight, *Institutions and Social Conflict* (Cambridge: Cambridge University Press, 1992); Jean Ensminger and Jack Knight, "Changing Social Norms: Common Property, Bridewealth, and Clan Exogamy," *Current Anthropology* 38, 1 (1997); Coleman and Mwangi, "Conflict, Cooperation, and Institutional Change."

45 Libecap, "Distributional Issues in Contracting for Property Rights," 7.

46 Ibid., 11. Others have focused on information problems that inhibit citizens' awareness of optimal policy moves, collective action problems, and credible commitment problems. Claude Ménard and Mary M. Shirley, eds., *Handbook of New Institutional Economics* (Berlin: Springer, 2008), 581; Lee Alston and Bernardo Mueller, "Property Rights and the State," in *Handbook of New Institutional Economics,* ed. Claude Ménard and Mary M. Shirley (Berlin: Springer, 2005), 582; Douglass C. North, *Structure and Change in Economic History* (New York: W.W. Norton, 1981).

47 Weimer, *Political Economy of Property Rights,* 10.

48 Daron Acemoglu, "Why Not a Political Coase Theorem? Social Conflict, Commitment, and Politics," *Journal of Comparative Economics* 31, 4 (2003): 622. For a discussion of the complications raised by commitment problems, see Levmore, "Two Stories," S430–31.

49 For example, Leroy Little Bear, "Aboriginal Rights and the Canadian Grundnorm," in *Arduous Journey: Canadian Indians and Decolonization,* ed. J.R. Ponting (Toronto: McClelland and Stewart, 1986); James Youngblood Henderson, "Mikmaw Tenure in Atlantic Canada," *Dalhousie Law Journal* 18 (1995).

50 Patrick Macklem, "First Nations Self-Government and the Borders of the Canadian Legal Imagination," *McGill Law Journal* 36 (1991); John Borrows, "Living between Water and Rocks: First Nations, Environmental Planning and Democracy," *University of Toronto Law Journal* 47, 4 (1997): 418.

51 Nicholas Blomley, "Disentangling Law: The Practice of Bracketing," *Annual Review of Law and Social Science* 10, 1 (2014); Nicholas Blomley, "The Ties That Blind: Making Fee Simple in the British Columbia Treaty Process," *Transactions of the Institute of British Geographers* 40, 2 (2014).

52 John Borrows, "The Durability of Terra Nullius: *Tsilhqot'in Nation v. British Columbia*," *University of British Columbia Law Review* 48, 3 (2015): 701.

53 *Guerin v The Queen*, [1984] 2 SCR 335, 379–80; *Delgamuukw v British Columbia*, [1997] 3 SCR 1010, para 145.

54 *Royal Proclamation, 1763,* reprinted in RSC 1985, App II, 1.

55 Banner, *How the Indians Lost Their Land,* 87.

56 Lavoie, "Why Restrain Alienation," 1005–8.

57 *Royal Proclamation, 1763.*

58 McNeil, "Self-Government," 477.

59 Ibid., 476, 487–88, 504–8.

60 Banner, *How the Indians Lost Their Land;* Stuart Banner, *Possessing the Pacific* (Cambridge, MA: Harvard University Press, 2007).

61 Banner, *How the Indians Lost Their Land,* 87.

62 Ibid.

63 Ibid., 89.

64 Ibid., 76.

65 Banner, *Possessing the Pacific,* 78.

66 Ibid., 76.

67 Ibid., 75, 78.

68 Olivia Dickason, *Canada's First Nations: A History of Founding Peoples from Earliest Times* (Oxford: Oxford University Press, 1997), 207. Many First Nations took, and continue to take, a different view of these historical treaty relationships – as ones that would "preserve rather than threaten their national integrity." Paul G. McHugh, *Aboriginal Societies and the Common Law: A History of Sovereignty, Status, and Self-Determination* (Oxford: Oxford University Press, 2004), 245.

69 McHugh, *Aboriginal Societies,* 182. McHugh also notes that these shifts in military power aided the transition of Indigenous peoples from "ally" to "subject" in Anglo-Canadian legal thought.

70 Dickason, *Canada's First Nations,* 220–21.

71 Ibid., 208.

72 Ibid., 211.

73 *An Act to Encourage the Gradual Civilization of the Indian Tribes in This Province, and to Amend the Laws Respecting Indians,* 1857, 20 Vict, c 26.

74 John S. Milloy, "The Early *Indian Acts:* Developmental Strategy and Constitutional Change," in *As Long as the Sun Shines and the Water Flows: A Reader in Canadian Native Studies,* ed. Ian L. Getty and Antoine S. Lussier (Vancouver: UBC Press, 1983), 58.

75 Robin Brownlie, "'A Better Citizen Than Lots of White Men': First Nations Enfranchisement – an Ontario Case Study, 1918–1940," *Canadian Historical Review* 87, 1 (2006): 32.

76 McHugh, *Aboriginal Societies,* 246.

77 Ibid.

78 Milloy, "Early *Indian Acts,*" 59.
79 *Indian Act,* SC 1918, c 26.
80 *Constitution Act, 1867,* 30–31 Vict, c 3 (UK), s 91(24).
81 *An Act for the Gradual Enfranchisement of Indians, the Better Management of Indian Affairs, and to Extend the Provisions of the Act 31st Victoria, c. 42,* SC 1869, c 6.
82 Dickason, *Canada's First Nations,* 225–26.
83 *Indian Act,* 1985, s 20(3).
84 Ibid., s 20(2).
85 Ibid., s 22.
86 Ibid., ss 18, 29, 89(1).
87 Ibid., s 25.
88 Ibid., s 24.
89 Ibid., ss 28(1)–(2), 58(1), 58(3).
90 Ibid., ss 37(2), 38(2). Designated lands are exempt from the prohibition on mortgage and seizure. Ibid., s 89(1.1).
91 Ibid., ss 39.1, 40.1(2).
92 Ibid., s 37(1). In *Derrickson v Kennedy*, [2006] 55 BCLR (4th) 123, 379 WAC 96 (CA), the Court of Appeal found that no surrender of reserve land is made or inferred by a lease granted to a non-band member under s 58(3) of the act.
93 *Indian Act,* 1985, s 39(1). This consent may still be deemed by a majority vote under ss 39(2)–(3).
94 Marena Brinkhurst and Anke Kessler, "Land Management on First Nations Reserves: Lawful Possession and Its Determinants," *Journal of Aboriginal Economic Development* 8, 2 (2013); Christopher Alcantara, "Individual Property Rights on Canadian Indian Reserves: The Historical Emergence and Jurisprudence of Certificates of Possession," *Canadian Journal of Native Studies* 23, 2 (2003): 393.
95 *Constitution Act, 1982,* being Schedule B to the *Canada Act, 1982* (UK) 1982, c 11, s 35(1).
96 *Delgamuukw.*
97 *Tsilhqot'in Nation v British Columbia*, [2014] 2 SCR 257.
98 Stuart Banner has likewise identified a shift from "ownership" to "occupancy" in colonial land policy. Banner, *How the Indians Lost Their Land,* 150.
99 Paul G. McHugh, *Aboriginal Title: The Modern Jurisprudence of Tribal Land Rights* (Oxford: Oxford University Press, 2011).
100 *Calder et al. v Attorney-General of British Columbia*, [1973] SCR 313.
101 *Delgamuukw,* para 113.
102 Ibid., paras 124–25.

103 *Tsilhqot'in Nation,* para 15. The court elaborated that "this means it cannot be alienated except to the Crown or encumbered in ways that would prevent future generations of the group from using and enjoying it. Nor can the land be developed or misused in a way that would substantially deprive future generations of the benefit of the land." *Tsilhqot'in Nation,* para 74.

104 Jennifer E. Dalton, "Aboriginal Title and Self-Government in Canada: What Is the True Scope of Comprehensive Land Claims Agreements," *Windsor Review of Legal and Social Issues* 22 (2006).

105 *Framework Agreement on First Nation Land Management* (signed in 1996), https://landsadvisoryboard.ca/wp-content/uploads/2018/11/Framework-Agreement-on-First-Nation-Land-Management-Dec-2018.pdf.

106 *First Nation Land Management Act,* SC 1999, c 24, s 13.3.

107 Government of Canada, Indigenous and Northern Affairs Canada, "First Nations Land Management – Operational and Developmental First Nations," http://www.aadnc-aandc.gc.ca/eng/1327165048269/1327165134401.

Chapter 3: Leaders and Land Reform

1 For example, Lee Alston and Gary Libecap, *Titles, Conflict, and Land Use: The Development of Property Rights and Land Reform on the Brazilian Amazon Frontier* (Ann Arbor: University of Michigan Press, 1999).

2 Benjamin E. Hermalin, "Toward an Economic Theory of Leadership: Leading by Example," *American Economic Review* (1998); Benjamin E. Hermalin, "Leading for the Long Term," *Journal of Economic Behavior and Organization* 62, 1 (2007).

3 Ahlquist and Levi, *In the Interest of Others.*

4 Ibid., Chapter 2.

5 Mariana Mota Prado and Michael J. Trebilcock, "Path Dependence, Development, and the Dynamics of Institutional Reform," *University of Toronto Law Journal* 59, 3 (2009).

6 A review of this literature is Jamie Baxter, "Leadership, Law and Development," *Law and Development Review* 12, 1 (2018). The following section draws on this review.

7 Lee Alston et al., *Brazil in Transition: Beliefs, Leadership, and Institutional Change* (Princeton, NJ: Princeton University Press, 2016), EPUB.

8 Lee Alston, "Beyond Institutions: Beliefs and Leadership," *Journal of Economic History* 77, 2 (2017).

9 Benjamin F. Jones and Benjamin A. Olken, "Do Leaders Matter? National Leadership and Growth since World War II," *Quarterly Journal of Economics* 120, 3 (2005): 839.

10 Robert Rotberg, *The Corruption Cure: How Citizens and Leaders Can Combat Graft* (Princeton, NJ: Princeton University Press, 2017).

11 For example, Margaret Levi and Brad Epperly, "Principled Principals in the Founding Moments of the Rule of Law," in *Global Perspectives on the Rule of Law,* ed. James Heckman, Robert L. Nelson, and Lee Cabatingan (London: Taylor and Francis, 2013).

12 Only rarely is this critique made explicit. Important exceptions are Adrian Leftwich, *Bringing Agency Back In: Politics and Human Agency in Building Institutions and States,* Synthesis and Overview Report, Research Paper 6, June (n.p.: Developmental Leadership Program, 2009), https://res.cloudinary.com/dlprog/image/upload/U8iUC5wKAxNQHSPMaHAjWXXUYff3ibNbzycWY9E5.pdf; Adrian Leftwich, "Beyond Institutions: Rethinking the Role of Leaders, Elites and Coalitions in the Institutional Formation of Developmental States and Strategies," *Forum for Development Studies* 37, 1 (2010).

13 Richard J. Samuels, *Machiavelli's Children: Leaders and Their Legacies in Italy and Japan* (Ithaca, NY: Cornell University Press, 2003), 2.

14 Richard Stubbs, "What Ever Happened to the East Asian Developmental State? The Unfolding Debate," *Pacific Review* 22, 1 (2009): 6; Adrian Leftwich, "Bringing Politics Back In: Towards a Model of the Developmental State," *Journal of Development Studies* 31, 3 (1995): 405–7.

15 Rotberg, *Corruption Cure,* 223.

16 Alston et al., *Brazil in Transition,* Chapter 7.

17 Ahlquist and Levi, "Leadership," 6–7.

18 Leftwich, "Beyond Institutions," 101–2.

19 Alston et al., *Brazil in Transition*, Chapter 7.

20 Ludger Helms, "Institutional Analysis," in *The Oxford Handbook of Political Leadership,* ed. R.A.W. Rhodes and Paul 't Hart (Oxford: Oxford University Press, 2014), 195.

21 Margaret Levi, "Why We Need a New Theory of Government," *Perspectives on Politics* 4, 1 (2006): 12.

22 Gérard Roland, "Understanding Institutional Change: Fast Moving and Slow Moving Institutions," *Studies in Comparative International Development* 38, 4 (2004).

23 Ensminger and Knight, "Changing Social Norms"; Fitzpatrick, "Evolution and Chaos"; Ryan Bubb, "The Evolution of Property Rights: State Law or Informal Norms?," *Journal of Law and Economics* 56, 3

(2013); Louis Putzel et al., "Formalization as Development in Land and Natural Resource Policy," *Society and Natural Resources* 28 (2015); Frank K. Upham, "The Paradoxical Roles of Property Rights in Growth and Development," *Law and Development Review* 8, 2 (2015).

24 Daniel Fitzpatrick and Andrew McWilliam, "Bright-Line Fever: Simple Legal Rules and Complex Property Customs among the Fataluku of East Timor," *Law and Society Review* 47, 2 (2013).

25 Dani Rodrik, "When Ideas Trump Interests: Preferences, Worldviews, and Policy Innovations," *Journal of Economic Perspectives* 28, 1 (2014): 190.

26 Samuels, *Machiavelli's Children,* 5.

27 Edward López and Wayne Leighton, *Madmen, Intellectuals, and Academic Scribblers: The Economic Engine of Political Change* (Stanford, CA: Stanford University Press, 2012), 24. For a discussion of "institutional entrepreneurs" in organizational theory, see Raghu Garud, Cynthia Hardy, and Steve Maguire, "Institutional Entrepreneurship as Embedded Agency: An Introduction to the Special Issue," *Organization Studies* 28, 7 (2007): 957.

28 Jaime Faustino and David Booth, "Development Entrepreneurship: How Donors and Leaders Can Foster Institutional Change," *Working Politically in Practice Series* (December 2014): 20.

29 López and Leighton, *Madmen,* 190–91.

30 Wim Naudé, "Entrepreneurship and Economic Development," in *International Development: Ideas, Experience, and Prospects,* ed. Bruce Currie-Adler et al. (Oxford: Oxford University Press, 2013), 3.

31 Alston et al., *Brazil in Transition,* Chapter 7.

32 Rodrik, "When Ideas Trump Interests," 198–99.

33 Riker and Sened, "A Political Theory of the Origin of Property Rights," 954–55.

34 Jay A. Conger and Rabindra N. Kanungo, "Charismatic Leadership in Organizations: Perceived Behavioral Attributes and Their Measurement," *Journal of Organizational Behavior* 15, 5 (1994).

35 Ahlquist and Levi, "Leadership," 8.

36 "Our task is to ... discover why a firm emerges at all in a specialized exchange economy." Ronald Coase, "The Nature of the Firm," *Economica* 4, 16 (1937): 390.

37 Armen A. Alchian and Harold Demsetz, "Production, Information Costs, and Economic Organization," *American Economic Review* 62, 5 (1972): 777.

38 Ibid., 778.

39 Bengt Holmstrom, "Moral Hazard in Teams," *Bell Journal of Economics* 13, 2 (1982).

40 Ahlquist and Levi, *In the Interest of Others,* Chapter 2; Levi and Epperly, "Principled Principals"; Douglass C. North, *Understanding the Process of Economic Change* (Princeton, NJ: Princeton University Press, 2005), 64.

41 Herbert A. Simon, *Models of Bounded Rationality: Empirically Grounded Economic Reason* (Cambridge, MA: MIT Press, 1982). Simon himself has described the theory of bounded rationality in terms that distinguish it from structural approaches to social change. See Herbert A. Simon, "Bounded Rationality in Social Science: Today and Tomorrow," *Mind and Society* 1, 1 (2000): 25: "Bounded rationality is simply the idea that the choices people make are determined not only by some consistent overall goal and the properties of the external world, but also by the knowledge that decision makers do and don't have of the world, their ability or inability to evoke that knowledge when it is relevant, to work out the consequences of their actions, to conjure up possible courses of action, to cope with uncertainty ... and to adjudicate among their many competing wants."

42 Vincent Ostrom and Elinor Ostrom, "Public Goods and Public Choices," in *Elinor Ostrom and the Bloomington School of Political Economy,* vol. 2, *Resource Governance,* ed. Daniel H. Cole and Michael D. McGinnis (Lanham, MD: Lexington Books, 2015). The construction here – which varies slightly from Levi and Ahlquist – assumes that output is equally divisible among each member of the group. While this might be accomplished through various mechanisms, I find evidence that at least some First Nations do this directly, for example, by issuing annual dividend payments to their members generated through band-operated enterprises.

43 Banner, "Transitions between Property Regimes," S362. The distinction between public and club goods in the present context is largely immaterial.

44 Note that this result obtains in the two-player setting. No attempt is made here to model a more general result.

45 See Benjamin E. Hermalin, "Leadership and Corporate Culture," in *Handbook of Organizational Economics,* ed. Robert Gibbons and John Roberts (Princeton, NJ: Princeton University Press, 2012), 441.

46 James Andreoni, "Leadership Giving in Charitable Fund-Raising," *Journal of Public Economic Theory* 8, 1 (2006): 3.

47 Ahlquist and Levi, *In the Interest of Others,* Chapter 2.

48 Ibid.

49 For a view on the role of political competition among leaders in development contexts, see Daron Acemoglu, Tristan Reed, and James

A. Robinson, "Chiefs: Economic Development and Elite Control of Civil Society in Sierra Leone," *Journal of Political Economy* 122, 2 (2014).

50 Ahlquist and Levi show that $R_{max} = (N-1)\sqrt{2E_{\theta}[\Delta V_{i}]}$. Ahlquist and Levi, *In the Interest of Others,* Chapter 2.

51 Ibid.

52 Ibid.

53 Ibid.

54 Ibid.

55 For a model about how more responsive procedural controls can give agents/politicians more freedom of action, see John Ferejohn, "Accountability and Authority: Toward a Theory of Political Accountability," in *Democracy, Accountability, and Representation,* ed. Adam Przeworski and Susan C. Stokes (Cambridge: Cambridge University Press, 1999), cited in Ahlquist and Levi, *In the Interest of Others,* Chapter 2. See also Margaret Levi, Audrey Sacks, and Tom Tyler, "Conceptualizing Legitimacy, Measuring Legitimating Beliefs," *American Behavioral Scientist* 53, 3 (2009).

56 Amy Kapczynski, "The Access to Knowledge Mobilization and the New Politics of Intellectual Property," *Yale Law Journal* 117 (2008): 860.

57 Giandomenico Majone, *Temporal Consistency and Policy Credibility: Why Democracies Need Non-Majoritarian Institutions,* European University Institute Working Papers RSC No 96/57 (Florence: European University Institute, 1996), 7.

Chapter 4: Save or Sell?

1 Brinkhurst and Kessler, "Land Management"; Mary Doidge, B. James Deaton, and Bethany Woods, "Institutional Change on First Nations: Examining Factors Influencing First Nations' Adoption of the Framework Agreement on First Nation Land Management," *Journal of Aboriginal Economic Development* 8, 2 (2013); Lavoie and Lavoie, "Land Regime Choice."

2 Brinkhurst and Kessler, ibid., 88–93; Doidge, Deaton, and Woods, ibid., 76–77.

3 "Westbank First Nation: Community, Leadership, Pride," *Canadian Business Journal* 5, 8 (2012): 173.

4 Robert Muckle, *The First Nations of British Columbia: An Anthropological Overview* (Vancouver: UBC Press, 1998), 33.

5 John R. Wagner, "Landscape Aesthetics, Water, and Settler Colonialism in the Okanagan Valley of British Columbia," *Journal of Ecological Anthropology* 12, 1 (2008): 24.

6 John E. Hall, *The Report of the Commission of Inquiry Concerning Certain Matters Associated with the Westbank Indian Band* (Ottawa: Canadian Government Publishing Centre, 1988), 5.

7 J.A.J. McKenna and Richard McBride, *Report of the Royal Commission on Indian Affairs for the Province of British Columbia (1913–1916),* (Victoria: Acme Press, 1916), 702, 716. In 1983, the Westbank First Nation reached a settlement with the federal government as compensation for reducing its land area.

8 Hall, *Report of the Commission of Inquiry,* 5; Robert White-Harvey, "Reservation Geography and the Restoration of Native Self-Government," *Dalhousie Law Journal* 17 (1994): 596.

9 Statistics Canada, "Tsinstikeptum 10, IRI [Census subdivision], British Columbia and British Columbia [Province] (table)" and "Tsinstikeptum 9, IRI [Census subdivision], British Columbia and British Columbia [Province] (table)," *Census Profile, 2016 Census,* Catalogue no. 98-316-X2016001 (Ottawa: Statistics Canada, 2017), https://www12.statcan.gc.ca/census-recensement/2016/dp-pd/prof/index.cfm?Lang=E. According to membership data from the Westbank First Nation website, 60 percent of its 855 members live on reserve, or approximately 5.7 percent of the total residential population. Westbank First Nation, "Population and Demographics," https://www.wfn.ca/our-community/about-westbank-first-nation/population-demographics.htm.

10 Roger Sugden and Keith Studies, "Economic Development of the BC Interior: A Case Study of Occupations in the Okanagan, 1881–1921," *BC Studies* 194 (2017): 65.

11 "Westbank First Nation: Community, Leadership, Pride."

12 Indigenous and Northern Affairs Canada, "First Nation Profiles: Population Characteristics – Westbank First Nation," http://fnp-ppn.aandc-aadnc.gc.ca/fnp/main/search/FNPopulation.aspx?BAND_NUMBER=601&lang=eng.

13 "Westbank First Nation: Community, Leadership, Pride."

14 *Westbank First Nation Self-Government Agreement between Her Majesty the Queen in Right of Canada and Westbank First Nation,* 2003, https://www.wfn.ca/docs/self-government-agreement-english.pdf.

15 *Westbank First Nation Self-Government Act,* SC 2004, c 17; *Westbank First Nation Constitution,* March 31, 2016.

16 *Westbank First Nation Self-Government Agreement between Her Majesty the Queen in Right of Canada and Westbank First Nation,* s 22(a).

17 *Constitution Act, 1982; Westbank First Nation Self-Government Agreement,* s 1(a). The agreement explicitly defines the self-governance rights of

the Westbank First Nation without prejudice to future land claims and treaty-making processes; see s 4(a).

18 *Westbank First Nation Self-Government Agreement,* s 87. Existing interests granted under the prior *Indian Act* land regime, including CP allotments and leases, remained in force under the new agreement (see s 88); *Westbank First Nation Constitution*, s 100.

19 *Westbank First Nation Land Use Law,* No 2007-01, s 2.2.

20 *Westbank First Nation Constitution,* s 103; *Westbank First Nation Allotment Law,* No 2006-03, s 3.1.

21 Allotments by agreement with individual community members are subject to approval by a majority of electors at a special meeting of community members, while allotments specifically for housing purposes are subject to a simplified procedure through a special commission established for this purpose: *Westbank First Nation Allotment Law,* ss 7.1, 11.2, 13. A more complex process requiring a community referendum exists for allotments made for the purpose of "raising revenue": *Westbank First Nation Allotment Law,* s 29.

22 *Westbank First Nation Constitution,* ss 104.1, 104.3–104.8, 104.9–104.11.

23 Ibid., ss 106.1, 108.4.

24 Ibid., ss 107.1–107.2. Mortgage interests are restricted to other members and to the First Nation itself.

25 Hall, *Report of the Commission of Inquiry*, 6.

26 Ibid., 8–9.

27 Ibid., 7–8.

28 Ibid., 6.

29 Ibid., 9.

30 John F. Leslie, "The Indian Act: An Historical Perspective," *Canadian Parliamentary Review* 25, 2 (2002): 26.

31 John F. Leslie, "The Policy Agenda of Native Peoples from World War II to the 1969 White Paper," in *Aboriginal Policy Research: Setting the Agenda for Change,* ed. Jerry P. White, Paul Maxim, and Dan Beavon (Toronto: Thompson Educational Publishing, 2013), 18–21.

32 H.B. Hawthorn, ed., *A Survey of the Contemporary Indians of Canada: Economic, Political, Educational Needs and Policies* (Ottawa: Government of Canada, Indian Affairs Branch, 1966).

33 Canada, Department of Indian Affairs and Northern Development, *Statement of the Government of Canada on Indian Policy, 1969* (Ottawa: Indian Affairs and Northern Development, 1969).

34 Leslie, "Policy Agenda," 22.

35 Hall, *Report of the Commission of Inquiry,* 11.

36 However, land interests held by non-community members appeared to have been subject to provincial real property taxes. J.W. Evans, *Some Indicators of Change: Westbank Indian Band (1971/72 to 1980/81)* (Vancouver: Indian and Northern Affairs Canada, 1982), 20.
37 For a discussion of the transaction costs associated with federal oversight of reserve lands, see Thomas Isaac, "First Nations Land Management Act and Third Party Interests," *University of Alberta Law Review* 42, 4 (2004); Christopher Alcantara, "Reduce Transaction Costs? Yes. Strengthen Property Rights? Maybe: The First Nations Land Management Act and Economic Development on Canadian Indian Reserves," *Public Choice* 132, 3–4 (2007).
38 Hall, *Report of the Commission of Inquiry,* 11.
39 Ibid., 14.
40 The two brothers appear to have spelled their surnames differently, as indicated in the text.
41 Evans, *Some Indicators of Change,* 25.
42 Ibid., 4; Hall, *Report of the Commission of Inquiry,* 15.
43 Evans, *Some Indicators of Change,* 6.
44 Library and Archives Canada, R1084-0-5-E, Commission of Inquiry Concerning Certain Matters Associated with the Westbank Indian Band fonds, "Transcript of Proceedings," vol. LXV, June 5, 1987, 9649–50.
45 Ibid., 9649.
46 Ibid., 9656–57.
47 Evans, *Some Indicators of Change,* 17.
48 Ibid., 18.
49 Ibid., 10.
50 Hall, *Report of the Commission of Inquiry,* 114.
51 Ibid., 115–16.
52 Ibid., 64, 116–21.
53 Ibid., 39.
54 Library and Archives Canada, Commission of Inquiry, 9652.
55 Evans, *Some Indicators of Change,* 12, 16–21.
56 Ibid., 12, 22.
57 Hall, *Report of the Commission of Inquiry,* x.
58 Ibid.
59 M.F. Nickason, *The Westbank Inquiry: Managing the Response of the Department of Indian and Northern Affairs* (Ottawa: Indian and Northern Affairs Canada, 1988), 3. See also Hall, *Report of the Commission of Inquiry,* xv.
60 Nickason, *The Westbank Inquiry,* 3.
61 Evans, *Some Indicators of Change,* 24–25.
62 Nickason, *The Westbank Inquiry,* 3.

63 Hall, *Report of the Commission of Inquiry,* 337–38.

64 Evans, *Some Indicators of Change,* 8.

65 Ibid., 7–8.

66 Hall, *Report of the Commission of Inquiry,* 119.

67 Ibid., 155.

68 Ibid., 114.

69 Canada, "Indian Lands Registry System (ILRS)," http://services.aadnc-aandc.gc.ca/ILRS_Public/home/home.aspx.

70 Indigenous and Northern Affairs Canada, "First Nation Profiles: Registered Population – Membertou," http://fnp-ppn.aandc-aadnc.gc.ca/fnp/main/search/FNRegPopulation.aspx?BAND_NUMBER=26&lang=eng.

71 Jacquelyn Thayer Scott, "'Doing Business with the Devil': Land, Sovereignty, and Corporate Partnerships in Membertou, Inc.," in *Self-Determination: The Other Path for Native Americans,* ed. Terry Anderson, Bruce L. Benson, and Thomas Flanagan (Stanford, CA: Stanford University Press, 2006), 246–47.

72 Membertou Reserve Band Council, "Consolidated Financial Statements," March 2017, 4.

73 Kelly Toughill, "Capitalism behind Success of Tiny Cape Breton Reserve," *Toronto Star,* March 17, 2004, A06.

74 *Re Indian Reserve, Sydney (City),* paras 10–11; Membertou First Nation, "Kings Road Reserve 100 Years Later," accessed November 16, 2017, http://www.membertou.ca/sites/default/files/KingsRoad_8Page%20Spread_final.pdf.

75 *Re Indian Reserve, Sydney (City),* para 34.

76 In fact, the Membertou CEO during this foundational period took a substantial pay cut to leave his law office and return to the community. Daniel Christmas, *IWCL Case Study: Membertou First Nation,* YouTube video, posted by Coady International Institute, July 21, 2011, https://www.youtube.com/watch?v=Z8SrNfDFFEQ&feature=related, 6:55. That same CEO earned between $95,000 and $150,000 in 2001; see Kelly Toughill, "Boardroom Finesse Buys Band Respect," *Toronto Star,* March 3, 2001, NAR.

77 Hugh Millward, "The Development, Decline, and Revival of Mining on the Sydney Coalfield," *Canadian Geographer* 28, 2 (1984): 182.

78 Laura Eggertson, "Getting Down to Business," *Toronto Star,* January 16, 2011, IN1.

79 Jon Tattrie, "Native Uprising," *Atlantic Business,* August 25, 2011, http://www.atlanticbusinessmagazine.net/article/native-uprising/.

80 Jacqueline King, "The Old and New Picture of Boston's Native Americans," *Bay State Banner,* November 16, 1978, 2; Janet Riddell, "Those

Non-Indian Indians: A Struggle for Recognition and Aid Confronts American Indians," *Boston Globe,* April 11, 1971, A3.

81 Joe Pilali, "Indian Council Seeking Funds for New Boston Headquarters," *Boston Globe,* December 21, 1973, 16.

82 King, "The Old and New Picture."

83 Eggertson, "Getting Down to Business."

84 Stephen Cornell et al., "Seizing the Future: Why Some Native Nations Do and Others Don't," in *Rebuilding Native Nations: Strategies for Governance and Development,* ed. Miriam Jorgensen (Tucson: University of Arizona Press, 2007), 315.

85 Christmas, *IWCL Case Study.*

86 Scott, "'Doing Business with the Devil,'" 262–64.

87 Ibid., 264.

88 Cited in ibid., 267.

89 Ahlquist and Levi, *In the Interest of Others,* Chapter 2.

90 *Constitution Act, 1982,* s 35.

91 *R v Sparrow,* [1990] 1 SCR 1075.

92 *Delgamuukw v British Columbia.*

93 *Haida Nation v British Columbia (Minister of Forests),* [2004] 3 SCR 511; *Rio Tinto Alcan Inc. v Carrier Sekani Tribal Council,* [2010] 2 SCR 650.

94 *R v Marshall,* [1999] 3 SCR 456; *R v Marshall* (reconsideration refused), [1999] 3 SCR 533. For a history of these treaties in the context of the *Marshall* case, see William Wicken, *Mi'kmaq Treaties on Trial: History, Land and Donald Marshall Junior* (Toronto: University of Toronto Press, 2001).

95 *Fisheries Act,* RSC 1985, c F-14.

96 Russel Barsh and James (Sa'ke'j) Youngblood Henderson, "Marshalling the Rule of Law in Canada: Of Eels and Honour," *Constitutional Forum* 11, 1 (1999): 1.

97 Royal Commission on the Donald Marshall, Jr., Prosecution (NS), *Royal Commission on the Donald Marshall, Jr., Prosecution: Digest of Findings and Recommendations* (Halifax: The Commission, 1989).

98 Bruce Wildsmith, "Vindicating Mi'kmaq Rights: The Struggle Before, During and After *Marshall,*" *Windsor Yearbook of Access to Justice* 19 (2001).

99 Bruce Wildsmith, counsel for the Union of Nova Scotia Indians in the *Marshall* case, asserts that Marshall's activities were an effort to get "back to his roots" and not part of a broader litigation strategy. Ibid., 216.

100 Terrance Paul, "Building Sustainable Economies: Approaches and Perspectives," Presentation at the Emerging Leaders seminar, Native

Nations Institute for Leadership, Management, and Policy, University of Arizona, Tucson, March 25, 2010, https://nnigovernance.arizona.edu/terrance-paul-building-sustainable-economies-membertou-first-nation.

101 Wildsmith, "Vindicating Mi'kmaq Rights," 216.

102 Ibid., 216–17.

103 *R v Marshall*, [1999] 3 SCR 456, paras 53–56.

104 Mark D. Walters, "Brightening the Covenant Chain: Aboriginal Treaty Meanings in Law and History after *Marshall*," *Dalhousie Law Journal* 24 (2001): 78.

105 *R v Marshall*, [1999] 3 SCR 456, paras 58–59.

106 *Union of Nova Scotia Indians v Maritimes and Northeast Pipeline Management Ltd.*, 1999 CanLII 8932 (FCA).

107 In public comments, Berndt Christmas observed that the litigation "sparked an interest in our community from a perception point of view that were [sic] there to do business, but we were also ready to go the extra mile if people weren't going to take us serious [sic]." Berndt Christmas, "First Nations Progression Model: The Use of Multiple Lines," speech to the Canadian Evaluation Society Conference, May 2002. Kelly Toughill's reporting also notes that Membertou's track record made it attractive for companies to avoid costly legal battles. Toughill, "Capitalism behind Success."

108 It may well be possible to characterize these litigation efforts as themselves part of leaders' rents based on a broader commitment to gaining recognition for Indigenous rights, but as this is broader in scope than my present focus on inalienability rules with respect to reserve lands, I leave it to future research and confine my analysis here to the role of litigation in equilibrium selection.

109 K. Brown et al., "'Membertou Always Wanted to Succeed': The Membertou Business Model," *Journal of Aboriginal Economic Development* 8, 1 (2012): 44.

110 Christmas, *IWCL Case Study*.

111 Brown et al., "'Membertou Always Wanted to Succeed,'" 44.

112 Christmas, *IWCL Case Study*, 13:30.

113 Scott, "'Doing Business with the Devil,'" 247, 265. Scott offers the first community referendum as an illustration of Membertou's "allegiance" to policies protecting communal ownership of land.

114 Ibid., 247.

115 Hal Higgins, "Membertou First Reserve in Atlantic Canada to Try Online Referendum," *CBC News*, April 22, 2016, http://www.cbc.ca/news/canada/nova-scotia/referendum-membertou-mi-kmaq-indigenous-voting-1.3548351.

116 Scott, "'Doing Business with the Devil,'" 260.
117 Evidence of John Paul, Membertou First Nation, to the House of Commons Standing Committee on Aboriginal Affairs and Northern Development, October 24, 2012, https://www.ourcommons.ca/DocumentViewer/en/41-1/AANO/meeting-46/evidence.
118 Ahlquist and Levi, *In the Interest of Others*.
119 Scott, "'Doing Business with the Devil,'" 259; *First Nations Financial Transparency Act,* SC 2013, c 7.
120 Brown et al., "'Membertou Always Wanted to Succeed,'" 37.
121 Scott, "'Doing Business with the Devil,'" 251.
122 Brown et al., "'Membertou Always Wanted to Succeed,'" 37.
123 *Membertou: Accountable to the Community,* YouTube video, posted by Centre for First Nations Governance, January 10, 2011, https://www.youtube.com/watch?v=GuHc-sONf4g&list=UU6Kmkt3MUlLgGT4vN4NVKWQ, 4:25–5:15.
124 Rachel Starks, *Managing Land, Governing for the Future: Finding the Path Forward for Membertou* (Dartmouth, NS: Atlantic Policy Congress of First Nations Chiefs Secretariat, 2013), 15.
125 Ibid., 15–16.
126 Daron Acemoglu and James A. Robinson, *Why Nations Fail: The Origins of Power, Prosperity, and Poverty* (London: Profile Books, 2012).

Chapter 5: Ideas and Interests in Uncertain Times

1 Jay A. Conger and Rabindra N. Kanungo, "Toward a Behavioral Theory of Charismatic Leadership in Organizational Settings," *Academy of Management Review* 12, 4 (1987): 637, citing in part R.J. House and Mary L. Baetz, "Leadership: Some Empirical Generalizations and New Research Directions," in *Research in Organizational Behavior,* ed. B.M. Staw (Greenwich, CT: JAI Press, 1979).
2 See generally J.R. Miller, *Compact, Contract, Covenant: Aboriginal Treaty-Making in Canada* (Toronto: University of Toronto Press, 2009). For a history of treaty negotiations in British Columbia, see Christopher MacKee, *Treaty Talks in British Columbia: Building a New Relationship* (Vancouver: UBC Press, 2010). For a history of the Nisga'a treaty, see Daniel Raunet, *Without Surrender, without Consent: A History of the Nisga'a Land Claims* (Vancouver: Douglas and McIntyre, 1996). Several good histories of the James Bay Cree treaty negotiations are: Wendy Moss, "The Implementation of the James Bay and Northern Quebec Agreement," in *Aboriginal Peoples and the Law: Indian, Metis and Inuit Rights in Canada,* ed. Bradford Morse (Montreal and Kingston: McGill-Queen's University Press, 1985); Boyce Richardson,

Strangers Devour the Land (White River Junction, VT: Chelsea Green Publishing, 2008); Sean McCutcheon, *Electric Rivers: The Story of the James Bay Project* (Montreal: Black Rose Books, 1991); Richard Salisbury, *A Homeland for the Cree Regional Development in James Bay, 1971–1981* (Montreal and Kingston: McGill-Queen's University Press, 2014).

3 Carole Blackburn, "Searching for Guarantees in the Midst of Uncertainty: Negotiating Aboriginal Rights and Title in British Columbia," *American Anthropologist* 107, 4 (2005); Blomley, "The Ties That Blind."

4 Cornelia Woll, *Firm Interests: How Governments Shape Business Lobbying on Global Trade* (Ithaca, NY: Cornell University Press, 2008), 8–11.

5 Ibid., 9. For further discussion, see Alston et al., *Brazil in Transition,* Chapter 7.

6 Rodrik, "When Ideas Trump Interests," 190. Knight's original work on risk and uncertainty is Frank H. Knight, *Risk, Uncertainty and Profit* (Boston: Houghton Mifflin, 1921).

7 Ahlquist and Levi, *In the Interest of Others,* Chapter 7.

8 Ibid.

9 Vivien A. Schmidt, "Discursive Institutionalism: The Explanatory Power of Ideas and Discourse," *Annual Review of Political Science* 11, 1 (2008); Vivien A. Schmidt, "Speaking of Change: Why Discourse Is Key to the Dynamics of Policy Transformation," *Critical Policy Studies* 5, 2 (2011); Vivien A. Schmidt, "Discursive Institutionalism: Understanding Policy in Context," in *Handbook of Critical Policy Studies*, ed. Frank Fischer, Douglas Torgerson, Anna Durnová, and Michael Orsini (Cheltenham, UK: Edward Elgar, 2015). For a critique challenging the commensurability between discursive institutionalism and other schools of institutionalism, see Colin Hay, "Ideas and the Construction of Interests," in *Ideas and Politics in Social Science Research,* ed. Daniel Béland and Robert Henry Cox (Oxford: Oxford University Press, 2011). For a critique that discursive institutionalism affords little attention to institutions, see Stephen Bell, "Where Are the Institutions? The Limits of Vivien Schmidt's Constructivism," *British Journal of Political Science* 42, 3 (2012).

10 Jal Mehta, "The Varied Roles of Ideas in Politics: From 'Whether' to 'How,'" in *Ideas and Politics in Political Science Research,* ed. Daniel Béland and Robert Henry Cox (Oxford: Oxford University Press, 2011), EPUB, Chapter 1.

11 Ibid., Chapter 1.

12 Schmidt, "Discursive Institutionalism: The Explanatory Power of Ideas and Discourse," 306.

13 Schmidt defines these different dimensions as "normative" and "cognitive." Ibid., 304.

14 Vivien A. Schmidt, "How, Where and When Does Discourse Matter in Small States' Welfare State Adjustment," *New Political Economy* 8, 1 (2003): 134.

15 Ibid., 137.

16 Harvey A. Feit, "Gifts of the Land: Hunting Territories, Guaranteed Incomes and the Construction of Social Relations in James Bay Cree Society," *Senri Ethnological Studies* 30 (1991): 224, 228–29.

17 Hans Carlson, *Home Is the Hunter: The James Bay Cree and Their Land* (Vancouver: UBC Press, 2014).

18 *Nisga'a Final Agreement,* Canada, British Columbia, and Nisga'a Nation, April 27, 1999, http://www.nnkn.ca/files/u28/nis-eng.pdf; Gary Fiegehen and Alex Rose, *Nisga'a: People of the Nass River* (Vancouver: Douglas and McIntyre, 1993).

19 Cole Harris, *Making Native Space: Colonialism, Resistance and Reserves in British Columbia* (Vancouver: UBC Press, 2007), 205; Hamar Foster, "Honouring the Queen's Flag: A Legal and Historical Perspective on the Nisga'a Treaty," *BC Studies* 120 (1998/99): 15–16.

20 Hamar Foster, Heather Raven, and Jeremy Webber, eds., *Let Right Be Done: Aboriginal Title, the Calder Case and the Future of Indigenous Rights* (Vancouver: UBC Press, 2007), 66.

21 Harris, *Making Native Space,* 249–50. See Appendix in Foster, Raven, and Webber, ibid., 241.

22 Foster, "Honouring the Queen's Flag," 22.

23 *Indian Act,* RSC 1927, c 98, s 141.

24 Joan Harper, *He Moved a Mountain: The Life of Frank Calder and the Nisga'a Land Claims Accord* (Vancouver: Ronsdale Press, 2013), Chapter 3.

25 *Calder et al. v Attorney-General of British Columbia.* For background on the case, see Foster, Raven, and Webber, *Let Right Be Done.*

26 Frank Calder regarded this result as a success. See Foster, Raven, and Webber, ibid., 45.

27 Alex Rose, *Spirit Dance at Meziadin: Chief Joseph Gosnell and the Nisga'a Treaty* (Madeira Park, BC: Harbour Publishing, 2001), 107–9, 143.

28 Ibid., 107–9, 166.

29 *Nisga'a Agreement in Principle,* 1996, https://www.crownpub.bc.ca/Product/Details/7655001512_S.

30 Douglas Sanders, "We Intend to Live Here Forever: A Primer on the Nisga'a Treaty," *University of British Columbia Law Review* 33, 1 (1999): 104–5; Rose, *Spirit Dance,* 175–200.

31 Taiaiake Alfred and Jeff Corntassel, "Being Indigenous: Resurgences against Contemporary Colonialism," *Government and Opposition* 40, 4 (2005); Neil Sterritt, "The Nisga'a Treaty: Competing Claims Ignored," *BC Studies* 120 (1998). Members of the community of Gingolx launched a court action against the federal government in April 2000, hoping to prevent ratification. Ross Hoffman and Andrew Robinson, "Nisga'a Self-Government: A New Journey Has Begun," *Canadian Journal of Native Studies* 30, 2 (2010): 399.

32 Overall returns of the referendum to ratify the NFA were 61 percent in favour, 23 percent opposed, and 15 percent abstaining. Harper, *He Moved a Mountain,* Chapter 16.

33 *Sga'nisim Sim'augit (Chief Mountain) v Canada (Attorney General)*, 2013 BCCA 49, para 5. The British Columbia Court of Appeal ruled in favour of the Nisga'a Nation.

34 Sanders, "We Intend to Live Here Forever," 103.

35 *Nisga'a Final Agreement,* c 2, para 23.

36 Ibid., c 2, para 25.

37 Ibid., c 3, para 4.

38 Ibid., c 3, paras 3–4.

39 *Nisga'a Nation Entitlement Act,* NLGSR 2000/12, as amended by the *Nisga'a Nation Entitlement Amendment Act, 2010*, NLGSR 2010/02, ss 2–2.1; *Nisga'a Village Entitlement Act,* NLGSR 2000/13, s 2.

40 *Nisga'a Nation Entitlement Act*, ss 3(1)–3(2); *Nisga'a Village Entitlement Act,* ss 3(1)–3(2).

41 *Nisga'a Landholding Transition Act,* NLGSR 2009/02, ss 2–3.

42 Ibid., s 4.

43 Harper, *He Moved a Mountain,* Chapter 3.

44 Ibid., Chapter 7.

45 "The Legacy of Frank Calder," *Times Colonist,* November 7, 2006; "Native Member Proposes Indians' Bill of Rights," *Victoria Times,* February 24, 1950; Harper, *He Moved a Mountain,* Chapter 3.

46 Harper, ibid., Chapter 4.

47 Canada, *Statement of the Government of Canada on Indian Policy, 1969*.

48 Harper, *He Moved a Mountain,* Chapter 9.

49 In a letter to Minister of Indian Affairs and Northern Development Jean Chretien in November 1969, Calder, citing resolutions from the 12th Annual Convention of the Nisga'a Tribal Council, wrote that "we must ensure that all British Columbians have equal rights and responsibilities under the Canadian Constitution." Cited in John Borrows, "Re-living the Present: Titles, Treaties, and the Trickster in British Columbia," *BC Studies* 120 (1998/99): 106.

50 Rose, *Spirit Dance,* 88–89.
51 Foster, Raven, and Webber, *Let Right Be Done,* 38.
52 Rose, *Spirit Dance,* 143–52.
53 Quoted in Tracie Scott, *Postcolonial Sovereignty? The Nisga'a Final Agreement* (Saskatoon: Purich Publishing, 2012), 140.
54 Schmidt, "How, Where and When," 137–38.
55 *The Constitution of the Nisga'a Nation,* October 9, 1998, art 36.
56 Ibid., art 31(2).
57 Hoffman and Robinson, "Nisga'a Self-Government," 401.
58 Ibid., 396–98, 402.
59 *James Bay and Northern Quebec Agreement and Complementary Agreements* (Ste-Foy, QC: Les Publications du Québec, 1998). Miller, *Compact, Contract, Covenant,* 257. The proposed project also encompassed large areas of Inuit land to the north of Cree territory.
60 Harvey A. Feit, "James Bay Cree Self-Governance and Land Management," in *We Are Here: Politics of Aboriginal Land Tenure,* ed. Edwin Wilmsen (Berkeley: University of California Press, 1989), 70; Stanley Warner and Raymond Coppinger, "Hydroelectric Power Development at James Bay: Establishing a Frame of Reference," in *Social and Environmental Impacts of the James Bay Hydroelectric Project,* ed. James F. Hornig (Montreal and Kingston: McGill-Queen's University Press, 1999), 20.
61 Billy Diamond, "Aboriginal Rights: The James Bay Experience," in *The Quest for Justice: Aboriginal Peoples and Aboriginal Rights,* ed. Menno Boldt and Anthony Long (Toronto: University of Toronto Press, 1985), 266; Warner and Coppinger, ibid., 26.
62 Diamond, ibid., 266. Population estimates at the time vary. Warner and Coppinger place the number between 5,000 and 6,000. Warner and Coppinger, ibid., 20. Diamond notes that the registered Cree population in 1971 was 5,638 persons. Diamond, ibid., 266. For a description of the watershed, see Hans Carlson, "A Watershed of Words: Litigating and Negotiating Nature in Eastern James Bay, 1971–75," *Canadian Historical Review* 85, 1 (2004): 63.
63 Richardson, *Strangers Devour the Land,* 82.
64 Carlson, *Home Is the Hunter,* 209.
65 Ibid.
66 Richardson, *Strangers Devour the Land,* 86.
67 Roy MacGregor, *Chief: The Fearless Vision of Billy Diamond* (Markham, ON: Penguin Books Canada, 1990), 44.
68 Ibid., 40–41, 45.
69 Ibid., 57–58, 65, 67; Richardson, *Strangers Devour the Land,* 82.
70 Diamond, "Aboriginal Rights," 267.

71 Warner and Coppinger, "Hydroelectric Power Development," 21–22; MacGregor, *Chief,* 68–69.

72 *James Bay Region Development Act,* SQ 1971, c 34.

73 *Kanatewat et al. v James Bay Development Corporation et al.*, 1973 CarswellQue, [1974] RP 38 (QCSC). For further history, see Moss, "Implementation," 685.

74 *James Bay Development Corporation et al. v Kanatewat et al.*, [1975] CA 166 (QC).

75 Arthur Ray, *Aboriginal Rights Claims and the Making and Remaking of History* (Montreal and Kingston: McGill-Queen's University Press, 2016); Miller, *Compact, Contract, Covenant,* 259–60; Diamond, "Aboriginal Rights," 273.

76 MacGregor, *Chief,* 73.

77 *James Bay and Northern Quebec Agreement.*

78 Miller, *Compact, Contract, Covenant,* 261.

79 Gouvernement du Québec and Grand Council of the Crees, *Agreement Concerning a New Relationship between le Gouvernement du Québec and the Crees of Québec (La Paix Des braves),* 2002, http://www.autochtones.gouv.qc.ca/relations_autochtones/ententes/cris/entente_cris_20020207.pdf; Government of Canada, Grand Council of the Crees, and Cree Nation Government, *Agreement on Cree Nation Governance between the Crees of Eeyou Istchee and the Government of Canada,* 2017 (*Cree Nation Governance Agreement*), https://www.rcaanc-cirnac.gc.ca/eng/1504798011685/1542989671051.

80 Carlson, *Home Is the Hunter,* 243. For several in-depth dialogues among Cree hunters in the early 1970s, see Harvey A. Feit, "Dialogues on Surviving: Eeyou Hunters' Ways of Engagement with Land, Governments, and Youth," in *Entangled Territorialities: Negotiating Indigenous Lands in Australia and Canada,* ed. Françoise Dussart and Sylvie Poirier (Toronto: University of Toronto Press, 2017).

81 Diamond, "Aboriginal Rights," 266.

82 Ibid., 280.

83 Lisa Palmer and Maureen Tehan, "Shared Citizenship and Self-Government in Canada: A Case Study of James Bay and Nunavik (Northern Quebec)," in *Settling with Indigenous People: Modern Treaty and Agreement-Making,* ed. Marcia Langton (Sydney: Federation Press, 2006), 20.

84 Ibid., 20.

85 Harvey A. Feit, "Neoliberal Governance and James Bay Cree Governance: Negotiated Agreements, Oppositional Struggles, and Co-governance," in *Indigenous Peoples and Autonomy: Insights for a Global Age,* ed. Mario Blaser et al. (Vancouver: UBC Press, 2010), 51–52.

86 MacGregor, *Chief,* 71.

87 Ibid., 115.
88 Carlson, *Home Is the Hunter,* xv.
89 MacGregor, *Chief,* 135.
90 Carlson, *Home Is the Hunter,* 205.
91 *James Bay and Northern Quebec Agreement,* s 11A; Robert Anderson, *Economic Development among the Aboriginal Peoples in Canada: The Hope for the Future* (North York, ON: Captus Press, 1999), 67.
92 Anderson, ibid., 67.
93 Gail Whiteman, "The Impact of Economic Development in James Bay, Canada: The Cree Tallymen Speak Out," *Organization and Environment* 17, 4 (2004).
94 See Hay, "Ideas and the Construction of Interests." For an alternative view, see Schmidt, "Speaking of Change."

Chapter 6: The Future of Inalienable Property

1 Priest, "Creating an American Property Law," 393.
2 Blomley, "The Ties That Blind"; Blomley, "Disentangling Law."
3 See Shmuel Noah Eisenstadt, *Max Weber on Charisma and Institution Building* (Chicago: University of Chicago Press, 1968), 18–27.
4 Baland and Platteau, "Division of the Commons," 647; William Blomquist, "A Political Analysis of Property Rights," in *Property in Land and Other Resources,* ed. Daniel Cole and Elinor Ostrom (Cambridge, MA: Lincoln Institute of Land Policy, 2011); Wyman, "From Fur to Fish," 129; Fitzpatrick, "Evolution and Chaos," 1002; Wyman, "Problematic Private Property," 146; Ménard and Shirley, *Handbook of New Institutional Economics,* 587; Shitong Qiao, "The Politics of Chinese Land: Partial Reform, Vested Interests and Small Property," *Columbia Journal of Asian Law* 29, 1 (2016); Roderick M. Hills Jr. and David Schleicher, "Planning an Affordable City," *Iowa Law Review* 101 (2016): 134–36; Kathryn Firmin-Sellers, "The Politics of Property Rights," *American Political Science Review* 89, 4 (1995).
5 Colin Scott, "Conflicting Discourses of Property, Governance and Development in the Indigenous North," in *In the Way: Indigenous Peoples, Life Projects and Globalization,* ed. Mario Blaser, Harvey Feit, and Glenn McRae (London: Zed Books, 2004), 310–11.
6 Simon Deakin, "The Corporation as Commons: Rethinking Property Rights, Governance and Sustainability in the Business Enterprise," *Queen's Law Journal* 37, 2 (2012): 368.
7 Ibid., 367.
8 Ibid., 374–75.

9 Elinor Ostrom, *Governing the Commons: The Evolution of Institutions for Collective Action* (Cambridge: Cambridge University Press, 1990); Elinor Ostrom, *Understanding Institutional Diversity* (Princeton, NJ: Princeton University Press, 2005); Elinor Ostrom and Xavier Basurto, "Crafting Analytical Tools to Study Institutional Change," *Journal of Institutional Economics* 7, 3 (2011).

10 43 USC s 1601 (1971).

11 Gary Anders and Kathleen Anders, "Incompatible Goals in Unconventional Organization: The Politics of Alaska Native Corporations," *Organization Studies* 7, 3 (1986): 215.

12 Thomas Thornton, "Alaska Native Corporations and Subsistence: Paradoxical Forces in the Making of Sustainable Communities," in *Sustainability and Communities of Place,* ed. Carl A. Maida (New York: Berghahn Books, 2007), 42–43.

13 Thomas Berger, *Village Journey: The Report of the Alaska Native Review Commission* (New York: Hill and Wang, 1985).

14 Thornton, "Alaska Native Corporations," 51.

15 Anders and Anders, "Incompatible Goals," 219.

16 Ibid., 219, citing work by Roger D. Blair and David L. Kaserman, "Ownership and Control in the Modern Corporation: Antitrust Implications," *Journal of Business Research* 11, 3 (1983): 334.

17 Gary N. Wilson and Christopher Alcantara, "Mixing Politics and Business in the Canadian Arctic: Inuit Corporate Governance in Nunavik and the Inuvialuit Settlement Region," *Canadian Journal of Political Science* 45, 4 (2012): 781–82.

18 Ahlquist and Levi, *In the Interest of Others,* Chapter 9.

19 Benjamin E. Hermalin and Michael S. Weisbach, "Information Disclosure and Corporate Governance," *Journal of Finance* 67, 1 (2012).

20 Espen Sjaastad and Ben Cousins, "Formalisation of Land Rights in the South: An Overview," *Land Use Policy* 26, 1 (2009): 4.

21 Taylor Brown, "Contestation, Confusion and Corruption: Market-Based Land Reform in Zambia," in *Competing Jurisdictions Settling Land Claims in Africa,* ed. Sandra Evers, Marja Spierenburg, and Harry Weis (Leiden: Brill, 2005), 88, 94; Nicholas J. Sitko and T.S. Jayne, "Structural Transformation or Elite Land Capture? The Growth of 'Emergent' Farmers in Zambia," *Food Policy* 48 (2014).

22 Saturnino M. Borras Jr. and Jennifer C. Franco, "Contemporary Discourses and Contestations around Pro-Poor Land Policies and Land Governance," *Journal of Agrarian Change* 10, 1 (2010); Laura German, George Schoneveld, and Esther Mwangi, "Contemporary Processes of Large-Scale Land Acquisition in Sub-Saharan Africa: Legal Deficiency or Elite Capture of the Rule of Law," *World Development* 48 (2013).

23 Mark D. Kielsgard and Lei Chen, "The Emergence of Private Property Law in China and Its Impact on Human Rights," *Asian-Pacific Law and Policy Journal* 15 (2014): 101–5; Hanoch Dagan and Michael A. Heller, "The Liberal Commons," *Yale Law Journal* 110, 4 (2001): 566.

24 Jong-sung You, "Land Reform, Inequality, and Corruption: A Comparative Historical Study of Korea, Taiwan, and the Philippines," *Korean Journal of International Studies* 12, 1 (2014); Jong-sung You, *Democracy, Inequality and Corruption: Korea, Taiwan and the Philippines Compared* (Cambridge: Cambridge University Press, 2015).

25 Fredrik Bynander and Paul 't Hart, "Leadership Success in Politics and Business: Converging Logics?," in *The Routledge Companion to Leadership,* ed. John Storey et al. (New York: Routledge, 2016).

26 Alston et al., *Brazil in Transition,* Chapter 7; Lee Alston and Bernardo Mueller, "Pork for Policy: Executive and Legislative Exchange in Brazil," *Journal of Law, Economics and Organization* 22, 1 (2005).

27 Levi and Epperly, "Principled Principals," 192.

28 Ahlquist and Levi, *In the Interest of Others,* Chapter 9.

29 Guy Grossman and W. Walker Hanlon, "Do Better Monitoring Institutions Increase Leadership Quality in Community Organizations? Evidence from Uganda," *American Journal of Political Science* 58, 3 (2014).

30 Tom Flanagan, "Corruption and First Nations in Canada," *Canadian Foreign Policy Journal* 23, 1 (2017).

31 *First Nations Financial Transparency Act,* ss 5–9.

32 Sean Jones, "The Myth of the First Nations Financial Transparency Act," *Globe and Mail,* November 6, 2015, https://www.theglobeandmail.com/report-on-business/rob-commentary/the-myth-of-the-first-nations-financial-transparency-act/article27125271/.

33 Pamela D. Palmater, "Stretched beyond Human Limits: Death by Poverty in First Nations," *Canadian Review of Social Policy* 65/66 (2011): 118–19.

34 Douglas Sanderson, "Overlapping Consensus, Legislative Reform and the Indian Act," *Queen's Law Journal* 39 (2014): 530.

35 Jones, "The Myth of the First Nations Financial Transparency Act."

36 John W. Bruce et al., *Land Law Reform: Achieving Development Policy Objectives* (Washington, DC: World Bank, 2006).

37 Martin Papillon and André Juneau, eds., *Aboriginal Multilevel Governance* (Montreal and Kingston: McGill-Queen's University Press, 2015).

38 Baxter, "Storytelling"; Jamie Baxter, "Indigenous Land Rights and the Politics of Property," in *Creating Indigenous Property: Power, Rights, and Relationships,* ed. Angela Cameron, Sari Graben, and Val Napoleon (Toronto: University of Toronto Press, 2020).

Bibliography

Legislation and Agreements

An Act for the Gradual Enfranchisement of Indians, the Better Management of Indian Affairs, and to Extend the provisions of the Act 31st Victoria, c. 42, SC 1869, c 6.

An Act to Encourage the Gradual Civilization of the Indian Tribes in This Province, and to Amend the Laws Respecting Indians, 1857, 20 Vict, c 26.

An Act to Give Effect to the Westbank First Nation Self Government Agreement, SC 2004, c 17.

Constitution Act, 1867, 30–31 Vict, c 3 (UK).

Constitution Act, 1982, being Schedule B to the *Canada Act, 1982* (UK) 1982, c 11.

The Constitution of the Nisga'a Nation, October 9, 1998.

First Nation Land Management Act, SC 1999, c 24.

First Nations Financial Transparency Act, SC 2013, c 7.

Fisheries Act, RSC 1985, c F-14.

Indian Act, SC 1918, c 26.

James Bay and Northern Quebec Agreement, 1975.

James Bay Region Development Act, SQ 1971, c 34.

Nisga'a Final Agreement, Canada, British Columbia, and Nisga'a Nation, April 27, 1999. http://www.nnkn.ca/files/u28/nis-eng.pdf.

Nisga'a Landholding Transition Act, NLGSR 2009/02.

Nisga'a National Entitlement Act, NLGSR 2000/12.

Nisga'a Village Entitlement Act, NLGSR 2000/13 (2016).

Royal Proclamation, 1763. Reprinted in RSC 1985, App II, 1.

Westbank First Nation Allotment Law, No 2006-03.

Westbank First Nation Constitution, March 31, 2016.

Westbank First Nation Land Use Law, No 2007-01.

Westbank First Nation Self-Government Agreement between Her Majesty the Queen in Right of Canada and Westbank First Nation, 2003. https://www.wfn.ca/docs/self-government-agreement-english.pdf.

Jurisprudence

Calder et al. v Attorney-General of British Columbia, [1973] SCR 313.
Delgamuukw v British Columbia, [1997] 3 SCR 1010.
Derrickson v Kennedy, [2006] 55 BCLR (4th) 123, 379 WAC 96 (CA).
Guerin v The Queen, [1984] 2 SCR 335.
Haida Nation v British Columbia (Minister of Forests), [2004] 3 SCR 511.
James Bay Development Corporation et al. v Kanatewat et al., [1975] CA 166 (QC).
Kanatewat et al. v James Bay Development Corporation et al., [1974] RP 38 (QCSC).
R v Marshall, [1999] 3 SCR 456.
R v Marshall (reconsideration refused), [1999] 3 SCR 533.
R v Sparrow, [1990] 1 SCR 1075.
Re Indian Reserve, Sydney (City), 1916 CarswellNat 37, 17 Ex CR 517, 42 DLR 314.
Rio Tinto Alcan Inc. v Carrier Sekani Tribal Council, [2010] 2 SCR 650.
Sga'nisim Sim'augit (Chief Mountain) v Canada (Attorney General), 2013 BCCA 49.
Tsilhqot'in Nation v British Columbia, [2014] 2 SCR 257.
Union of Nova Scotia Indians v Maritimes and Northeast Pipeline Management Ltd., 1999 CanLII 8932 (FCA).

Secondary Sources

Abramowicz, Michael. "On the Alienability of Legal Claims." *Yale Law Journal* 114 (2005): 697–779.
Acemoglu, Daron. "Why Not a Political Coase Theorem? Social Conflict, Commitment, and Politics." *Journal of Comparative Economics* 31, 4 (2003): 620–52.
Acemoglu, Daron, Simon Johnson, and James A. Robinson. "Institutions as a Fundamental Cause of Long-Run Growth." In *Handbook of Economic Growth,* vol. 1A, ed. Philippe Aghion and Steven N. Durlauf, 1A:385–472. Amsterdam: Elsevier, 2005.
Acemoglu, Daron, Tristan Reed, and James A. Robinson. "Chiefs: Economic Development and Elite Control of Civil Society in Sierra Leone." *Journal of Political Economy* 122, 2 (2014): 319–68.

–. *Why Nations Fail: The Origins of Power, Prosperity, and Poverty*. London: Profile Books, 2012.
Ahlquist, John, and Margaret Levi. *In the Interest of Others: Organizations and Social Activism*. Princeton, NJ: Princeton University Press, 2013. EPUB.
–. "Leadership: What It Means, What It Does, and What We Want to Know About It." *Annual Review of Political Science* 14 (2011): 1–24.
Alcantara, Christopher. "Individual Property Rights on Canadian Indian Reserves: The Historical Emergence and Jurisprudence of Certificates of Possession." *Canadian Journal of Native Studies* 23, 2 (2003): 391–424.
–. "Reduce Transaction Costs? Yes. Strengthen Property Rights? Maybe: The First Nations Land Management Act and Economic Development on Canadian Indian Reserves." *Public Choice* 132, 3–4 (2007): 421–32.
Alchian, Armen A., and Harold Demsetz. "Production, Information Costs, and Economic Organization." *American Economic Review* 62, 5 (1972): 777–95.
Alexander, Gregory S. "Governance Property." *University of Pennsylvania Law Review* 160, 7 (2012): 1853–87.
Alfred, Taiaiake, and Jeff Corntassel. "Being Indigenous: Resurgences against Contemporary Colonialism." *Government and Opposition* 40, 4 (2005): 597–614.
Aligică, Paul Dragoş, and Peter Boettke. "The Two Social Philosophies of Ostroms' Institutionalism." *Policy Studies Journal* 39, 1 (2011): 29–49.
Alston, Lee. "Beyond Institutions: Beliefs and Leadership." *Journal of Economic History* 77, 2 (2017): 353–72.
Alston, Lee, and Gary Libecap. *Titles, Conflict, and Land Use: The Development of Property Rights and Land Reform on the Brazilian Amazon Frontier*. Ann Arbor: University of Michigan Press, 1999.
Alston, Lee, Marcus André Melo, Bernardo Mueller, and Carlos Pereira. *Brazil in Transition: Beliefs, Leadership, and Institutional Change*. Princeton, NJ: Princeton University Press, 2016. EPUB.
Alston, Lee, and Bernardo Mueller. "Pork for Policy: Executive and Legislative Exchange in Brazil." *Journal of Law, Economics and Organization* 22, 1 (2005): 87–114.
–. "Property Rights and the State." In *Handbook of New Institutional Economics,* ed. Claude Ménard and Mary M. Shirley, 573–90. Berlin: Springer, 2005.
Alt, James E., and Kenneth A. Shepsle. *Perspectives on Positive Political Economy*. Cambridge: Cambridge University Press, 1990.
Anders, Gary, and Kathleen Anders. "Incompatible Goals in Unconventional Organization: The Politics of Alaska Native Corporations." *Organization Studies* 7, 3 (1986): 213–33.

Anderson, Robert. *Economic Development among the Aboriginal Peoples in Canada: The Hope for the Future*. North York, ON: Captus Press, 1999.

Andolfatto, David. "A Theory of Inalienable Property Rights." *Journal of Political Economy* 110, 2 (2002): 382–93.

Andreoni, James. "Leadership Giving in Charitable Fund-Raising." *Journal of Public Economic Theory* 8, 1 (2006): 1–22.

Aragón, Fernando M. "Do Better Property Rights Improve Local Income? Evidence from First Nations' Treaties." *Journal of Development Economics* 116 (2015): 43–56.

Arthur, Brian. *Increasing Returns and Path Dependence in the Economy*. Ann Arbor: University of Michigan Press, 1994.

Ault, David E., and Gilbert L. Rutman. "The Development of Individual Rights to Property in Tribal Africa." *Journal of Law and Economics* 22, 1 (1979): 163–82.

Bailey, Ian. "B.C. Nisga'a Allow Members to Purchase Reservation Land." *Globe and Mail,* November 15, 2013, A6.

Baland, Jean-Marie, and Jean-Philippe Platteau. "Division of the Commons: A Partial Assessment of the New Institutional Economics of Land Rights." *American Journal of Agricultural Economics* 80, 3 (1998): 644–50.

Banner, Stuart. *How the Indians Lost Their Land: Law and Power on the Frontier*. Cambridge, MA: Harvard University Press, 2005.

–. *Possessing the Pacific*. Cambridge, MA: Harvard University Press, 2007.

–. "Transitions between Property Regimes." *Journal of Legal Studies* 31, S2 (2002): S359–71.

Barsh, Russel, and James (Sa'ke'j) Youngblood Henderson. "Marshalling the Rule of Law in Canada: Of Eels and Honour." *Constitutional Forum* 11, 1 (1999): 1–18.

Bates, Robert, Avner Greif, Margaret Levi, Jean-Laurent Rosenthal, and Barry Weingast. *Analytical Narratives*. Princeton, NJ: Princeton University Press, 1998.

Baxter, Jamie. "Indigenous Land Rights and the Politics of Property." In *Creating Indigenous Property: Power, Rights, and Relationships,* ed. Angela Cameron, Sari Graben, and Val Napoleon. Toronto: University of Toronto Press, 2020.

–. "Leadership, Law and Development." *Law and Development Review* 12, 1 (2018): 119–58.

–. "Property, Information and Institutional Design." *Journal of Aboriginal Economic Development* 8, 2 (2013): 55–69.

–. "Storytelling, Social Movements, and the 'Evolution' of Indigenous Land Tenure." *Australian Indigenous Law Review* 18, 1 (2014): 65–76.

Baxter, Jamie, and Michael Trebilcock. "Formalizing Land Tenure in First Nations: Evaluating the Case for Reserve Tenure Reform." *Indigenous Law Journal* 7, 2 (2009): 45–122.

Bell, Abraham, and Gideon Parchomovsky. "The Evolution of Private and Open Access Property." *Theoretical Inquiries in Law* 10, 1 (2009): 77–102.

–. "Property Lost in Translation." *University of Chicago Law Review* 80, 2 (2013): 515–73.

Bell, Stephen. "Where Are the Institutions? The Limits of Vivien Schmidt's Constructivism." *British Journal of Political Science* 42, 3 (2012): 714–19.

Berger, Thomas. *Village Journey: The Report of the Alaska Native Review Commission*. New York: Hill and Wang, 1985.

Berneshawi, Suzanne. "Resource Management and the Mi'kmaq Nation." *Canadian Journal of Native Studies* 17, 1 (1997): 115–48.

Blackburn, Carole. "Searching for Guarantees in the Midst of Uncertainty: Negotiating Aboriginal Rights and Title in British Columbia." *American Anthropologist* 107, 4 (2005): 586–96.

Blair, Roger D., and David L. Kaserman. "Ownership and Control in the Modern Corporation: Antitrust Implications." *Journal of Business Research* 11, 3 (1983): 333–43.

Blomley, Nicholas. "Disentangling Law: The Practice of Bracketing." *Annual Review of Law and Social Science* 10, 1 (2014): 133–48.

–. "The Ties That Blind: Making Fee Simple in the British Columbia Treaty Process." *Transactions of the Institute of British Geographers* 40, 2 (2014): 168–79.

Blomquist, William. "A Political Analysis of Property Rights." In *Property in Land and Other Resources,* ed. Daniel Cole and Elinor Ostrom, 369–87. Cambridge, MA: Lincoln Institute of Land Policy, 2011.

Borras, Saturnino M. Jr., and Jennifer C. Franco. "Contemporary Discourses and Contestations around Pro-Poor Land Policies and Land Governance." *Journal of Agrarian Change* 10, 1 (2010): 1–32.

Borrows, John. *Canada's Indigenous Constitution*. Toronto: University of Toronto Press, 2010.

–. "The Durability of Terra Nullius: *Tsilhqot'in Nation v. British Columbia*." *University of British Columbia Law Review* 48, 3 (2015): 701–42.

–. "Living between Water and Rocks: First Nations, Environmental Planning and Democracy." *University of Toronto Law Journal* 47, 4 (1997): 417–68.

–. *Recovering Canada: The Resurgence of Indigenous Law*. Toronto: University of Toronto Press, 2002.

–. "Re-living the Present: Titles, Treaties, and the Trickster in British Columbia." *BC Studies* 120 (1998/99): 99–108.

Brinkhurst, Marena, and Anke Kessler. "Land Management on First Nations Reserves: Lawful Possession and Its Determinants." *Journal of Aboriginal Economic Development* 8, 2 (2013): 78–95.

Brown, K., M. Finney, M. Doucette, J.E. Tulk, N. Bernard, and Y.I. Yuan. "'Membertou Always Wanted to Succeed': The Membertou Business Model." *Journal of Aboriginal Economic Development* 8, 1 (2012): 32–48.

Brown, Taylor. "Contestation, Confusion and Corruption: Market-Based Land Reform in Zambia." In *Competing Jurisdictions Settling Land Claims in Africa,* ed. Sandra Evers, Marja Spierenburg, and Harry Weis, 79–102. Leiden: Brill, 2005.

Brownlie, Robin. "'A Better Citizen Than Lots of White Men': First Nations Enfranchisement – an Ontario Case Study, 1918–1940." *Canadian Historical Review* 87, 1 (2006): 29–52.

Bruce, John W., Renée Giovarelli, Leonard Rolfes Jr., David Bledsoe, and Robert Mitchell. *Land Law Reform: Achieving Development Policy Objectives*. Washington, DC: World Bank, 2006.

Bubb, Ryan. "The Evolution of Property Rights: State Law or Informal Norms?" *Journal of Law and Economics* 56, 3 (2013): 555–94.

Buchanan, James, and Gordon Tullock. *The Calculus of Consent: Logical Foundations of Constitutional Democracy*. Ann Arbor: University of Michigan Press, 1962.

Bynander, Fredrik, and Paul 't Hart. "Leadership Success in Politics and Business: Converging Logics?" In *The Routledge Companion to Leadership,* ed. John Storey, Jean Hartley, Jean-Louis Denis, Paul 't Hart, and David Ulrich. New York: Routledge, 2016.

Canada, Department of Indian Affairs and Northern Development. *Statement of the Government of Canada on Indian Policy, 1969*. Ottawa: Indian Affairs and Northern Development, 1969.

Carlson, Hans. *Home Is the Hunter: The James Bay Cree and Their Land*. Vancouver: UBC Press, 2014.

–. "A Watershed of Words: Litigating and Negotiating Nature in Eastern James Bay, 1971–75." *Canadian Historical Review* 85, 1 (2004): 63–84.

Cherry, Mark. *Kidney for Sale by Owner: Human Organs, Transplantation, and the Market*. Washington, DC: Georgetown University Press, 2016.

Christmas, Berndt. "First Nations Progression Model: The Use of Multiple Lines." Speech to the Canadian Evaluation Society Conference, May 2002.

Christmas, Daniel. *IWCL Case Study: Membertou First Nation*. YouTube video, posted by Coady International Institute, July 21, 2011. https://www.youtube.com/watch?v=Z8SrNfDFFEQ&feature=related.

Coase, Ronald. "The Nature of the Firm." *Economica* 4, 16 (1937): 386–405.

Coleman, Eric A., and Esther Mwangi. "Conflict, Cooperation, and Institutional Change on the Commons." *American Journal of Political Science* 59, 4 (2015): 1–11.

Coleman, Jules L. *The Practice of Principle*. Oxford: Oxford University Press, 2001.

Conger, Jay A., and Rabindra N. Kanungo. "Charismatic Leadership in Organizations: Perceived Behavioral Attributes and Their Measurement." *Journal of Organizational Behavior* 15, 5 (1994): 439–52.

–. "Toward a Behavioral Theory of Charismatic Leadership in Organizational Settings." *Academy of Management Review* 12, 4 (1987): 637–47.

Cornell, Stephen, Miriam Jorgensen, Joseph P. Kalt, and Katherine Spilde Contreras. "Seizing the Future: Why Some Native Nations Do and Others Don't." In *Rebuilding Native Nations: Strategies for Governance and Development,* ed. Miriam Jorgensen, 296–320. Tucson: University of Arizona Press, 2007.

Dagan, Hanoch, and Michael A. Heller. "The Liberal Commons." *Yale Law Journal* 110, 4 (2001): 549–623.

Dagan, Tsilly, and Talia Fisher. "Rights for Sale." *Minnesota Law Review* 96 (2012): 90–140.

Dalton, Jennifer E. "Aboriginal Title and Self-Government in Canada: What Is the True Scope of Comprehensive Land Claims Agreements." *Windsor Review of Legal and Social Issues* 22 (2006): 29–78.

Davidson, Nestor M., and Rashmi Dyal-Chand. "Property in Crisis." *Fordham Law Review* 78, 4 (2010): 1607–60.

Davis, Kevin E., and Michael J. Trebilcock. "Legal Reforms and Development." *Third World Quarterly* 22, 1 (2010): 21–36.

Deakin, Simon. "The Corporation as Commons: Rethinking Property Rights, Governance and Sustainability in the Business Enterprise." *Queen's Law Journal* 37, 2 (2012): 339–81.

Demsetz, Harold. "Toward a Theory of Property Rights." *American Economic Review* 57, 2 (1967): 347–59.

–. "Toward a Theory of Property Rights II: The Competition between Private and Collective Ownership." *Journal of Legal Studies* 31, S2 (2002): S653–72.

Diamond, Billy. "Aboriginal Rights: The James Bay Experience." In *The Quest for Justice: Aboriginal Peoples and Aboriginal Rights,* ed. Menno Boldt and Anthony Long, 265–85. Toronto: University of Toronto Press, 1985.

Dickason, Olivia. *Canada's First Nations: A History of Founding Peoples from Earliest Times*. Oxford: Oxford University Press, 1997.

Doidge, Mary B., James Deaton, and Bethany Woods. "Institutional Change on First Nations: Examining Factors Influencing First Nations' Adoption of the Framework Agreement on First Nation Land Management." *Journal of Aboriginal Economic Development* 8, 2 (2013): 70–78.

Drees, Marilyn F. "Do State Legislatures Have a Role in Resolving the Just Compensation Dilemma? Some Lessons from Public Choice and Positive Political Theory." *Fordham Law Review* 66 (1997): 787–841.

Eberts, Mary. "Still Colonizing after All These Years." *University of New Brunswick Law Journal* 64 (2013): 123–59.

Eggertson, Laura. "Getting Down to Business." *Toronto Star,* January 16, 2011, IN1.

Eggertsson, Thráinn. *Economic Behavior and Institutions: Principles of Neo-institutional Economics*. Cambridge: Cambridge University Press, 1990.
–. "Opportunities and Limits for the Evolution of Property Rights Institutions." In *Property in Land and Other Resources,* ed. Daniel H. Cole and Elinor Ostrom, 13–36. Cambridge: Lincoln Institute of Land Policy, 2012.
Eisenstadt, Shmuel Noah. *Max Weber on Charisma and Institution Building*. Chicago: University of Chicago Press, 1968.
Ellickson, Robert C. "Property in Land." *Yale Law Journal* 102 (1993): 1315–400.
Ensminger, Jean, and Jack Knight. "Changing Social Norms: Common Property, Bridewealth, and Clan Exogamy." *Current Anthropology* 38, 1 (1997): 1–24.
Epstein, Richard A. "Why Restrain Alienation?" *Columbia Law Review* 85, 5 (1985): 970–90.
Evans, J.W. *Some Indicators of Change: Westbank Indian Band (1971/72 to 1980/81)*. Vancouver: Indian and Northern Affairs Canada, 1982.
Farber, Daniel A. "Public Choice Theory and Legal Institutions." In *The Oxford Handbook of Law and Economics,* ed. Francesco Parisi, 1:181–201. Oxford: Oxford University Press, 2017.
Faustino, Jaime, and David Booth. "Development Entrepreneurship: How Donors and Leaders Can Foster Institutional Change." *Working Politically in Practice Series* (December 2014).
Feder, Gershon, and David Feeny. "Land Tenure and Property Rights: Theory and Implications for Development Policy." *World Bank Economic Review* 5, 1 (1991): 135–53.
Feder, Gershon, and Raymond Noronha. "Land Rights Systems and Agricultural Development in Sub-Saharan Africa." *World Bank Research Observer* 2, 2 (1987): 143–69.
Feit, Harvey A. "Dialogues on Surviving: Eeyou Hunters' Ways of Engagement with Land, Governments, and Youth." In *Entangled Territorialities: Negotiating Indigenous Lands in Australia and Canada,* ed. Françoise Dussart and Sylvie Poirier, 25–50. Toronto: University of Toronto Press, 2017.
–. "Gifts of the Land: Hunting Territories, Guaranteed Incomes and the Construction of Social Relations in James Bay Cree Society." *Senri Ethnological Studies* 30 (1991): 223–68.
–. "James Bay Cree Self-Governance and Land Management." In *We Are Here: Politics of Aboriginal Land Tenure,* ed. Edwin Wilmsen, 68–98. Berkeley: University of California Press, 1989.
–. "Neoliberal Governance and James Bay Cree Governance: Negotiated Agreements, Oppositional Struggles, and Co-governance." In *Indigenous*

Peoples and Autonomy: Insights for a Global Age, ed. Mario Blaser, Ravi De Costa, Deborah McGregor, and William D. Coleman, 49–79. Vancouver: UBC Press, 2010.

Fennell, Lee Anne. "Adjusting Alienability." *Harvard Law Review* 122 (2009): 1403–65.

Ferejohn, John. "Accountability and Authority: Toward a Theory of Political Accountability." In *Democracy, Accountability, and Representation,* ed. Adam Przeworski and Susan C. Stokes, 131–53. Cambridge: Cambridge University Press, 1999.

Fiegehen, Gary, and Alex Rose. *Nisga'a: People of the Nass River.* Vancouver: Douglas and McIntyre, 1993.

Firmin-Sellers, Kathryn. "The Politics of Property Rights." *American Political Science Review* 89, 4 (1995): 867–81.

Fitzpatrick, Daniel. "Evolution and Chaos in Property Right Systems: The Third World Tragedy of Contested Access." *Yale Law Journal* 115, 5 (2006): 996–1048.

Fitzpatrick, Daniel, and Andrew McWilliam. "Bright-Line Fever: Simple Legal Rules and Complex Property Customs among the Fataluku of East Timor." *Law and Society Review* 47, 2 (2013): 311–43.

Flanagan, Thomas, Christopher Alcantara, and André Le Dressay. *Beyond the Indian Act: Restoring Aboriginal Property Rights.* Montreal and Kingston: McGill-Queen's University Press, 2010.

Flanagan, Tom. "Corruption and First Nations in Canada." *Canadian Foreign Policy Journal* 23, 1 (2017): 15–31.

Foot, Richard. "Nisga'a Take First, Wary Steps toward Private Land Ownership." *Victoria Times Colonist*, August 15, 2010, A12.

Foster, Hamar. "Honouring the Queen's Flag: A Legal and Historical Perspective on the Nisga'a Treaty." *BC Studies* 120 (1998/99): 11–36.

Foster, Hamar, Heather Raven, and Jeremy Webber, eds. *Let Right Be Done: Aboriginal Title, the Calder Case and the Future of Indigenous Rights.* Vancouver: UBC Press, 2007.

Garud, Raghu, Cynthia Hardy, and Steve Maguire. "Institutional Entrepreneurship as Embedded Agency: An Introduction to the Special Issue." *Organization Studies* 28, 7 (2007): 957–69.

German, Laura, George Schoneveld, and Esther Mwangi. "Contemporary Processes of Large-Scale Land Acquisition in Sub-Saharan Africa: Legal Deficiency or Elite Capture of the Rule of Law." *World Development* 48 (2013): 1–18.

Graben, Sari. "Lessons for Indigenous Property Reform: From Membership to Ownership on Nisga'a Lands." *University of British Columbia Law Review* 47, 2 (2014): 399–442.

Greif, Avner. *Institutions and the Path to the Modern Economy: Lessons from Medieval Trade*. Cambridge: Cambridge University Press, 2006.

Grossman, Guy, and W. Walker Hanlon. "Do Better Monitoring Institutions Increase Leadership Quality in Community Organizations? Evidence from Uganda." *American Journal of Political Science* 58, 3 (2014): 669–86.

Hall, John E. *The Report of the Commission of Inquiry Concerning Certain Matters Associated with the Westbank Indian Band*. Ottawa: Canadian Government Publishing Centre, 1988.

Harper, Joan. *He Moved a Mountain: The Life of Frank Calder and the Nisga'a Land Claims Accord*. Vancouver: Ronsdale Press, 2013. EPUB.

Harris, Cole. *Making Native Space: Colonialism, Resistance and Reserves in British Columbia*. Vancouver: UBC Press, 2007.

Hasen, Richard L. "Vote Buying." *California Law Review* 88, 5 (2000): 1323–72.

Hawthorn, H.B., ed. *A Survey of the Contemporary Indians of Canada: Economic, Political, Educational Needs and Policies*. Ottawa: Government of Canada, Indian Affairs Branch, 1966.

Hay, Colin. "Ideas and the Construction of Interests." In *Ideas and Politics in Social Science Research,* ed. Daniel Béland and Robert Henry Cox, 65–82. Oxford: Oxford University Press, 2011.

Hazlett, Thomas W. "Assigning Property Rights to Radio Spectrum Users: Why Did FCC License Auctions Take 67 Years?" *Journal of Law and Economics* 41, S2 (1998): 529–76.

Heller, Michael A. "The Boundaries of Private Property." *Yale Law Journal* 108, 6 (1999): 1163–223.

Helms, Ludger. "Institutional Analysis." In *The Oxford Handbook of Political Leadership,* ed. R.A.W. Rhodes and Paul 't Hart, 195–209. Oxford: Oxford University Press, 2014.

Henderson, James Youngblood. "Mikmaw Tenure in Atlantic Canada." *Dalhousie Law Journal* 18 (1995): 196–294.

Hermalin, Benjamin E. "Leadership and Corporate Culture." In *Handbook of Organizational Economics,* ed. Robert Gibbons and John Roberts, 432–78. Princeton, NJ: Princeton University Press, 2012.

–. "Leading for the Long Term." *Journal of Economic Behavior and Organization* 62, 1 (2007): 1–19.

–. "Toward an Economic Theory of Leadership: Leading by Example." *American Economic Review* (1998): 1188–206.

Hermalin, Benjamin E., and Michael S. Weisbach. "Information Disclosure and Corporate Governance." *Journal of Finance* 67, 1 (2012): 195–233.

Higgins, Hal. "Membertou First Reserve in Atlantic Canada to Try Online Referendum." *CBC News,* April 22, 2016. http://www.cbc.ca/news/canada/nova-scotia/referendum-membertou-mi-kmaq-indigenous-voting-1.3548351.

Hills, Roderick M. Jr., and David Schleicher. "Planning an Affordable City." *Iowa Law Review* 101 (2016): 91–136.

Hoffman, Ross, and Andrew Robinson. "Nisga'a Self-Government: A New Journey Has Begun." *Canadian Journal of Native Studies* 30, 2 (2010): 387–405.

Holmstrom, Bengt. "Moral Hazard in Teams." *Bell Journal of Economics* 13, 2 (1982): 324–40.

Hopper, Tristin. "B.C. First Nation Leads Historic and Controversial Move toward Aboriginal Private Home Ownership." *National Post,* November 8, 2013, https://nationalpost.com/news/canada/b-c-first-nation-leads-historic-and-controversial-move-toward-aboriginal-private-home-ownership.

–. "Homes of Their Own: Starting With Three Houses, Nisga'a Nation Realizes Dream of Privatizing Native Land." *National Post*, November 9, 2013, A4.

House, R.J., and Mary L. Baetz. "Leadership: Some Empirical Generalizations and New Research Directions." In *Research in Organizational Behavior,* ed. B.M. Staw, 399–401. Greenwich, CT: JAI Press, 1979.

Indigenous and Northern Affairs Canada. "First Nation Profiles: Registered Population– Membertou," http://fnp-ppn.aandc-aadnc.gc.ca/fnp/main/search/FNRegPopulation.aspx?BAND_NUMBER=26&lang=eng.

–. "First Nation Profiles: Population Characteristics – Westbank First Nation," http://fnp-ppn.aandc-aadnc.gc.ca/fnp/main/search/FNPopulation.aspx?BAND_NUMBER=601&lang=eng.

Isaac, Thomas. "First Nations Land Management Act and Third Party Interests." *University of Alberta Law Review* 42, 4 (2004): 1047–60.

Jones, Benjamin F., and Benjamin A. Olken. "Do Leaders Matter? National Leadership and Growth since World War II." *Quarterly Journal of Economics* 120, 3 (2005): 835–64.

Jones, Sean. "The Myth of the First Nations Financial Transparency Act." *Globe and Mail,* November 6, 2015. https://www.theglobeandmail.com/report-on-business/rob-commentary/the-myth-of-the-first-nations-financial-transparency-act/article27125271/.

Kantor, Shawn Everett. "Razorbacks, Ticky Cows, and the Closing of the Georgia Open Range: The Dynamics of Institutional Change Uncovered." *Journal of Economic History* 51, 4 (1991): 861–86.

Kapczynski, Amy. "The Access to Knowledge Mobilization and the New Politics of Intellectual Property." *Yale Law Journal* 117 (2008): 804–85.

Kielsgard, Mark D., and Lei Chen. "The Emergence of Private Property Law in China and Its Impact on Human Rights." *Asian-Pacific Law and Policy Journal* 15 (2014): 94–134.

King, Jacqueline. "The Old and New Picture of Boston's Native Americans." *Bay State Banner,* November 16, 1978, 2.

Knight, Frank H. *Risk, Uncertainty and Profit.* Boston: Houghton Mifflin, 1921.

Knight, Jack. *Institutions and Social Conflict.* Cambridge: Cambridge University Press, 1992.

Krier, James E. "The Tragedy of the Commons, Part Two." *Harvard Journal of Law and Public Policy* 15 (1992): 325–47.

Lavoie, Malcolm. "Why Restrain Alienation of Indigenous Lands?" *University of British Columbia Law Review* 49, 3 (2016): 997–1060.

Lavoie, Malcolm, and Moira Lavoie. "Land Regime Choice in Close-Knit Communities: The Case of the First Nations Land Management Act." *Osgoode Hall Law Journal* 54 (2017): 559–607.

Leftwich, Adrian. "Beyond Institutions: Rethinking the Role of Leaders, Elites and Coalitions in the Institutional Formation of Developmental States and Strategies." *Forum for Development Studies* 37, 1 (2010): 93–111.

–. *Bringing Agency Back In: Politics and Human Agency in Building Institutions and States.* Synthesis and Overview Report, Research Paper 6, June. n.p.: Developmental Leadership Program, 2009. https://res.cloudinary.com/dlprog/image/upload/U8iUC5wKAxNQHSPMaHAjWXXUYff3ibNbzycWY9E5.pdf.

–. "Bringing Politics Back In: Towards a Model of the Developmental State." *Journal of Development Studies* 31, 3 (1995): 400–27.

"The Legacy of Frank Calder." *Times Colonist,* November 7, 2006.

Leslie, John F. "The Indian Act: An Historical Perspective." *Canadian Parliamentary Review* 25, 2 (2002): 23–27.

–. "The Policy Agenda of Native Peoples from World War II to the 1969 White Paper." In *Aboriginal Policy Research: Setting the Agenda for Change,* ed. Jerry P. White, Paul Maxim, and Dan Beavon, 15–28. Toronto: Thompson Educational Publishing, 2013.

Levi, Margaret. "Why We Need a New Theory of Government." *Perspectives on Politics* 4, 1 (2006): 5–19.

Levi, Margaret, and Brad Epperly. "Principled Principals in the Founding Moments of the Rule of Law." In *Global Perspectives on the Rule of Law,* ed. James Heckman, Robert L. Nelson, and Lee Cabatingan, 192–209. London: Taylor and Francis, 2013.

Levi, Margaret, Audrey Sacks, and Tom Tyler. "Conceptualizing Legitimacy, Measuring Legitimating Beliefs." *American Behavioral Scientist* 53, 3 (2009): 354–75.

Levmore, Saul. "Two Stories about the Evolution of Property Rights." *Journal of Legal Studies* 31, S2 (2002): S421–51.

Libecap, Gary D. *Contracting for Property Rights*. Cambridge: Cambridge University Press, 1993.

–. "Distributional Issues in Contracting for Property Rights." *Journal of Institutional and Theoretical Economics* 145, 1 (1989): 6–24.

Little Bear, Leroy. "Aboriginal Rights and the Canadian Grundnorm." In *Arduous Journey: Canadian Indians and Decolonization,* ed. J.R. Ponting, 243–59. Toronto: McClelland and Stewart, 1986.

López, Edward, and Wayne Leighton. *Madmen, Intellectuals, and Academic Scribblers: The Economic Engine of Political Change*. Stanford, CA: Stanford University Press, 2012.

Lowry, William R. *Preserving Public Lands for the Future: The Politics of Intergenerational Goods*. Washington, DC: Georgetown University Press, 1998.

Lubell, Mark, Richard C. Feiock, and Edgar E. Ramirez de la Cruz. "Local Institutions and the Politics of Urban Growth." *American Journal of Political Science* 53, 3 (2009): 649–65.

MacGregor, Roy. *Chief: The Fearless Vision of Billy Diamond*. Markham, ON: Penguin Books Canada, 1990.

MacKee, Christopher. *Treaty Talks in British Columbia: Building a New Relationship*. Vancouver: UBC Press, 2010.

Macklem, Patrick. "First Nations Self-Government and the Borders of the Canadian Legal Imagination." *McGill Law Journal* 36 (1991): 382–456.

Majone, Giandomenico. *Temporal Consistency and Policy Credibility: Why Democracies Need Non-Majoritarian Institutions*. European University Institute Working Papers RSC No 96/57. Florence: European University Institute, 1996.

Mashaw, Jerry L. "Public Law and Public Choice: A Critique and Rapprochement." In *Research Handbook on Public Law and Public Choice,* ed. Daniel A. Farber and Anne Joseph O'Connell, 1–30. Cheltenham: Edward Elgar, 2010.

McChesney, Fred S. "Rent Extraction and Rent Creation in the Economic Theory of Regulation." *Journal of Legal Studies* 16, 1 (1987): 101–18.

McCutcheon, Sean. *Electric Rivers: The Story of the James Bay Project*. Montreal: Black Rose Books, 1991.

McHugh, Paul G. *Aboriginal Societies and the Common Law: A History of Sovereignty, Status, and Self-Determination*. Oxford: Oxford University Press, 2004.

–. *Aboriginal Title: The Modern Jurisprudence of Tribal Land Rights*. Oxford: Oxford University Press, 2011.

McKenna, J.A.J., and Richard McBride. *Report of the Royal Commission on Indian Affairs for the Province of British Columbia (1913–1916)*. Victoria: Acme Press, 1916.

McNeil, Kent. "Self-Government and the Inalienability of Aboriginal Title." *McGill Law Journal* 47 (2002): 473–510.

Mehta, Jal. "The Varied Roles of Ideas in Politics: From 'Whether' to 'How.'" In *Ideas and Politics in Political Science Research,* ed. Daniel Béland and Robert Henry Cox. Oxford: Oxford University Press, 2011. EPUB.

Membertou: Accountable to the Community. YouTube video, posted by Centre for First Nations Governance, January 10, 2011. https://www.youtube.com/watch?v=GuHc-sONf4g&list=UU6Kmkt3MUlLgGT4vN4NVKWQ.

Membertou First Nation. "Kings Road Reserve 100 Years Later," accessed November 16, 2017. http://www.membertou.ca/sites/default/files/KingsRoad_8Page%20Spread_final.pdf.

Ménard, Claude, and Mary M. Shirley, eds. *Handbook of New Institutional Economics*. Berlin: Springer, 2008.

Merrill, Thomas W. "Introduction: The Demsetz Thesis and the Evolution of Property Rights." *Journal of Legal Studies* 31, S2 (2002): S331–38.

Merrill, Thomas W., and Henry E. Smith. "Optimal Standardization in the Law of Property: The *Numerus Clausus* Principle." *Yale Law Journal* 110 (2000): 1–70.

Miller, J.R. *Compact, Contract, Covenant: Aboriginal Treaty-Making in Canada*. Toronto: University of Toronto Press, 2009.

Milloy, John S. "The Early *Indian Acts:* Developmental Strategy and Constitutional Change." In *As Long as the Sun Shines and the Water Flows: A Reader in Canadian Native Studies,* ed. Ian L. Getty and Antoine S. Lussier, 56–64. Vancouver: UBC Press, 1983.

Millward, Hugh. "The Development, Decline, and Revival of Mining on the Sydney Coalfield." *Canadian Geographer* 28, 2 (1984): 180–85.

Moe, Terry. "Vested Interests and Political Institutions." *Political Science Quarterly* 130, 2 (2015): 277–318.

Moss, Wendy. "The Implementation of the James Bay and Northern Quebec Agreement." In *Aboriginal Peoples and the Law: Indian, Metis and Inuit Rights in Canada,* ed. Bradford Morse, 684–94. Montreal and Kingston: McGill-Queen's University Press, 1985.

Moustakas, John. "Group Rights in Cultural Property: Justifying Strict Inalienability." *Cornell Law Review* 74 (1989): 1179–227.

Muckle, Robert. *The First Nations of British Columbia: An Anthropological Overview*. Vancouver: UBC Press, 1998.

Napoleon, Val. "Thinking About Indigenous Legal Orders." In *Dialogues on Human Rights and Legal Pluralism,* ed. René Provost and Colleen Sheppard, 229–45. Berlin: Springer, 2012.

Nash, Jonathan Remy. "Economic Efficiency versus Public Choice: The Case of Property Rights in Road Traffic Management." *Boston College Law Review* 49 (2008): 673–739.

"Native Member Proposes Indians' Bill of Rights." *Victoria Times,* February 24, 1950.

Naudé, Wim. "Entrepreneurship and Economic Development." In *International Development: Ideas, Experience, and Prospects,* ed. Bruce Currie-Adler, Ravi Kanbur, David M. Malone, and Rohinton Medhora, 311–22. Oxford: Oxford University Press, 2013.

Nickason, M.F. *The Westbank Inquiry: Managing the Response of the Department of Indian and Northern Affairs.* Ottawa: Indian and Northern Affairs Canada, 1988.

North, Douglass C. *Structure and Change in Economic History.* New York: W.W. Norton, 1981.

–. *Understanding the Process of Economic Change.* Princeton, NJ: Princeton University Press, 2005.

North, Douglass C., and Robert Paul Thomas. *The Rise of the Western World: A New Economic History.* Cambridge: Cambridge University Press, 1973.

Ostrom, Elinor. "Beyond Markets and States: Polycentric Governance of Complex Economic Systems." *American Economic Review* 100 (2010): 641–72.

–. *Governing the Commons: The Evolution of Institutions for Collective Action.* Cambridge: Cambridge University Press, 1990.

–. *Understanding Institutional Diversity.* Princeton, NJ: Princeton University Press, 2005.

Ostrom, Elinor, and Xavier Basurto. "Crafting Analytical Tools to Study Institutional Change." *Journal of Institutional Economics* 7, 3 (2011): 317–43.

Ostrom, Vincent, and Elinor Ostrom. "Public Goods and Public Choices." In *Elinor Ostrom and the Bloomington School of Political Economy.* Vol. 2, *Resource Governance,* ed. Daniel H. Cole and Michael D. McGinnis, 3–36. Lanham, MD: Lexington Books, 2015.

Ostrom, Vincent, Charles Tiebout, and Robert Warren. "The Organization of Government in Metropolitan Areas: A Theoretical Inquiry." *American Political Science Review* 55, 4 (1961): 831–42.

Palmater, Pamela D. "Matnm Tel-Mi'Kmawi: I'm Fighting for My Mi'Kmaw Identity." *Canadian Journal of Native Studies* 33, 1 (2013): 147–67.

–. "Stretched beyond Human Limits: Death by Poverty in First Nations." *Canadian Review of Social Policy* 65/66 (2011): 112–27.

Palmer, Lisa, and Maureen Tehan. "Shared Citizenship and Self-Government in Canada: A Case Study of James Bay and Nunavik (Northern Quebec)." In *Settling with Indigenous People: Modern Treaty and Agreement-Making,* ed. Marcia Langton, 19–43. Sydney: Federation Press, 2006.

Papillon, Martin, and André Juneau, eds. *Aboriginal Multilevel Governance.* Montreal and Kingston: McGill-Queen's University Press, 2015.

Pasternak, Shiri. "How Capitalism Will Save Colonialism: The Privatization of Reserve Lands in Canada." *Antipode* 47, 1 (2015): 179–96.

Paul, Terrance. "Building Sustainable Economies: Approaches and Perspectives." Presentation at the Emerging Leaders seminar, Native Nations Institute for Leadership, Management, and Policy, University of Arizona, Tucson, March 25, 2010. https://nnigovernance.arizona.edu/terrance-paul-building-sustainable-economies-membertou-first-nation.

Pilali, Joe. "Indian Council Seeking Funds for New Boston Headquarters." *Boston Globe,* December 21, 1973, 16.

Prado, Mariana Mota, and Michael J. Trebilcock. "Path Dependence, Development, and the Dynamics of Institutional Reform." *University of Toronto Law Journal* 59, 3 (2009): 341–80.

Priest, Claire. "Creating an American Property Law: Alienability and Its Limits in American History." *Harvard Law Review* 120, 2 (2006): 385–459.

Putzel, Louis, Alice B. Kelly, Paolo Omar Cerutti, and Yustina Artati. "Formalization as Development in Land and Natural Resource Policy." *Society and Natural Resources* 28 (2015): 453–72.

Qiao, Shitong. "The Politics of Chinese Land: Partial Reform, Vested Interests and Small Property." *Columbia Journal of Asian Law* 29, 1 (2016): 70–113.

Radin, Margaret Jane. *Contested Commodities.* Cambridge, MA: Harvard University Press, 1996.

–. "Market-Inalienability." *Harvard Law Review* 100, 8 (1987): 1849–937.

Raunet, Daniel. *Without Surrender, without Consent: A History of the Nisga'a Land Claims*. Vancouver: Douglas and McIntyre, 1996.

Ray, Arthur. *Aboriginal Rights Claims and the Making and Remaking of History*. Montreal and Kingston: McGill-Queen's University Press, 2016.

Richardson, Boyce. *Strangers Devour the Land.* White River Junction, VT: Chelsea Green Publishing, 2008.

Riddell, Janet. "Those Non-Indian Indians: A Struggle for Recognition and Aid Confronts American Indians." *Boston Globe,* April 11, 1971, A3.

Riker, William H., and Itai Sened. "A Political Theory of the Origin of Property Rights: Airport Slots." *American Journal of Political Science* 35, 4 (1991): 951–69.

Rodrik, Dani. "When Ideas Trump Interests: Preferences, Worldviews, and Policy Innovations." *Journal of Economic Perspectives* 28, 1 (2014): 189–208.

Roland, Gérard. "Understanding Institutional Change: Fast Moving and Slow Moving Institutions." *Studies in Comparative International Development* 38, 4 (2004): 109–31.

Rose, Alex. *Spirit Dance at Meziadin: Chief Joseph Gosnell and the Nisga'a Treaty*. Madeira Park, BC: Harbour Publishing, 2001.

Rose, Carol. "Property as Storytelling: Perspectives from Game Theory, Narrative Theory, Feminist Theory." *Yale Journal of Law and the Humanities* 2 (1990): 37–57.

Rose-Ackerman, Susan. "Inalienability." In *The New Palgrave Dictionary of Economics and the Law,* ed. Peter Newman, 2:268–73. London: Macmillan, 1998.

–. "Inalienability and the Theory of Property Rights." *Columbia Law Review* 85, 5 (1985): 931–69.

–. "Law and Economics: Paradigm, Politics, or Philosophy." In *Law and Economics,* ed. Nicholas Mercuro, 233–58. Boston: Kluwer Academic Publishers, 1989.

Rotberg, Robert. *The Corruption Cure: How Citizens and Leaders Can Combat Graft*. Princeton, NJ: Princeton University Press, 2017.

Royal Commission on the Donald Marshall, Jr., Prosecution (NS). *Royal Commission on the Donald Marshall, Jr., Prosecution: Digest of Findings and Recommendations*. Halifax: The Commission, 1989.

Salisbury, Richard. *A Homeland for the Cree Regional Development in James Bay, 1971–1981*. Montreal and Kingston: McGill-Queen's University Press, 2014.

Samuels, Richard J. *Machiavelli's Children: Leaders and Their Legacies in Italy and Japan*. Ithaca, NY: Cornell University Press, 2003.

Sanders, Douglas. "We Intend to Live Here Forever: A Primer on the Nisga'a Treaty." *University of British Columbia Law Review* 33, 1 (1999): 103–28.

Sanderson, Douglas. "Overlapping Consensus, Legislative Reform and the Indian Act." *Queen's Law Journal* 39 (2014): 511–50.

Sandler, Todd. "Intergenerational Public Goods: Transnational Considerations." *Scottish Journal of Political Economy* 56, 3 (2009): 353–70.

Schmidt, Vivien A. "Discursive Institutionalism: The Explanatory Power of Ideas and Discourse." *Annual Review of Political Science* 11, 1 (2008): 303–26.

–. "Discursive Institutionalism: Understanding Policy in Context." In *Handbook of Critical Policy Studies*, ed. Frank Fischer, Douglas Torgerson, Anna Durnová, and Michael Orsini, 171–89. Cheltenham, UK: Edward Elgar, 2015.

–. "How, Where and When Does Discourse Matter in Small States' Welfare State Adjustment." *New Political Economy* 8, 1 (2003): 127–46.

–. "Speaking of Change: Why Discourse Is Key to the Dynamics of Policy Transformation." *Critical Policy Studies* 5, 2 (2011): 106–26.

Scott, Colin. "Conflicting Discourses of Property, Governance and Development in the Indigenous North." In *In the Way: Indigenous Peoples,*

Life Projects and Globalization, ed. Mario Blaser, Harvey Feit, and Glenn McRae, 299–312. London: Zed Books, 2004.

Scott, Jacquelyn Thayer. "'Doing Business with the Devil': Land, Sovereignty, and Corporate Partnerships in Membertou, Inc." In *Self-Determination: The Other Path for Native Americans,* ed. Terry Anderson, Bruce L. Benson, and Thomas Flanagan, 242–72. Stanford, CA: Stanford University Press, 2006.

Scott, Tracie. *Postcolonial Sovereignty? The Nisga'a Final Agreement.* Saskatoon: Purich Publishing, 2012.

Shepsle, Kenneth. *Analyzing Politics: Rationality, Behavior, and Institutions.* New York: W.W. Norton, 2010.

Shoemaker, Jessica A. "Complexity's Shadow: American Indian Property, Sovereignty, and the Future." *Michigan Law Review* 115, 4 (2016): 487–552.

–. "Like Snow in the Spring Time: Allotment, Fractionation, and the Indian Land Tenure Problem." *Wisconsin Law Review* 4 (2003): 729–88.

Simon, Herbert A. "Bounded Rationality in Social Science: Today and Tomorrow." *Mind and Society* 1, 1 (2000): 25–39.

–. *Models of Bounded Rationality: Empirically Grounded Economic Reason.* Cambridge, MA: MIT Press, 1982.

Singer, Joseph William. "The Ownership Society and Takings of Property: Castles, Investments, and Just Obligations." *Harvard Environmental Law Review* 30 (2006): 309–38.

Sitko, Nicholas J., and T.S. Jayne. "Structural Transformation or Elite Land Capture? The Growth of 'Emergent' Farmers in Zambia." *Food Policy* 48 (2014): 194–202.

Sjaastad, Espen, and Ben Cousins. "Formalisation of Land Rights in the South: An Overview." *Land Use Policy* 26, 1 (2009): 1–9.

Smith, Henry E. "Exclusion versus Governance: Two Strategies for Delineating Property Rights." *Journal of Legal Studies* 31, S2 (2002): S453–87.

–. "Property as Complex Interaction." *Journal of Institutional Economics* 13, 4 (2017): 809–14.

Starks, Rachel. *Managing Land, Governing for the Future: Finding the Path Forward for Membertou.* Dartmouth, NS: Atlantic Policy Congress of First Nations Chiefs Secretariat, 2013.

Sterk, Stewart. "Restraints on Alienation of Human Capital." *Virginia Law Review* 79, 2 (1993): 383–460.

Sterritt, Neil. "The Nisga'a Treaty: Competing Claims Ignored." *BC Studies* 120 (1998): 73–98.

Storella, Alison. "It's Selfie-Evident: Spectrums of Alienability and Copyrighted Content on Social Media." *Boston University Law Review* 94 (2014): 2045–88.

Stubbs, Richard. "What Ever Happened to the East Asian Developmental State? The Unfolding Debate." *Pacific Review* 22, 1 (2009): 1–22.

Sugden, Roger, and Keith Studies. "Economic Development of the BC Interior: A Case Study of Occupations in the Okanagan, 1881–1921." *BC Studies* 194 (2017): 65–89.

Tattrie, Jon. "Native Uprising." *Atlantic Business,* August 25, 2011. http://www.atlanticbusinessmagazine.net/article/native-uprising/.

Taylor, James. *Stakes and Kidneys: Why Markets in Human Body Parts Are Morally Imperative*. Burlington, VT: Ashgate, 2005.

Thornton, Thomas. "Alaska Native Corporations and Subsistence: Paradoxical Forces in the Making of Sustainable Communities." In *Sustainability and Communities of Place,* ed. Carl A. Maida, 41–62. New York: Berghahn Books, 2007.

Toughill, Kelly. "Boardroom Finesse Buys Band Respect." *Toronto Star,* March 3, 2001, NAR.

–. "Capitalism behind Success of Tiny Cape Breton Reserve." *Toronto Star,* March 17, 2004, A06.

Trebilcock, Michael J., and Paul-Erik Veel. "Property Rights and Development: The Contingent Case for Formalization." *University of Pennsylvania Journal of International Law* 30, 2 (2008): 397–481.

Upham, Frank K. "The Paradoxical Roles of Property Rights in Growth and Development." *Law and Development Review* 8, 2 (2015): 253–69.

Vermeule, Adrian. "The Invisible Hand in Legal and Political Theory." *Virginia Law Review* 96, 6 (2010): 1417–52.

Wagner, John R. "Landscape Aesthetics, Water, and Settler Colonialism in the Okanagan Valley of British Columbia." *Journal of Ecological Anthropology* 12, 1 (2008): 22–38.

Walters, Mark D. "Brightening the Covenant Chain: Aboriginal Treaty Meanings in Law and History after *Marshall*." *Dalhousie Law Journal* 24 (2001): 75–138.

Warner, Stanley, and Raymond Coppinger. "Hydroelectric Power Development at James Bay: Establishing a Frame of Reference." In *Social and Environmental Impacts of the James Bay Hydroelectric Project,* ed. James F. Hornig, 19–38. Montreal and Kingston: McGill-Queen's University Press, 1999.

Weimer, David L. *The Political Economy of Property Rights: Institutional Change and Credibility in the Reform of Centrally Planned Economies*. Cambridge: Cambridge University Press, 1997.

"Westbank First Nation: Community, Leadership, Pride." *Canadian Business Journal* 5, 8 (2012): 168–75.

White-Harvey, Robert. "Reservation Geography and the Restoration of Native Self-Government." *Dalhousie Law Journal* 17 (1994): 587–611.

Whiteman, Gail. "The Impact of Economic Development in James Bay, Canada: The Cree Tallymen Speak Out." *Organization & Environment* 17, 4 (2004): 425–48.

Wicken, William. *Mi'kmaq Treaties on Trial: History, Land and Donald Marshall Junior*. Toronto: University of Toronto Press, 2001.

Wildsmith, Bruce. "Vindicating Mi'kmaq Rights: The Struggle Before, During and After *Marshall*." *Windsor Yearbook of Access to Justice* 19 (2001): 203–42.

Williamson, Oliver. *The Economic Institutions of Capitalism: Firms, Markets, Relational Contracting*. New York: Free Press, 1985.

Wilson, Gary N., and Christopher Alcantara. "Mixing Politics and Business in the Canadian Arctic: Inuit Corporate Governance in Nunavik and the Inuvialuit Settlement Region." *Canadian Journal of Political Science* 45, 4 (2012): 781–804.

Woll, Cornelia. *Firm Interests: How Governments Shape Business Lobbying on Global Trade*. Ithaca, NY: Cornell University Press, 2008.

Wyman, Katrina. "From Fur to Fish: Reconsidering the Evolution of Private Property." *New York University Law Review* 80 (2005): 117–240.

–. "Problematic Private Property: The Case of New York Taxicab Medallions." *Yale Journal on Regulation* 30 (2013): 125–87.

You, Jong-sung. *Democracy, Inequality and Corruption: Korea, Taiwan and the Philippines Compared*. Cambridge: Cambridge University Press, 2015.

–. "Land Reform, Inequality, and Corruption: A Comparative Historical Study of Korea, Taiwan, and the Philippines." *Korean Journal of International Studies* 12, 1 (2014): 191–224.

Index

Note: Page numbers with (i) refer to diagrams.